INSIDE COLLEGE

Undergraduate Education
for the Future

INSIDE COLLEGE

Undergraduate Education for the Future

Ronald D. Simpson
and
Susan H. Frost

Foreword by
Sven Groennings, Ph.D.

INSIGHT BOOKS
PLENUM PRESS • NEW YORK AND LONDON

Library of Congress Cataloging in Publication Data

Simpson, Ronald D.
  Inside college: undergraduate education for the future / Ronald D. Simpson and
Susan H. Frost; foreword by Sven Groennings.
    p.   cm.
  "Insight books."
  Includes bibliographical references (p.) and index.
  ISBN 0-306-44504-2
  1. Education, Higher—United States. I. Frost, Susan H. II. Title.
LA227.4.S56   1993
378.73—dc20   93-27880
                                                                             CIP

ISBN 0-306-44504-2

To Charlotte, Jennifer, Timothy, and Dianne Simpson;
and Randall, Susannah, and Charles Frost,
for their love and support during this project and throughout
our professional careers

Foreword

Everyone looks forward to undergraduate education because it brings into one's life the stimulation of new people and ideas and the development of skills and potential. Higher education also prepares the student for employment and participatory citizenship and offers substantial financial return on personal investment. As a social and economic good, undergraduate education is important not only to students and parents, but also to government, taxpayers, and corporations that profit from having sophisticated workers and prosperous consumers. Therefore, both individuals and society have a stake in successful undergraduate education.

The stake in higher education is growing in the knowledge-based economy. Eighty percent of all U.S. goods and services compete with those from other countries, and eighty percent of the value of U.S. goods and services depend on the skills and knowledge of our work force. Competition is based on high technology, sophisticated services, and advanced knowledge. Knowledge is the key to productivity, competitiveness, and our standard of living.

Undergraduate education is a requirement for half of all jobs created in this decade. By the year 2000, semiskilled manufacturing workers will account for only ten percent of all U.S. employees. The new work force will reflect the diversity of the country; more than half of all college students are currently women. Higher education for the greatest feasible number, including all minority groups, is essential to the nation's future.

Just as our population and work force are changing, colleges and universities are in transition. They are reexamining their objectives, reforming curricula, developing new approaches to learning. At the same time that they are getting ready to educate a new work force, budget crises are contributing to concerns about costs, and government and business leaders, students, parents, and taxpayers are insisting that institutions account for their use of funds to improve learning.

Although these issues influence learning, students see college as much more than a place to explore educational objectives, reformed curricula, and learning approaches. The impact of college on students extends far beyond courses and degrees. Students become part of a college environment, and faculty, and especially peers, shape their values, attitudes, beliefs, and motivation. Informal learning through activities, cross-cultural contacts, and personal relationships is powerful.

Students are in charge of their educational opportunities and need to begin the college experience with a realistic sense of the advantages the undergraduate years offer. Students are wise to think carefully about how choices are defined at the beginning of college and how opportunities change during the course of study. Students who think about options and make wise choices build on who they are and what they hope to achieve.

Four choices merit particularly careful thought. The first is the major field of study. It is important to understand the nature of various disciplines—what one studies and how—as well as how various courses are related to one another and where they lead, and to bear in mind that the choice of major is subject to change.

Second, relationships are matters of choice. Students can, for example, choose to know other students from different backgrounds and interests, join social, musical, or religious groups, participate in sports, volunteer for community service, or exchange views with members of the faculty in formal or informal settings. As students make such choices, they should keep in mind that the faculty is a source of guidance and insight.

Third, students must decide whether or not to participate in shaping their own education. Certainly we benefit in proportion to our involvement and participation in education. Some students seek, for example, summer internships to complement their studies, so that their coursework informs their activities, and their activities make their formal education more meaningful. In addition, such experiences can provide distinctive credentials.

The fourth area of choice is how students choose to gain international knowledge. Communication, management, labor, commerce, governmental relations, environmental and security concerns, the arts, and all the professions from journalism to engineering will be more internationally connected in the future. Therefore, employers will increasingly expect new workers to have international knowledge. Students who set out to learn how the global economy affects individuals, communities, and professional fields will bring a much needed perspective to their first job.

Making the most of undergraduate opportunities requires strategic thinking—the earlier the planning, the better. Students should be purposeful and create unique agendas. Since personal development involves change, it is not surprising that interests sometimes change; therefore it is worthwhile to take stock from time to time.

We are beginning a new era—one that requires fresh insight into learning and new educational policy in many institutions. Students, parents, business and political leaders, and college faculty and administrators should participate in these changes.

Inside College: Undergraduate Education for the Future, coming at a time of enormous change, provides a powerful and clearly written view of college for all who are or should be interested in undergraduate education. *Inside College* asks the right questions, presents useful data, and brings together important perspectives. This book will benefit many constituencies as they define expectations and make choices that shape the future of undergraduate education for both individuals and our society.

Sven Groennings, Ph.D., president of Knowledge Network for All Americans, leads research on education policy. He has served as American Express Company's vice president for education, director of the Fund for the Improvement of Postsecondary Education in the U.S. Department of Education, and a professor of higher education.

Preface

Each fall 14 million students—perhaps the most valuable U.S. resource—enroll in college. In doing so, these students are investing not only in their own future, but in the future of our nation and our world. For their investment of time, money, and effort, graduates receive what *Time* magazine described in its 1993 college guide as "the hottest of educational tickets"—a U.S. diploma.

Despite *Time*'s view, numerous authors, researchers, and commentators have recently blamed U.S. education, and more specifically U.S. higher education, for many of society's ills. Some attacks have come from people outside the system: Reporter Charles Sykes, in *Profscam: Professors and the Demise of Higher Education*, indicts college and university professors for having abandoned their students for a university culture where good teachers are not only unrewarded, they are penalized. Other outsiders join Sykes in condemning the current state of affairs and the future of the academy.

Still others attack higher education from the inside. The late Professor Allan Bloom expressed grave concern about the state of college and university learning in his book, *The Closing of the American Mind*. According to Bloom, the U.S. campus lacks direction, distinction, and challenge. Other insiders criticize the current university climate, and some even foresee a higher education revolution by the year 2000.

These and similar commentaries help shape public opinion and provide impetus for our look at today's undergraduate enterprise. As college professors and administrators, we know that popular critical reviewers tell only part of the higher education story. We began our study expecting to find that various colleges and universities offer students a respectable number of opportunities to participate in high-quality learning experiences. We find however that many innovations exist—so many that we, too, are tempted to use the word revolutionary. In short we have come to believe that teaching and learning are gaining new positions of importance in the United States and elsewhere.

In *Inside College*, we view higher education from the inside: We examine the opinions of critics and the predictions of futurists; we look at issues that define higher learning and explore the challenges of the new century. This book is organized into three parts: Part I examines the current international and national parameters that define higher education and explores such questions as (1) what facts and perceptions influence today's human capital needs; (2) educationally, where do we stand in the global marketplace; and (3) will we be viable competitors in the year 2000?

Part II considers the heart of the matter: students and their learning experiences. Diversity, change, and global orientation, the new common denominators, are examined to determine how these constants can be incorporated into exemplary learning experiences.

Part III discusses access, the all-important route to opportunity. Before students benefit from college, they must understand college costs and how to manage them. They also need to understand the array of opportunities available on college campuses. We hear from students who have succeeded in creating unique learning opportunities for themselves.

We conclude with a look into the future. Rather than viewing college as the end of formal education or the beginning of professional experience, we see college as a vital connecting point between the structured learning environment of the classroom and the unstructured learning environment of the larger world. Today's college students must prepare for dynamic futures, and they must do so with tomorrow's needs in mind. To contribute to timely definitions of these needs, we have invited leading scholars and practitioners to share their views on the challenges facing colleges and universities. Throughout *Inside College*, their essays provide insight into the issues.

As students and practitioners of higher education, parents, and teachers, we understand the new undergraduate enterprise. Although college and university administrators, faculty members, business and political leaders, and parents will find this book valuable, we tell the story with students in mind. While we call the new commitment to learning revolutionary, benefits are not apparent to everyone. For those who discover new opportunities and claim them, excellent learning challenges await.

In this book, we raise many questions, and we answer most of them. Perhaps the most important questions remain unanswered, but they define the challenge of new investigations and continued progress in higher learning in the United States.

Ronald D. Simpson
Susan H. Frost

Athens, Georgia and Gainesville, Georgia

Acknowledgments

We experienced unparalleled support from our institutions, The University of Georgia and Emory University, and a host of individuals while writing this book. Vice President William Prokasy at The University of Georgia and Vice Provost Mel Lockhart at Emory University were characteristically supportive of this academic endeavor. The following higher education and business leaders, researchers, and teachers who accepted our invitation to present their views and findings here bring unparalleled range and depth of expertise and experience to the book. In alphabetical order they are Mary Atwater, The University of Georgia; Betty Jean Craige, The University of Georgia; John P. Crecine, Georgia Institute of Technology; Vince Dooley, The University of Georgia; Billy E. Frye, Emory University; John N. Gardner, University of South Carolina; Fred Hargadon, Princeton University; Thomas K. Hearn, Jr., Wake Forest University; James T. Laney, Emory University; Sherry H. Penney and Jean MacCormack, University of Massachusetts at Boston; R. Eugene Rice, Antioch College; Sheryl L. Santos, Arizona State University; John Sculley, Apple Computer, Inc.; Dianne W. Strommer, the University of Rhode Island; Patrick T. Terenzini, the Pennsylvania State University; Joab Thomas, the Pennsylvania State University; and Philip Winstead, Furman University.

The views and experiences of successful students are important also. The following students, asked to contribute not because of honors or awards received but because they are creating outstanding college experiences for themselves, are Elizabeth Anderson, Harvard University; Larry Battertin, Colorado State University; Dorothy Harris Blaise, East Carolina University; John S. Darden, Washington and Lee University; William Desmond, Loyola College; Theresa DiRaimo, University of Rhode Island; Susannah Frost, The University of Georgia; Valerie Goetz, Stanford University; Catherine Little, The University of Georgia; and JoAnn McKenzie, Emory University.

We interviewed other students and used their insights to present wide-ranging student perspectives. Among those interviewed are Gabrielle Chaput, Brenau University; Julius Cruz, Emory University; Neva Daley, Yale University; Amy Griswold, the University of North Carolina at Chapel Hill; Theresa Kelly, Valencia Community College; Mike McKenzie, a graduate of Georgia Institute of Technology; and Dorothy Preston, Indiana University. Others requested not to be identified. We appreciate the candor, thoughtfulness, and energy of all these students. All direct quotes are the remarks of real people. In a few cases where direct quotes are not used, we have merged the experiences of two or more people to portray a real-life situation.

We thank those who helped in many other ways. Karen Anderson, Richard Bestwick, Sheila Buckmaster, John Grandin, Marnie Hogan, Eleanor Hutchens, Karen Kalivoda, Patricia Kalivoda, Susan Kelley, Norman Kuel, Brian Martine, Nancy Moore, Walton Moore, Ron Nelson, Cathy Nix, Deborah Olsen, Lyda Porter, Ellen Rogers, Claire Swann, Fred Volkwein, and Richard Yarborough pointed out important sources of information and identified and put us in touch with students.

Margaret Anderson, Gina Dress, Tom Dyer, Frank Gillespie, William Jackson, JoAnn McKenzie, Katie Smith, Anne Sturtevant, and Dan Walls provided collegial support and rich ideas. Ray Tripp read part of the draft. Marcy Alexander, Karen Fain, Jay Funderburk, Steve Hatfield, Michael Johnson, Kelly McDougal, Sue Moore, Nyta Richardson, and Lori Stepat provided clerical and technical support. William Desmond graciously allowed us to use portions of his column appearing in *The New York Times* and *The Evening Sun*.

Throughout the conceptual and production stages, we were fortunate to have the guidance of Insight Books editors Norma Fox and Frank Darmstadt. Both enlarged our vision with their beneficial comments on the drafts. Our good friend and colleague, Sven Groennings, read several sections of the manuscript, made imaginative suggestions, and agreed to write the Foreword. Our spouses, Charlotte Simpson and Randall Frost, were always in our corner, as were our children Jennifer and Timothy Simpson and Susannah and Charles Frost. Finally two people deserve special thanks—Pat Curtin and Cecile Herrin, who typed and edited countless versions of the manuscript and worked overtime on many occasions. To all these people, we extend our deepest appreciation.

 Contents

PART II: TEACHING AND LEARNING

PART III: INVESTING IN THE FUTURE

PART I

COLLEGE

Perceptions and Reality

1 ⬛ The Legacy of Higher Learning

Emerging in not much more than two centuries as an incredibly successful experiment in human freedom and self-government, the United States is a land of enormous diversity. It is also a land of enormous opportunity. Today U.S. children differ more from one another than ever before, yet any one of them can become a scientist, a senator, or even president. Adults in the United States are no less flexible: Whereas in the past they selected a career for life, today they embark on new endeavors. Although such patterns of achievement are as diverse as the individuals pursuing them, most include learning and, more specifically, higher learning. Once considered a prerogative of the privileged, a college education is now within the reach of all segments of the U.S. population.

In important ways, the development of U.S. higher education reflects the development of the population. Like the original colonists, the first college students had similar backgrounds and similar goals; consequently they studied the same curriculum. Today the rich social histories, complex systems of governance, distinct personalities, and diverse curricula that define Harvard and the more that 3500 other colleges and universities in the United States mirror the evolving mix of the nation.[1] How can colleges and universities address the needs of so many different individuals? Before we investigate this important question, we must understand the history of U.S. higher education.

3

The Puritans settled the Massachusetts Bay Colony in 1630, then established Harvard College in 1636. That they opened a college in the wilderness only 6 years after erecting shelter, churches, and a framework of government seems amazing. Their effort reflected their belief that an educated citizenry and a lettered clergy were basic requirements for an ordered society.[2]

Soon other English settlers joined the Puritans in providing higher learning in the New World. The colleges we now know as William and Mary, Yale, Princeton, The University of Pennsylvania, Columbia, Brown, Rutgers, and Dartmouth—all established before 1776—had different systems of governance but offered a standard curriculum of Greek and Latin languages and literature. Their students were sons of aristocratic settlers preparing to manage the affairs of their world. Other young colonists did not imagine attending college, which was considered necessary to society, but not to the people.[3]

By 1770 new and powerful ideas of nationalism dominated the thoughts of the colonists, and college students were no exception. Young men looked with hostility on privilege. They wanted to attend college and demanded a curriculum that prepared them to be citizens of the new republic. Many colleges expanded their offerings to meet the student's needs, but self-made men who characterized the new nation had little use for higher learning. In 1771 only 63 students graduated from Harvard. They constituted the largest class to graduate for the next 40 years.[4]

After the Revolutionary War, Americans altered their view of higher education. Rather than merely preparing the sons of aristocrats for their father's life-style, perhaps college could provide a way of getting ahead. The curriculum, too, was in motion, and visionaries like Thomas Jefferson brought courses of study in line with the future. New state universities offered classes in law, politics, chemistry, anatomy, and medicine. Nineteen new colleges, more than twice as many as had been founded in the past 150 years in the United States, opened their doors between 1782 and 1802. Although religious denominations founded some of these schools, communities supported the grass-roots endeavors.

The colleges not only made higher education available to people of modest means, they also strengthened local economies and became centers of community learning. By 1820 colleges were more than a collection of faculty, students, and buildings; they represented a way of life. Based on the notion that students could benefit from living close to faculty members and other students, the "collegiate way" became a college tradition.[5]

A few years later, higher education faced another turning point. In a country redefined by the Civil War, the narrowly drawn curriculum no longer served the needs of the country or its citizens. Technological and scientific knowledge demanded new courses of study, women demanded to be included, and new kinds of leaders understood that wealth could support a broader concept of higher learning. The 1862 Morrill Land Grant Act expanded the university's role by making available public lands and federal dollars to every state school. In return agriculture was added to the curriculum. By 1890 the Industrial Revolution brought modernization to all aspects of life, and soon steel mills, mines, factories, and international merchandising dominated the economy. The United States became a world power, and the U.S. research university was born.[6]

Resulting from the blend of three educational philosophies— utility, liberal culture, and research—the emergence, and then dominance, of U.S. research universities marked the beginning of a new era in higher education. Much as the colonial colleges reflected the English model of liberal learning, research universities, such as Johns Hopkins, Chicago, and Clark, resembled German institutions. They emphasized research to gain new knowledge, not teaching undergraduates. In 1900 they formed the Association of American Universities (A.A.U.) to standardize requirements for the Ph.D., strengthen its credibility in Europe, and bolster the standards of weaker institutions. Soon universities commanded most of the social resources available to higher education. Although they did not completely eclipse liberal arts colleges, universities took their place as vital contributors to the development of the country and the world.[7]

During this time, another long-held but unorganized mission of higher education also became more well defined. From the earliest days, when colonial college students prepared themselves to serve society, the notion of public service was alive on college campuses. A century later, James Angell, president of The University of Michigan, viewed higher education as a necessity, not a luxury, and worked with other state university leaders to enable graduates of public high schools to attend college. By 1900 state universities had reached out to the public in other ways. In Wisconsin, for example, faculty members worked through extension services to address the problems of society. Soon professors at other schools followed their example, and by the 1920s, the service ideal enjoyed wide support from public and private universities.[8]

In 1920 the future of higher education was bright. Significant numbers of new millionaires, created during the Industrial Revolution, became major benefactors of research. New knowledge increased exponentially during the 1920s and 1930s, but still the profound implications of university research were not apparent. Not even in 1936, when Harvard celebrated the three hundredth anniversary of its founding, did the renowned scholars and public

---

Philosopher Richard Rorty has asked whether modern democratic institutions, which emphasize individual freedom and personal rights, also can foster a sense of common purpose. At the heart of this question lies the deeper one of whether our institutions have the wherewithal to prepare the people our society needs as visionaries, clear-eyed leaders, and moral exemplars, or whether individual wants and aspirations have pushed the common good irretrievably to the background. Perhaps no institution in our society more poignantly focuses this issue than the university, which has, on the one hand, a bedrock foundation of freedom of inquiry and speech and, on the other hand, a high mission of protecting the public trust.

James T. Laney, president, Emory University
from *Annual Report of the President*, Emory University 1989–1990

figures who commented on the future of higher education predict the events that would transform Harvard and other academies into the influential institutions they have become.[9]

Today the oversight is understandable. In 1936 only 5 percent of the population graduated from college. The work of scholars attracted little support from the federal government and only minimal attention abroad. But World War II brought new perceptions of the usefulness of higher education. When threatened, the United States looked to its universities for answers to difficult questions concerning national defense and later, economic development. By 1945 a broader range of the population was attending college, and institutions had a dual mission: They existed not only to teach students but to foster new knowledge.[10]

Following World War II, with the founding of the National Science Foundation, the research mission of higher education continued to grow. The blending of public and private funds on both public and private campuses led to the observation that institutions were becoming more like one another, not increasingly diverse. But colleges and universities were facing new challenges. From World War II to the 1970s, the traditional-age college student population swelled; by the 1980s their number was declining. Adults filled vacant seats in classrooms, but each year more students of all ages needed more substantial amounts of financial aid to cover the increasing cost of college. In the 1980s national committees of scholars identified other perilous conditions: Undergraduates were not involved in learning; their professors ignored them, directing their attention to research instead.

Using data from the 1990 census, experts predict that the pool of traditional-age college students will increase during the last half of the decade and the next century. By 2002 more than 16 million students are expected to attend U.S. colleges and universities.[11] Students come to college with new and different needs, and many find their needs unmet. Financial crises threaten efforts to improve undergraduate teaching. The country and the world need new and inspired leaders to meet the next century. We depend on higher education to prepare them. Much is left to be done.

COLLEGE: INVESTING IN TOMORROW

Thus far we have discussed college as a system of higher education, using such global terms as shared missions and common dilemmas. Now we turn our attention to college at the individual level and focus not on themes and trends, but on students.

Quite unlike the elementary and high school experiences of many U.S. citizens, college experiences are defined by breadth and by variety; in fact no two colleges or universities are quite the same. Many variables contribute to their unique characters, making each one distinct.

At Berkeley students walking down Telegraph Avenue notice more than a few graying, long-haired hippies who make their living by selling tie-dyed T-shirts, jewelry, and other crafts. Students purchase their wares but wonder why these anachronisms have remained attached to the university since 1968. At Pennsylvania State University in the spring, eight out of ten students wear Penn State sweat shirts, Penn State caps, Penn State shorts, or all three. They enjoy a warm Saturday by moving the furniture—plants, rugs, and all—out of the fraternity houses and relaxing in the sunshine. Others play volleyball under the elms or jump for charity on trampolines on College Street. There is nothing quite like a football game at The University of Michigan, where fans gather with over 100,000 of their closest friends to cheer the Big Blue to victory. Saturday night in Baton Rouge when the Louisiana State University Tigers take the field is equally exciting. The latter two universities offer sharp contrasts to the atmosphere of a Harvard–Dartmouth game in Harvard Stadium. Here friendly birds surround the players as they move down the field. The stands are not full, but the mood is joyful. The Emory quadrangle is even more serene as students walk with brisk purpose to their classes.

Orderly campuses of liberal arts colleges, where gifted scholars and talented leaders are consistently produced, define still other college scenes. Here successful students devote hours to studying that contribute only to survival in small classes. Quiet conversations are part of the weekday routine at Washington and Lee, Spelman, Pomona, or Carleton. But on weekends, a different story unfolds as parties and other social activities provide a change of pace.

Midsized state colleges and universities compose an equally important segment of the system and form, in many ways, the backbone of U.S. higher education. They admit, educate at a reasonable cost, and graduate thousands of students each year. Ball State, Eastern New Mexico, Appalachian State, Southeastern Missouri State, and Northern Iowa, for example, offer a solid education and valuable opportunities for involvement to students of all ages. In addition they enrich regional business, cultural, and agricultural communities.

Other educational opportunities are available at 2-year or community colleges for students who prefer to stay close to home, work part-time, or address academic deficiencies in a controlled environment. Faculty members at these institutions are primarily engaged in teaching and therefore design programs with students in mind. The quality of teaching is often noticeably high.

Much of the strength of U.S. higher education lies in its diversity. Given the range of choices, even the most thoughtful high school senior may select a college or university assuming that his/her most challenging decision has been made. Looking back, however, most find that choosing a college or university was only the first of many decisions that lead to a college degree.

ONE STUDENT'S STORY

In May, 1991, William Desmond was one of about 2000 high school seniors whose mailbox contained a package from Harvard. The envelope was a thick one, containing his acceptance letter, course catalogs, financial aid information, and an extra bit of exciting news. Not only was Desmond admitted to Harvard, but he had been accepted as a Harvard scholar. The packet was his reward for the 30 pages of admissions forms he had submitted along with numerous essays and a $50 application fee. Princeton and Yale soon responded with similar rewards.

But Desmond, a bright young man from Baltimore, did not chose Harvard, Princeton, or Yale. Although he admits to feeling like a fool even to question the worth of places like Harvard, he chose a small liberal arts college—Loyola of Baltimore—right in his hometown. Desmond chose Loyola because he sensed its quiet commitment to the individual. He explained his views in columns that appeared in *The New York Times* and Baltimore's *The Evening Sun*.[12]

Although Desmond's decision about where to attend college was behind him, the subject was far from closed. Soon incredulous respondents were asking why he had declined to invest in the Ivy League. Was cost a factor? Even though Desmond had been named a Presidential Scholar and prestigious schools offered generous scholarships, respondents noted that his parents taught at Loyola, qualifying him for tuition waivers. Although Desmond had invited questions about his decision by writing his columns, why all the interest in one young man's decision about where to attend college?

William Desmond's story is a real and not unusual commentary on the intricacies of higher education. Incredible options, pressures, and pitfalls confront college-bound students, many of whom make a most important decision when they are least equipped to do so. Considering this, did Desmond make the right choice? Perhaps he will never know, but a more useful question concerns the decisions he will make in college. If Desmond studies diligently, plans carefully, and becomes involved in his college experiences, he will most likely be a successful graduate of whatever college or university he attends. If he explores the opportunities available to him, he can create unique learning experiences for himself and be well prepared for the future.

When my friends and teachers heard of my acceptance [to Harvard], they showered me with praise. At parties, strangers would lift their eyebrows in admiration, or so I fancied. Normally overlooked, I suddenly became the "one who got into Harvard." All urged me not to lose such an opportunity.

But as my initial euphoria faded, I began to wonder. I wondered about schools that send out admission packages that cost $3 to mail and which seem like advertisements to impress a customer. A strange way to begin a college education! I was puzzled why my peers were so thunderstruck by the name of a school they knew little about. Many were clearly convinced that attending one of these elite universities would automatically guarantee a good life afterward.

One's worth increases in proportion to the college one chooses; one's future is predicted accordingly, and parents' love is measured in terms of the money they are willing to sacrifice for tuition. Resisting such pressures is difficult. I almost came to believe that in a smaller school I would be sticking myself on a secondary road, passing up the more ambitious fast lane. I felt like a fool even to question the worth of places like Harvard.

William Desmond, high school senior
from "Tell Harvard I'm Not Home," *The Evening Sun* (21 May 1991)

Desmond's story relates his introduction to the undergraduate enterprise. His legacy flows from the Puritans who founded Harvard, from those who made higher learning available to a broad segment of the U.S. population, and from those who continue to nurture its excellence. Our brief look at this legacy suggests that past challenges and the system's response to them have defined its development. Indeed themes and trends continue to influence the present and shape the future. But today's students cannot wait for trends to emerge. They need an in-depth look at today's issues and tomorrow's requirements before they attempt to make the most of their college years.

2　What Critics Say About Higher Education

Since 1984 a new national pastime has emerged that can be described in several ways—the critical review of higher education in the United States, issuing report cards on the condition of postsecondary learning, and taking potshots at a revered part of the U.S. scene for fun and profit. Discussions of higher education have appeared in books, reports from official organizations, and articles in periodicals. There are pure opinion pieces on the topic, meticulously researched scholarly offerings, and something in between. Some discussions reflect the views of college and university insiders, while others have been written by outside observers. Most chronicle the negative, and a few offer universal solutions for unnamed people to put in place. Some list plans for recovery, leaving no question in readers' minds about just who needs to get busy.

THE NATIONAL PICTURE

The discourse began in 1984 when two national reports on the state of higher education appeared. Written by committee members of education organizations, the reports gave official notice that all was not well in the ivory tower. The first report, sponsored by the National Institute for Education (NIE), examined the overall condition of higher education in the United States. Its title describes its action plan. *Involvement in Learning: Realizing the Potential of American Higher Education* responded to *A Nation at Risk: The Imperative for Educational Reform*, a widely read study of primary and secondary education. *Involvement in Learning* presents the decline of undergraduate education in this country and contains many warnings. Although students should be involved in their education, they are not; although faculty members should interact frequently with student, they do not. And although higher education should transfer knowledge about society and its economy to students, teach a curriculum with both breadth and depth, and offer excellence without extravagance, it does not. Greater student involvement, increased emphasis on the freshman and sophomore years, and an assessment of stated academic and social standards are some of the report's recommendations.

The National Endowment for the Humanities (NEH) also sponsored a study in 1984. In *To Reclaim a Legacy: A Report on the Humanities in Higher Education*, William Bennett, former U.S. Secretary of Education, and his study group looked at higher education in the humanities. In Bennett's view, few college graduates know enough about their civilization or their culture. Bennett blames teachers at all levels for this lack and calls for reshaping the undergraduate curricula. Bennett's requirements for an educated person are central to his plan. He advocates a return to traditional texts and emphasizes the importance of a core curriculum.

Integrity in the College Curriculum: A Report to the Academic Community followed the next year. Issued by the Association of American Colleges (AAC), this report points to the faculty's in role curriculum decay. The AAC finds that undergraduate courses lack structure and suggests incorporating a framework in the curriculum that includes processes, methods, and modes to develop understanding and judgement.

In 1987 the Carnegie Foundation for the Advancement of Teaching issued a different kind of report. In *College: The Undergraduate Experience in America*, Ernest Boyer, author and president of the foundation took an empirical approach. After questioning 5000 faculty members and 4500 undergraduate students across the country, Boyer documented widespread deficiencies, such as poor transition from high school to college, inadequate orientation to college, and lack of purpose in the curriculum. He advises colleges and universities to provide a balance between individual interests and shared concerns. In conclusion, Boyer offers "A Guide to a Good College," a series of questions for students and parents to ask when choosing a college or university—Does the college have clearly stated goals about the undergraduate experience? Is a coherent curriculum in place? Is good teaching valued as well as research? Do students see a connection between what they learn and how they live? Answers to these and Boyer's many other questions are critical because they reveal much about what a college or university has to offer undergraduates.

OTHER CRITIQUES REACH THE PUBLIC

Formal education organizations sponsored these reports. Consequently they translate into official opinions about the direction colleges and universities should take. While the results of such studies are important, the findings rarely reach the public; however, all critical reviews of higher education in the 1980s did not remain on library shelves or in government offices. Individual writers also spoke up, and some of them reached significant segments of the population.

In 1987 Allan Bloom, a philosophy professor at the University of Chicago, achieved celebrity status when he wrote an essay on the state of U.S. education. *The Closing of the American Mind: How Higher Education Has Failed Democracy and Impoverished the Souls of Today's Students* has no footnotes and no list of references; it merely documents Bloom's opinions about the state of undergraduate learning. Even so, it was number one on the *Publisher's Weekly* best seller list for 33 weeks.

According to Bloom, the U.S. university is no longer distinctive. Students find plenty to do, but courses do not relate to them or to each other. Instead professors use their subject matter to compete with their colleagues, thereby denying students valuable opportunities to learn about the mysteries of the universe or about their own self-motivation. Specifically Bloom charges that the breadth of the curriculum and the proliferation of trendy composite courses weaken undergraduate learning. In Bloom's view, the curriculum is not substantial enough to occupy three years of undergraduate study, much less the traditional four.[1]

The former president of Harvard, Derek Bok, is another inside commentator on academe. In *Higher Learning*, Bok's more optimistic view of the academy, he asks how well U.S. research universities are educating their students and how they can improve. Major universities enroll the most gifted high school graduates, vital national resources whose university learning is important to all citizens. By nature research institutions are autonomous, competitive, and responsive, and to some extent, competition is healthy: It pushes professors and administrators to perform better in the eyes of the many constituencies judging them. The need to respond to these constituencies protects the university from the danger of being controlled by a single group. Decentralized management encourages innovation, produces experimental teaching methods, and addresses the needs of diverse groups.[2]

What then is the problem at our larger, more prestigious institutions? According to Bok, U.S. universities enjoy more power and influence than ever before. Never have they been so attractive to students of all ages and nationalities; never have they had the modern technological advantages of today. Yet are universities managing the explosion of knowledge with success? Do their leaders have the confidence of the people? Are they contributing to the solutions of national problems? According to Bok, the future depends on answers to these questions.

Somewhere between Bloom's popular and damning description of the academy and Bok's more objective look at high learning, we find several volumes that shed light on particular problems, raise compelling questions, and suggest specific, sometimes radical, solutions. Most take aim at the professoriate and its

It's a lot tougher to gain admission to Princeton now than it was back in 1960, not because the "standards" for admission have changed (relatively speaking) but because the number of applicants who "meet those standards" has increased enormously over the years. Put another way, while the size of the entering freshman class increased 41 percent between 1960 and 1988, the number of applicants increased by 221 percent! Many of the best schools now offer students far more advanced preparation in various fields, and, that being the case, Princeton's faculty now have come to expect more by way of advanced preparation on the part of their students. But it is also true that some "golden era" in the past remains the benchmark against which any current generation of student seems always (and unreasonably) to be found wanting. (I am reminded of the T-shirts worn by some over-40 rowers: "The Older We Get, The Better We Were.")

Fred Hargadon, dean of admission, Princeton University
from "Chances for Admission, Then and Now," *PAW* (20 Dec. 1989)

commitment, or lack of it, to good teaching. Perhaps the most scathing commentaries are those written by a journalist who looks at higher education from the outside. In *ProfScam: Professors and the Demise of Higher Education* and *The Hollow Men: Politics and Corruption in Higher Education*, Charles Sykes describes in vivid detail what he sees as the rot at the core of the university.[3]

In his bill of indictment, Sykes is quite clear about the villains' identity: The faculty has destroyed university learning. Faculty members are overpaid, underworked, unapproachable, uncommunicative, and unavailable; they leave students in the care of slavelike teaching assistants while they pursue their own interests and justify their flight from the classroom with mundane research.[4]

Sykes identifies the source of this problem as former radical students who have become Marxist professors, shrill feminists, and the like. He is alarmed that Dartmouth President James Freedman would cite the emphasis on Western civilization as a menace to the understanding of students who will eventually shape the future. In Sykes's view, Western tradition is the root of democracy; how can it be preserved if "cultural amnesia" is allowed? Sykes blames faculty members for fragmented, politically motivated curricula. He applauds the recently organized National Association of Scholars, but he doubts its ability to balance the popular leftist scholarship of the Modern Language Association.[5]

Underscoring Sykes's view that leftist intellectuals make up the faculties of research institutions, economist Martin Anderson, a fellow at a leading conservative research institute and author of *Impostors in the Temple*, also blames the professoriate for the ills of the academy. Faculty, he charges, relax in near-socialist universities and enjoy job security, high pay, and a system of peer review that protects them from the typical controls of the marketplace while they produce irrelevant research. In support of his argument, Anderson condemns the scholarship of disciplines with which he does not seem to be familiar. He is a critic who believes that only a reformation will save U.S. higher education.[6]

Roger Kimball is a higher education outsider who agrees with Sykes's characterization of today's faculty members. Kimball is managing editor of *The New Criterion*, a critical publication in the arts. In *Tenured Radicals: How Politics Has Corrupted Our Higher Education*, Kimball identifies today's tenured professors and academic deans as yesterdays' student radicals who 20 years ago attempted to destroy the physical aspects of the academy; today they attack from within. According to Kimball, a state of crisis prevails in the humanities departments of many schools where feminists, advocates of "oppression studies," and other politically motivated groups work to destroy traditional humanistic study. Unlike Sykes, Kimball does not confine his criticism to major universities. He finds radical menus in even the most prestigious liberal arts colleges.[7]

In 1990 a higher education insider went on record as agreeing with Sykes's and Kimball's indictment of the professoriate. In *Killing the Spirit: Higher Education in America*, Page Smith, historian and founding provost of the University of California at Santa

Cruz, offers a more tempered but equally depressing view of the academy. Like Kimball, Smith relates today's problems to charges against academe made by students in the 1964–1969 era: Faculties at elite universities and others who imitate them have abandoned teaching; classroom instruction continues to take second place to research.[8]

Why do universities permit this imbalance? Smith speculates that they have come to depend on enormous federal grants, such as those from the military–industrial complex. Instead of the vibrant academic communities aspiring college students, their parents, and contributing alumni envision, today's universities are collections of isolated specialists who hardly communicate with one another. Students are left to part-time faculty, graduate assistants, and visiting professors who teach without permanent appointments; consequently they direct their energies to perpetual job-hunting activities.

Smith joins Bloom and Kimball in mourning the demise of the humanities. According to Smith, universities had "cast out" all nonscientific investigations by 1900; to survive, many areas of study, such as psychology and sociology, became experimental. The "ancient and classic human concerns," such as love, courage, and passion, were excluded, leaving the U.S. university spiritually arid. A tireless lust for the new, excessive specialization, the quest of knowledge for its own sake, denial of a universal moral structure, greed, and the problems of immensity contribute to the impoverishment of the U.S. university.[9] All in all, Smith presents a lucid but discouraging picture of not only our heritage but our future. He suggests that United States' long love affair with higher learning is at an end.

BOYER'S POSITIVE VIEW

In the face of such widespread criticism, is there a more encouraging picture? While most of the charges leveled by Bloom, Bok, Sykes, Kimball, and Smith have their basis in truth, could these present only a part of the picture? Another part is shown by

When evaluating what one hears or reads about higher education, it is well to keep in mind some fundamental differences in the ways by which we come to believe what is true. Basically, we come to knowledge through one or more of the following methods: tenacity, authority, reason, or the method of science.

With the method of tenacity, we believe something to be true simply because we have always believed it, whether or not there is evidence to support our belief. Indeed, we may hold some beliefs even in the face of evidence to the contrary. Knowledge from authority is given. We believe something because we are told by respected, authoritative sources that it is true. The most obvious examples are religious—the Bible, the Koran, the Talmud. But other authorities also make substantial contributions to what we know: parents, teachers, experts in a field, and so on.

Some knowledge comes to us because "it stands to reason." Given certain assumptions or premises, the conclusion follows inexorably: if $A = B$ and $B = C$, then A must $= C$—no doubt about it! No doubt, that is, as long as we're willing to accept propositions 1 and 2. If we reject one or both, the third's claim to truth is empty.

The fourth way of knowing, the scientific method, seeks to identify those "truths" that exist independently of the knower's beliefs, biases, or preferences. The scientific method seeks "truths" that can be demonstrated to be true (or at least probably true), through observation or experience (empirical evidence), and that can be verified as true (or probably true) by other independent observers. It is precisely on this point where opinions and beliefs part company with research findings and research-based conclusions.

Some of the criticisms of higher education in the United States are based on the personal beliefs and opinions of the critics. Allan Bloom's *The Closing of the American Mind* is an example. Other critiques have a somewhat stronger claim to The Truth in that they are based on research findings, the validity and adequacy of which is open to scrutiny by friends and foes alike and, presumably, which can be replicated and verified by other, independent researchers. Boyer's critique is an example of research-based criticism. Although even the most rigorous and "scientific" investigation of what is and is not the case in the real world is subject to the bias of the researcher who designs the study, because conclusions based on evidence gathered using the scientific method can be examined and evaluated by independent observers they possess a greater believability that a claim based on one of the other three sources.

Finally, it is important to understand the nature and constraints on the scientific method. Science is inherently cumulative. No study "proves" or "disproves" a hypothesis, proposition, or claim about what is true. Research evidence tends to support or not a claim about the truth, but it does not "prove" anything. The validity of a truth claim is strengthened or weakened to the extent that scientific evidence supports or fails to support the claim. Thus, it behooves us to be wary of investing too much faith in any single study and to remain skeptical of claims to the truth that are based more on belief than on empirical evidence.

Patrick T. Terenzini, professor and senior scientist, Center for the Study of Higher Education, The Pennsylvania State University, and coauthor with Ernest T. Pascarella of *How College Affects Students: Findings and Insights from Twenty Years of Research*

Ernest Boyer, author of *College: The Undergraduate Experience in America*.[10] To respond to students' concerns about the priority of teaching in colleges and universities, Boyer asked faculty members across the country how they spend their time and which activities they prize most highly. He discovered that although undergraduates are aggressively recruited, they lose in a system where good teaching is seldom rewarded and faculty members who spend time advising students risk not being awarded tenure and promotion. Boyer sees the present as our time of greatest need for connecting the work of the academy to challenges on the national level. The rich diversity and potential of U.S. higher education cannot be fully realized if colleges and universities adopt narrowly defined campus missions or inappropriately restricted systems of faculty reward. Research needs are critical but so is renewed commitment to teaching and service.

Boyer's *Scholarship Reconsidered: Priorities of the Professoriate* offers an enlarged view of academic research, for which Boyer prefers the term scholarship, long used to define a variety of creative work. Boyer defines modern scholarship as encompassing (1) discovery, or traditional research; (2) integration, or making connections across disciplines; (3) application, or defining and solving problems; and (4) teaching, or educating and attracting future scholars. Boyer's definition celebrates the distinctiveness of faculty talent and supports rewards not only for talented researchers but also for those gifted at integrating, applying, and transmitting knowledge.[11]

Boyer's data refute the opinions of Smith, Kimball, and others. For example, Boyer questioned faculty members and administrators about their loyalty and sense of community on campus. From 1984 to 1989, the percentage of faculty members who reported that the institution was very important to them increased from 29 percent to 40 percent. Ninety-six percent of the college presidents surveyed in 1989 professed a strong belief in the importance of community.[12] Perhaps these findings foreshadow a move toward the collegiate atmosphere found lacking by authors in the mid-1980s.

HIGHER LEARNING IN THE NEW CENTURY

What then will be the next step in undergraduate education? Clearly today's issues compel both institutions and undergraduates to find fresh approaches to college and university learning. But are the critics contributing to new directions? According to Bloom, the U.S. family no longer discusses ideas. How can college teaching be effective when learning is not valued at home? Bloom poses an important question, but his answer is somewhat less engaging. His only serious solution, a return to the Great Books, ignores many unalterable realities. To be relevant, the curriculum must address the diverse needs of today's student population, whose members are not familiar with Western traditions.

Sykes, on the other hand, offers solutions, but he is the least qualified of the critics to examine the professoriate. His off-base attack on those teaching undergraduates, called "muckraking journalism"[13] by one reviewer, reveals his narrow view of the relationship between the campus and society.[14] In contrast to Sykes, scholars describe the vital and indispensable connection between teaching and research as a basic feature of universities, where new knowledge contributes to the ongoing development of the disciplines. Thus research reinforces the teaching mission. For example, in an investigation of 27 academic departments at the State University of New York at Albany, researchers found that undergraduate majors in departments composed of instructors actively engaged in research have higher levels of academic fit and intellectual development than majors in departments composed of instructors who are less active researchers.[15] These findings suggest that quality in teaching and research go hand in hand.

Kimball's argument also ignores the facts. When he writes of student radicals as a phenomenon of the past, Kimball disregards both current events and up-to-date research. Not unlike their parents in the 1960s, many of today's college students are activists; for example, in 1990 protesters at the University of California at Berkeley marched on the chancellor's office to demand that the university establish departments of gay/lesbian/bisexual studies, and when questioned about activism, record numbers of college freshmen said they participated in demonstrations in high school and expect to do so in college.[16]

Kimball's tenet that yesterday's student radicals have become today's professional destructionists is unsubstantiated: Some observers feel that career interests dominate today's academicians, who look for perks, higher salaries, and personal prestige, not opportunities to take radical and visible stands for social upheaval.[17]

Critics notwithstanding, Boyer calls the 1990s the decade of undergraduate education. His broader view of research ratifies important differences among institutions, recognizes the diversity of talent within the professoriate, and may help faculty members direct their professional lives more meaningfully. With Boyer's findings in mind, colleges and universities could begin to define their own motives rather than conform to external pressures for prestige. Undergraduate institutions could stop trying to imitate research universities and instead take pride in teaching. Diversity could replace uniformity as the goal and the spirit of U.S. higher learning.

How can institutions, teachers, students and parents respond to this call? The answer to this question depends on future life-styles and work in this country and the world. Many authors, business leaders, psychologists, and educators foresee a more complex and global society, increased reliance on science and technology, and economic decline for the United States. Some believe that the U.S. educational system lacks the ability to meet the demands of a society where everyone belongs to a minority group, children no longer enjoy better life-styles than their parents, and the velocity of change is increasing.

A high school graduate in 1993 will be 35 years old in 2010. By 2000 half of all college students will be 25 years old or older. They will have been born before 1975, but their futures belong in the new century. How is change defining the society in which they will live? What kind of college experiences will prepare them to be productive in this society? In Chapter 3, we take a close look at some projections about living and learning in the future.

3 ![graduation cap icon] The New Millennium: Where Do Trends and Learning Meet?

What does the future hold for today's college students? On countless campuses, planning committees, administrative teams, and enrollment managers seek answers to this question and then anticipate the needs their finding imply. Students and their parents seek answers to the question, since choosing a college, a major, or even a professor determines a part of a student's future, thereby rendering informed and relevant choices critical. Business and political leaders also seek answers because skill levels of future employees, opinions of future voters, and earning power of future taxpayers hang in the balance. Tomorrow's prosperity rests on the shoulders of today's college students. As contributing adults, what will their world look like? How can higher education best prepare them to define and achieve success?

TOMORROW'S FORECAST: AN ESSENTIAL PLANNING TOOL

As we approach the twenty-first century, a new type of expert is emerging to give clues about tomorrow. Predictably these experts are called futurists, and their forecasts are made by using the past to predict the future as a logical extension of the past. One futurist, Don Reynolds, sees himself as a historian of events that have not yet happened. He stretches his imagination by analyzing technological, demographic, and economic trends. Of course futurists do no always agree. Sometimes they reach different conclusions about trends, policy, and global concerns, but it is possible to use the work of several futurists to produce a composite of tomorrow.

Predictions of people not known specifically as futurists are also important. Experts in the field, policy setters, and researchers have clues about new developments. In Chapter 3 we consider the ideas of many thinkers as we look at the tomorrows of today's college students. We begin with trends that foreshadow some larger questions about the future, then we consider specific predictions about life-style, business, and education.

A GLOBAL PICTURE

In 1990 John Naisbitt and Patricia Aburdene announced the dawn of a new era. In their best seller *Megatrends 2000*, Naisbitt and Aburdene predicted that the global economy would boom and the arts would experience a renaissance; free market socialism would emerge; and global life-styles and cultural nationalism would mix to define new living patterns. In framing their predictions, Naisbitt and Aburdene acknowledged the metaphoric and spiritual significance of the millennium and recognized its power to evoke positive visions and terrifying nightmares about the future.[2]

While Naisbitt and Aburdene might be the most visible U.S. futurists, they are not alone. Others define such coming trends as shifts in thinking about peace, democratic free enterprise, and environmental responsibility. In the future most human endeavors, systems, and institutions will become more complex; and science and technology will drive the forces of change. In addition, the importance of the United States will decline, and U.S. educational systems will not improve rapidly enough to meet the country's needs. Some futurists believe that colleges and universities have poor potential for change. As drop-out rates increase, businesses will assume an even greater responsibility for educating employees. More optimistic writers predict an increase in intellectual competence. In their view, creativity and how to learn from error will define new approaches to education.[3]

LIVING AND WORKING IN THE NEW CENTURY

How will we recognize the twenty-first century? For one thing, life-styles will be different for people of all ages. Increasing numbers of children will be born to unmarried mothers, and more than half of all children will live with single parents.[4] Most children will never know a time when their mother did not work outside the home. These children and their counterparts in more traditional family settings will grow up with computers and face increasingly complex issues as teenagers. Such children must be skilled in thinking, analyzing, and challenging themselves, since most will have multiple careers as adults and find it necessary to reeducate themselves throughout life.

Naisbitt and Aburdene call the 1990s the decade of women in leadership. By the year 2000, more that 80 percent of U.S. women between the ages of 25 and 54 will be in the work force, and the rest will be out of work only temporarily.[5] Women will be the prototypical information age workers, much as men were typical workers in the industrial age. As technologically skilled employees, women will be premium commodities.

Early in the new century, women will finally attain positions of real leadership in the corporate and political United States. Increasing numbers of women will own businesses and define a new corporate image. They will value independence, not bureaucracy, balance multiple priorities, and lead by exemplifying excellence.[6] They will continue to be the family's principal care-giver.

What do trends concerning children and women mean for the male population? By 2010 everyone will be a member of some minority group; thus coworkers will be less like one another than now. White males already constitute less than half the labor force, but by 2000, 28 percent of all new workers will be white women; 21 percent will be minority women, and 21 percent will be minority males. Only 9 percent of new workers will be white males.[7] Increasing numbers of men and women will find limited opportunities for advancement in corporate settings. They will leave their jobs in middle age to start new businesses; their new professions will require them to enroll in college to learn new skills. By 2000 half of all college students will be over age 25.

New corporate attitudes will accompany the work force of the next century. Increasing numbers of single parents of both sexes, a scarcity of skilled labor, and the high cost of job training will encourage employers to do all they can to retain valuable contributors in the work place. In 1991 a congressional committee convened to consider the growing needs of working fathers across the country, and IBM expanded the workday to allow employees to meet family and other personal responsibilities. Policy changes such as these will be commonplace as employers seek ways of increasing productivity and try to help employees maintain a nurturing family environment.

Employers will also require a globally competitive work force. Fast-paced technology, expanding information needs, and growing computer capabilities will dictate ongoing corporate job training for all levels of workers. Few people will enter college at 18 and graduate with all the skills needed for a lifetime of productive work.

In addition to new internal policies, corporations will have new views about working with others to increase competitiveness. Rosabeth Moss Kanter, Harvard Business School professor and adviser to many Fortune 500 companies, sees the years ahead as good ones for dreamers and visionaries as barriers to innovation disappear and business leaders reshape their corporations for global competition. Corporations of the future will not be based on layers of status but on the current contributions of individuals. Through strategic partnerships and global alliances, companies will work together to extend influence without increasing size. Maximizing intellectual capital will be critically important, and

> The problem from an education standpoint is that we really aren't preparing people for a world in which they'd change careers four or five times in a lifetime. It will be a world in which the most successful people are those who can deal with ideas, who can look at things from many perspectives.
>
> And yet in education today, as in business, we have been moving more toward specialization. Specialization can contravene personal creativity. We have to be able to tilt the county toward the individual and open the minds of students while they're in universities to become generalists and not specialists. We've got to prepare people with conceptual skills, so that they can be skeptical and contrast and compare different ideas.
>
> College is the last place in which to be pragmatic. College is a time when people should be most inquisitive and exposed to ideas. The last thing to be doing there is training for a career. I'm in favor of more liberal education and less specialization, with the idea that people can get that late on the job. But they never get a chance in later life to be exposed to the broad agenda of experiences that college offers.
>
> John Sculley, chairman, Apple Computer, Inc. from "A Perspective on the Future," *Change* (Mar./Apr. 1988)

leaders who can convince others to work together productively will be valued.[8]

LEARNING IN THE NEW CENTURY

And what part will higher education play in the year 2000 and beyond? Our clues about the future suggest that old educational habits may be outdated. In the information age of the twenty-first century, most jobs will require some form of postsecondary education, but college will be expensive, so creative financing will be necessary. Many students will work after high school to earn tuition money, or they will attend college part-time while working. Even though future students will be older and more purposeful when they begin, they will not prepare for lifetime careers as undergraduates. Fluid styles of living and changing job requirements will result in people having several careers. The value of a liberal arts education, with its emphasis on critical thinking and problem solving, will become apparent as people educate and reeducate themselves to remain current in the work place and to maximize their retirement years, which medical research promises to extend.

Unfortunately critics of higher education do not describe a system that is expanding to meet these needs; instead they cast doubt on the academy's ability to renew itself in a timely manner. Inside observers describe the 1980s as an unfinished academic revolution during which federally funded student loans encouraged unprecedented access to college. Institutions changed to accommodate differences in ethnicity, age, gender, income, attendance patterns, and physical ability. Now needs created by the revolution must be met so that colleges and universities not only admit but also reach underrepresented student populations, rethink the curriculum with all students in mind, and create challenging climates in the academic community.[9]

Such changes take time, and today's students cannot afford to wait for broad-based remedies that may or may not be in place for the next generation of learners. Today's students need immediate and effective answers about how to find coherence, relevance, and quality in today's undergraduate experience.

Other constituencies, too, need answers. The demand for college-educated contributors at all levels of the work force are increasing, and each year U.S. businesses spend $25 billion teaching employees skills they should bring to the work place.[10] At the same time, countless numbers of parents mortgage homes, juggle multiple jobs, and save for years to send their children to college. Business leaders and parents, as well as students themselves, have a vested interest in undergraduate education.

UNDERGRADUATE ISSUES: 1990s DEFINITIONS
FOR TWENTY-FIRST CENTURY SOLUTIONS

What then is the remedy for students, parents, and business leaders? For each of these groups, the problems are immediate, and appropriate solutions depend on understanding higher education issues, of which diversity, the mandate to improve teaching and learning, and embracing globalization are but three.

Diversity

To usher in the 1900s, Martha Minow, a Harvard professor of law, spoke to a national group of college and university attorneys about the trends and norms she expected to define the new decade. If the 1970s were the "me" generation and the 1980s where the "mean" generation, Minow proposed that the 1990s become the decade of distinction. According to Minow, distinction can be accomplished if neutrality, equality, and tolerance define new norms for higher education. Although admirable, these norms cannot be achieved without real effort. Equality will remain elusive until individuals consider others' views and acknowledge the limits of their own perspectives. Neutrality will not be possible until people search for initially unknown perspectives and collaborate with one another to disseminate them. Tolerance will be realized when individuals challenge the unstated norms of academic communities and understand what it takes to make others feel included.[11]

With these statements, Minow captures the essence of the diversity issue and joins a host of others who comment on important differences that influence higher education. For example, Boyer encourages diversity by asking institutions to challenge the norms of the academy and to adopt different viewpoints about faculty productivity. Instead of forcing community college faculty members into molds more appropriate for university professors,

Boyer suggests that colleges and universities ratify different measures of excellence. By contrast, Sykes denounces diversity, calling it an "all purpose mantra" for political issues in the college classroom.

In the context of higher education, what are the diversity issues and what do they mean to students? Perhaps the most obvious ones concern student populations. Changing demographics, the principal influence on higher education since 1970,[12] make diversity a critical issue. Today on the campuses of large and small, public and private institutions, adult students, members of ethnic minority groups, international students, students who are academically unprepared for college, and students with disabilities join with traditional-age, majority students to make up the most complex student population ever enrolled. Even within homogeneous subpopulations, gender, socioeconomic, and intellectual differences exist.

Students from different circumstances have different needs and bring different challenges to classrooms and residence halls. Institutions must find ways to meet their needs, offer a high-quality yet relevant curriculum, and still keep college affordable— a tall order, but not an entirely new one. Laurence Veysey named "diversity of mind" the most striking characteristic of those who designed the U.S. university to accommodate the "dissonant attitudes" of its leaders.[13] To remain relevant and truly distinctive, the academy must continue to accommodate the individual backgrounds, needs, and attitudes of students so different as to be unimaginable by early leaders. In the process, the integrity and relevance of the baccalaureate degree must be assured.

Mandate to Improve Teaching and Learning

According to the Commonwealth of Virginia's Commission on the University of the Twenty-first Century, the next generation of universities will not be collections of buildings but networks of resources linked either electronically or physically. The commission's statement is not so surprising as the list of resources, including not only equipment and space, but teachers, students, and information. Commission members recognize the growing importance of interdisciplinary approaches and recommend rewards for interdisciplinary research and teaching, good teaching in general, advising, and contributing to curriculum reform.[14] As noted in Chapter 2, others join the commonwealth in urging increased emphasis on good teaching: Authors Bloom, Bok, Kimball, Smith, and Sykes find fault with the scant attention professors give undergraduates, and business leaders focus on resurrecting education at all levels.[15] Boyer urges higher education leaders to build recognition for teaching, advising, and other opportunities for individual interaction with undergraduates into the reward systems of academe.

Fortunately we have optimistic news to report on this front. Today many colleges and universities do not just plan for the future, they welcome the teaching and learning challenge. Over 1000 institutions actively promote instructional excellence and faculty development in the United States. Their efforts address our human capital needs and maximize our most precious resource—the individual intellect.

Embracing Globalization

In the last few years, it has become apparent that the United States must create cultural, educational, and economic links to be productive in a shrinking world. In fact futurists name the global economy as an overarching trend of the new millennium. They see all national economies as part of a surging global structure where individuals who can produce new ideas and new technology will be valued as leaders and workers. The new requirements for excellence are already becoming clear, and many U.S. businesses are demanding job-specific international competencies from employees at all levels.

How do we prepare students to succeed in the new competitive environment? Richard J. Wood, president of Earlham College, sees higher education as an untapped resource. According to Wood, even though the United States participates in the global economy, we have yet to change undergraduate education to reflect our participation. The resources—faculty and students— are in place, but significant global education is still a secondary consideration. Wood sees the task of U.S. colleges and universities as one of educating individuals who can work with people from other cultures to resolve multidimensional issues.[16] Others echo Wood's sentiments and work to internationalize the curriculum. Colleges and universities, business and government leaders, and students should view their work as critical to the future of the United States because to remain at present levels of globalization is to fall behind. Exciting opportunities abound for students who seek a worldwide view, but first they must understand the world stage.

THE INDIVIDUAL: STAR OF THE NEW MILLENNIUM

It is said that more new knowledge has been accumulated since 1950 than in all the years before that time. Most of us have no trouble believing this statement. Before 1950 televisions were marvelous new toys; now they may be near the bottom of the technology totem pole. Our world is truly expanding faster than we can learn about it, and the situation has staggering implications for the college curriculum.

While the effect of the knowledge explosion on the college curriculum is profound, it is not new. When the first U.S. colleges opened their doors, elective courses were unnecessary. Students did not have to choose what to learn because all knowledge considered appropriate for the baccalaureate degree could be mastered in four years. All students (white, male, and in comfortable financial positions) were expected to master a prescribed classical course of study. Then in the nineteenth century, elective systems evolved to allow students to choose some of their classes. Specialization followed and by 1900, most students (by this time some were women, few were African-American) selected an area of study, or a major, and prepared for a lifetime career.

Today we face another changing situation. Knowledge is accumulating so rapidly that long-term career preparation in college is obsolete and continued learning is essential. In fact many people not only update their knowledge in one field, but they change fields altogether. A surgeon may become a high school teacher, a college professor may become a financial adviser, and an attorney may enter the ministry. It is becoming common to find students of all ages attending college to prepare for a career change.

Now baccalaureate learning not only involves teaching facts, but teaching learning processes. Well-educated people must be open to new cultures, new ideas, and new technologies and remain current in the work place and in the world by learning to learn on their own. This twenty-first century requirement acknowledges the personal needs of students as well as the professional requirements of the marketplace.

The new requirements for higher education also reflect one of Naisbitt and Aburdene's millennial megatrends—the triumph of the individual. Indeed the individual is emerging as the most important player in the new millennium, and this is good news for today's college students. Perhaps more than ever before, it is possible to construct coherent and relevant individual paths to learning in college. This statement may surprise those who view universities, and even some small colleges, as student mills. After all university classes of 300 students are not unusual, and liberal arts colleges admit 60 students to freshman biology sections; students take computerized tests and academic advising is not required and sometimes seems unavailable. But these very circumstances offer opportunities for learning. Students who investigate their institution's offerings, discover opportunities and then select the in-class and out-of-class programs most appropriate for them are winners. The educational experiences they create for themselves are unique to their needs and their future plans, and they learn in the very process of creating these experiences. Such challenges offer students an arena in which to practice skills they will need to become tomorrow's collaborators and innovators.

According to Kanter, the next century will be a time for dreamers and visionaries. We share her view; we also believe that higher education is the place to prepare for dreams and visions. This country and the world will need them for future success.

PART II

TEACHING AND LEARNING

4 ⬛ Who Goes to College and Why

Anyone who shares a mailbox with a college-bound high school senior knows that U.S. colleges and universities spend hundreds of thousands of dollars each year to recruit 18-year olds. But high school seniors have represented a shrinking segment of the college-bound population, as predictors of demographic trends warned. Nevertheless college enrollment is at an all-time high because many adults, international students, students who are not prepared academically, and students with disabilities are attending college. In 1993 the number of traditional-age college students began increasing again, but today they are strikingly different from the past. Members of ethnic minority groups are enrolling in significant numbers, a growing trend. The resulting student mix has created a new and important undergraduate profile as illustrated in Figure 4.1.

DIVERSITY: A RICH DIFFERENCE

Changing demographics have been named the principal external influence on higher education since 1970.[1] Indeed the number of 18- and 19-year-olds in the United States decreased over 10 percent between 1975 and 1985, causing forecasters to predict that some colleges and universities would not survive into the 1980s while others would adjust their programs to accommodate fewer

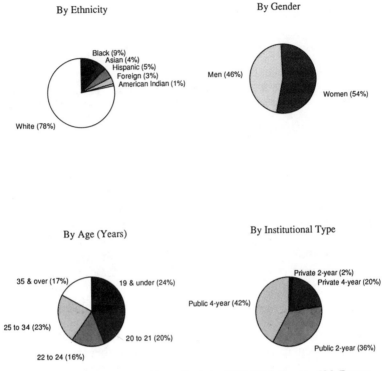

By Ethnicity

By Gender

By Age (Years)

By Institutional Type

Figure 4.1. Undergraduate Enrollment Statistics (1990–1991). SOURCE: U.S. Department of Education

students. Fortunately the predictions proved false; the number of 18- and 19-year-olds in college in 1985 was only 1 percent less than those in 1975. In fact, total college enrollment rose steadily from 1976 to 1986. Why were forecasters wrong? Because traditional-age college students enrolled at a much higher rate in 1985 than in 1975 and colleges and universities altered their educational programs to accommodate a number of new constituencies.[2]

There are several explanations for these trends. For many in the United States a college education became a valuable and attainable asset in the late 1970s and early 1980s. With fewer young people to vie for places in the classroom, a broader range of students enrolled in college. In spite of increasing costs, college became more affordable because families had fewer children. Also the mere prediction of declining numbers influenced enrollment as colleges and universities reacted to the gloomy forecast by doing everything they could to attract students. They welcomed adults, who enrolled in college to be trained or retrained for the ever-changing job market. They increased efforts to recruit traditional-age students, and in some cases, they lowered admissions standards.

Looking back we see that students are the winners in the demographics game, since they were strongly recruited as the college-age population declined. Even though the college-age population is increasing again, colleges continue to recruit aggressively and work to retain their diverse student bodies. As a result, most university students are exposed to multicultural and international points of view in almost any class; students at small colleges establish friendships with students from ethnic groups, age groups, and nationalities different from their own. As a student at an Ivy League university who grew up in Wisconsin noted,

> We talked a lot about diversity at first. Not just racial diversity but even the diversity that comes from going to a public versus a private high school. Getting together in groups to discuss diversity was mandatory, but I learned a lot. This school is a good place to become more tolerant. It has really been exciting.

Today diversity is a hallmark of the college student population, whereas 20 years ago, most college students were much like each other. Almost all were white Americans; over half were 18–24 year old males who attended college full-time and lived in college housing.[3] Currently 54 percent of all college students are women, and almost 20 percent are African-American, Hispanic, Asian-American, or American Indian. About 3 percent are international students, and 7 percent have disabilities. More that 30 percent of undergraduates are over 24, while some are in their seventies.[4]

> I've often thought that the most relevant information I could provide a faculty member about an incoming freshman would be their year of birth. Given comparable academic preparation and credentials, what really distinguishes one generation of students from another are the quite different historical time lines that mark and characterize their respective precollege years.
>
> Fred Hargadon, dean of admission, Princeton University from "Chances for Admission, Then and Now," *PAW* (20 Dec. 1989)

Such diversity offers rich rewards to students who have opportunities to work and live with peers whose cultures, abilities, and interests differ from their own.[5] Although many authors criticize today's college experience as inferior to that of the past, inquiring students can find extraordinary learning opportunities in diversity.

In Chapter 4, we discuss a number of population groups, all of which make important contributions to U.S. higher education (see Figure 4.2) by celebrating their differences.

FRESHMEN: THEIR COMMON DENOMINATOR IS CHANGE

Parents, especially fathers, of many traditional-age college students were college students themselves 25 years ago. As male baby boomers, they composed the largest group of college students in U.S. history. "How different can the university be from when I was there," asked one soon-to-be-educated father? His freshman daughter, who entered the state university from which he had graduated in 1967, answered, "For one thing, no one knows or cares where you are, who is in your room, or if you ever study. The issues here are big ones, Dad, like will your date rape you and give you AIDS." After one term, her father agreed that college life has changed in unimaginable ways. (See Chapter 9 for a discussion of health and wellness on campus.)

In 1969, 57 percent of all college freshmen were men, and 90

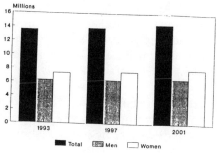

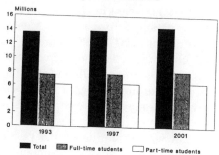

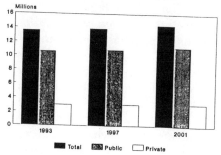

Figure 4.2. Undergraduate Enrollment Projections for the Years 1993, 1997, and 2001. SOURCE: U.S. Department of Education

percent were white. Baby boomers with high scores on the Scholastic Aptitude Test (SAT) competed for a limited number of places in college classes. Not surprising, as freshmen, they rated themselves higher in academic ability than freshmen do today. Baby boomers were also more inclined to attend school full-time, take courses that challenged their academic skills, and major in liberal arts areas.[6]

Today more than half of all freshmen are women, and almost 20 percent are members of ethnic minority groups. While they rate themselves higher in drive to achieve, leadership skills, and intellectual self-confidence than students 25 years ago, today's freshmen post lower entering test scores and plan to take fewer challenging courses than did their parents.[7]

When asked what motivated his peers, one California freshman said without hesitation "future income. Most take a specific path to a particular destination—making money." Research supports this student's observation. Freshmen in the 1990s are characterized by the desire to be better-off financially than students in 1980. Although the former are politically conservative, they approve of abortion and casual sex; however they do not lack social conscience. More than ever before, freshman consider social values important and want to influence the political structure. They intend to contribute to a clean environment and think the government should control pollution. More than twice as many freshmen in 1990 as in 1969 participated in demonstrations in high school and plan to continue demonstrating in college. These trends suggest that today's freshmen are dissatisfied with existing conditions in the United States and intend to influence the U.S. way of life.[8]

Although today's freshman population is quite different from that of the last generation, one constant remains important for first-year college students. Change is the hallmark of freshman year. Many freshmen undergo the most significant changes of their lives. Some students manage change of this magnitude with little difficulty. Others find the process so stressful that their success in college is threatened.[9] Later chapters address college programs designed to support students as they make the transition from high school to college. For now it is important to note that the dynamics of transition can make the difference between a successful and an unsuccessful college experience. Students who adopt the college community readily go on to complete general education requirements, choose majors, and design their future life-styles. Those who do not adjust may leave college before attaining their goals.

ADULTS: LEARNING AGAINST THE ODDS

As the number of traditional-age freshmen declined, the number of adult students increased. In 1990 the 5.5 million adults who enrolled in college reported various reasons for doing so—to remain current in the work force, support rising standards of living, or take advantage of life-long learning opportunities. Changing norms for women in the work place have influenced many of them to attend college to prepare for a career outside the home.

About 40 percent of all students who earn college credit are adults.[10] Eighty-eight percent of adult students are white; 71 percent are employed full-time; 63 percent are married; and 58 percent are women. Projections suggest that more and more adults will return to college in the 1990s. By the year 2000, 75 percent of the work force will have to be retrained for their jobs.[11] Although many adults will enroll in college for job training, they may learn much more and graduate with a new focus for their lives.

Fortunately timely research on adult development has influenced the college experiences of today's adult students. In the past psychologists believed that human beings developed throughout adolescence and remained basically the same afterwards. Today newer theories of adult development show that far from reaching a point of no change and no growth, adults progress through developmental stages much like children and adolescents. These stages have distinct characteristics and engender needs that can be addressed through formal education.

Laurent Daloz, a ground-breaking researcher in the field of adult development, observed in 1986 that we all change with age. The question is, how does this change occur?[12] By linking change to development, Daloz defines development not as change only, but as change with direction. When so defined, change can be properly guided by education.

Like freshmen, adult students are at transition points in their lives. Such transition points usually occur between periods of stability, and some adults, especially those in midlife, seek to give meaning to life through higher education.[13] Colleges and universities that recognize the developmental process in adult students and plan programs to meet their needs can enhance adult students' success.[14]

Although many institutions make impressive efforts to meet the needs of adults, institutions define adult students in different ways. Some use an age-related definition and classify all students over age 24 or 25 as adults. Others define adult students by the time they have been away from formal education and thus consider those who have been away from school for 2 years or more as adult students.[15]

Most adult students work full- or part-time. Unlike traditional-age students, they do not identify education as their primary concern in life. Most look for a manageable "fit" of family, work, school, and community responsibilities.

"Before I went back to school," said the mother of two with a part-time job, "I thought I had all the bases covered—the car pools, the shopping, the laundry, my work responsibilities. Then my mother-in-law asked me when I would study. I was shocked. I had not thought about this at all, and it turned out to be the hardest part to manage." While the juggling act can be stressful, many adults say that returning to college is an exciting adventure quite different from the traditional-age undergraduate experience. One 42 year old remarked, "I feel good. I feel positive about my accomplishments. For once I am doing something I really want to do for me—not for anyone else. I came back because I had the experience for upper level management, but not the degree. Now I will have both."

Traditional-age undergraduate students usually identify the campus culture as the focus point for their lives during college and consider full participation in college as an important part of the educational experience; most adults do no enjoy this luxury. While adult students form close relationships with faculty and other students of all ages, the relationships differ from those of younger students because they are centered around course content and classroom experiences. Academic matters, problems of mobility, managing multiple life roles, integrating a wide range of responsibilities, and finding support within the college concern adult students, who also worry about how to relate to traditional-age students in the classroom.[16]

Many adults anticipate that job responsibilities, lack of time, not enjoying their studies, lack of confidence in their abilities, and difficult course work will be significant barriers to achievement in college. Job responsibilities usually prove to be more significant barriers than anticipated, while a lack of confidence is less troublesome than expected.[17] Most adult students agree with Theresa Kelly, a 34-year-old Valencia Community College student, who feels that using time productively is the biggest challenge. "Before coming back to college I thought things would fall into place. But I am constantly juggling class, my kids, and studying. Time management skills are important. Younger students need to manage time also. Adult students don't have time. Younger students don't appreciate the time they have."

Although adult students worry about how they relate to younger students, they often bring valuable perspectives to the classroom. Traditional-age undergraduates appreciate the fascinating real world view of adults, who offer eye-witness accounts of events younger students know only as history lessons.[18]

When adults decide to enter college for the first time or to return after several years away from campus, they are in many ways bucking the system.[19] To be successful, they must focus on the transition process and new ways of receiving college services. Some institutions recognize these needs and adjust programs to serve adults; others may soon join them, since forecasts indicate that the adult student population will continue to grow. Dorothy

Preston, a particularly thoughtful adult undergraduate at Indiana University, is studying to address the needs of the swelling market for adult education. "My double major in adult education and sociology is preparing me to advise business and government about the future learning needs of their employees. I want to help them cope in the twenty-first century."

ETHNIC MINORITIES: GROWING POPULATIONS

During the 1980s the U.S. population grew at a slower rate than in any decade since the Great Depression, yet minority populations expanded at 2–14 times the rate of the corresponding nonminority populations. Since this trend is expected to continue, collectively, minority populations will make up one-third of the U.S. population by the year 2000.[20]

This prediction has important implications for the United States in general and for higher education specifically, since despite their increasing number, African-Americans and Hispanics remain underrepresented in colleges and universities.[21]

Statistics highlight these enrollment trends (see Table 4.1). While the total number of African–American and Hispanic youths is increasing, the increase in African–American representation is considerably smaller than the increase in other ethnic minority populations. The percentage of Hispanic enrollment shows a much larger increase, while Asian–American enrollment has almost doubled. Collectively minority enrollment is about 20 percent. As colleges work to identify the needs of all students and design programs to meet their needs, it is necessary to consider the special characteristics of the larger minority groups.

African-Americans: A Population in Jeopardy

The African-American population comprises 12 percent of the U.S. population. Although the number of African-Americans

TABLE 4.1. College Student Enrollment by Ethnic Group:
A 10-Year Change in Total Enrollment (1980–1990)

Ethnic Group	1980 (thousands)	1990 (thousands)	10-Year Change (%)
White	9,833	10,675	+8.6
African-American	1,107	1,223	+10.5
Hispanic	472	758	+60.6
Asian-American	286	555	+94.1
American Indian	84	103	+22.6
Foreign	305	397	+30.2
Total Enrollment	12,087	13,710	+13.4

SOURCE: U.S. Department of Education.

grew more than 13 percent in the 1980s, compared to an overall population growth rate of 9.8 percent, there has been a steady decline in college attendance among African-Americans from a high point in 1980. Why do so few African-American high school graduates attend college? Even though they are more academically able now than in the past, increasing numbers select options other than college after high school. Many enlist in the armed services, especially the navy and the air force, while others attend vocational or technical schools to receive direct job training. Undoubtedly such programs offer positive alternatives to college, so the question is whether or not colleges and universities should be concerned about the declining number of African-Americans on campus? The answer is a resounding yes! Although African-American teenagers did not lose ground in the 1980s, they are still disadvantaged by most social indicators when compared to whites.[22]

As the pool of white youths has declined, colleges and universities have intensified efforts to recruit African–American students to fill classrooms and residence halls. Once enrolled, African–American students who set goals for themselves, become involved on campus, and develop positive relationships

Multicultural education is an idea, a reform movement, and a process to alter educational structures so that all students possess an equitable chance to learn and achieve. Even though the multicultural education movement began with social scientists, the important tenets of multicultural education do not just belong in social science, history, and literature courses. The important concepts of pluralism, assimilation, stereotype, prejudice, discrimination, power, equity, culture, beliefs, and values are vital to all disciplines taught in higher education, even science and mathematics. It is important for all students to realize that the paradigms used by scientists and mathematicians are based on belief and value systems, and the contributing scientists and mathematicians have come from different cultural backgrounds.

On predominantly white campuses, students are being asked to interact with students from different cultures from throughout the world. Their higher education experiences provide them opportunities to gain the knowledge and develop the skills necessary to interact with these students. College and university students need not only awareness and sensitivity but knowledge and skills provided by multicultural strands interwoven throughout the disciplines in order to be successful in the twenty-first century.

Mary Atwater, professor, School of Teacher Education, The University of Georgia

with faculty members tend to be successful. A healthy balance of challenge and support, opportunities for friendship, participation in campus life, and a sense of academic progress are critical ingredients for success.[23] One young woman who graduated from a small high school in New York City and stayed in the northeast for college advises other African–American students to "be open to new ideas, new people. Don't limit yourself to one ethnic group." Successful African-American students also understand the historical context through which they gained access to college, learn to act as advocates for themselves, and develop a cultural identity on campus.

To improve the college experience for African-American students, effective programs should begin with short-term enrichment experiences on college campuses for high school students. Interaction can be expanded during the senior year in hope of identifying the strengths and weaknesses of future college freshmen.[24] Systematic orientation and involvement with faculty members, especially African-American instructors, can result in positive college experiences for African-American students.

Hispanics: Underrepresented on Campus

Even though more Hispanic students attend college now than in the past, Hispanics are still underrepresented on campus. Of the 22 million Hispanics in the United State, only 758,000 went to college in 1990. This figure is alarming: While Hispanics are on their way to becoming the largest minority group in the United States, they remain educationally disadvantaged. Only half of all Hispanic students who enter kindergarten graduate from high school, and only one-third of them enroll in college.[25]

Hispanic students bring to college an especially strong identity with home and family life. They are often the first members of their families to attend college, and their adjustment can be more difficult than for other minorities. Like African-American students, Hispanics need a supportive college community to aid the adjustment process. Because they may also be academically underprepared for college work, some choose community colleges for a low-cost education that provides remediation while they continue to live at home. Unfortunately many Hispanic students in community colleges never transfer to 4-year institutions, and fewer Hispanic than white transfer students graduate.

College graduates most often have good high school preparation, effective study habits, and high self-esteem. They are well educated, affluent, and enter college directly after high school.

They live on campus and receive financial aid if they need it.[27] Conversely Hispanic students often attend low-income minority schools with poor achievement records. Many lack motivation and goals. They are emotionally unequipped to cope with college, and they live at home. Hispanic students often do not know how to find out about financial aid, and many must work to support themselves and their families. In addition they have no models on which to pattern a successful college experience.

Hispanic students report that Hispanic role models on campus, especially in faculty positions, can make a significant difference in their college career. Many successful students give credit to a particular person who took a special interest in them or offered encouragement. These students agree that adult role models encourage students to develop positive self-concepts, especially on predominantly white campuses. In turn successful minority students can become models for siblings and young members of their ethnic groups. Unfortunately faculty role models are scarce, and many students never find mentors or friends who take personal interest in Hispanic students' academic success.[28] "No, I have never had a Hispanic professor" said a senior at a private college on the West Coast. "It would make a difference, though. I would like to get my Ph.D. and perhaps teach. It would really help to see someone who has made it doing this."

Asian-Americans: Not Always the Whiz Kids

As a group, Asian-American college students are quite different from African-American or Hispanic students. Many Asian-American students are high achievers in school; indeed the fact that they are characterized as whiz kids has led to a public perception that Asian-American students do not need the educational services usually made available to members of other minority groups. Asian-Americans believe that higher education leads to social mobility and count on college to help them become part of U.S. life. At times sociologists impede their progress by identifying them as a group not plagued with the social problems of other ethnic minorities.[29]

In 1990 the 7.2 million Asian-Americans in the United States constituted 2.9 percent of the total population. The count has more than doubled since 1980, reflecting a growth rate (107 percent) far outdistancing that of the Hispanic population (53 percent), the African-American population (13 percent), and the U.S. population as a whole (9.8 percent).[30] Immigration accounts for about two-thirds of the growth rate. From 1970 to 1980, 1.6 million Asian-Americans came to the United States; from 1981 to 1988, 1.75 Asian-Americans were admitted, making them the largest group to enter the United States legally in a year. Although the term Asian-American describes a highly diverse segment of the population, including Asian Indians, Chinese, Filipinos, Japanese, Koreans, and Vietnamese, Asian-Americans share one important characteristic: They identify a college degree as a means of mobility in a society that may otherwise restrict their success. "My family wants me to prepare for something specific," observes a private university student whose family is from the Philippines, "but I want to find something I can be happy doing."

Evidence of the dedication of Asian-American students is reflected in their high school and college graduation rates. Sixty-seven percent of the total U.S. population over age 24 graduates from high school, compared to over 75 percent of all Asian-Americans. Only 16.2 percent of the total population over age 24 graduates from college, while more than 33 percent of the Asian-Americans over age 24 have a college degree.[31] In 1980, 286,000 Asian-Americans attended colleges and universities as undergraduates; by 1990 this figure was 555,000. In other words, Asian-Americans increased their participation in higher education by almost 100 percent in 10 years.[32] In 1986 only 2 percent of the Asian-American high school seniors who entered college in 1980 reported that they left college without receiving at least a bachelors degree.[33]

Most Asian-American students major in technical fields,

such as engineering, the physical sciences, or mathematics, and they may need to improve their communication skills through the arts and humanities courses. Most Asian-Americans choose public over private universities, and in some cases, they constitute a sizable portion of their freshman class.[34] But most Asian-American students consider themselves members of a minority group much like African-Americans or Hispanics, and they need the same services as other "at-risk" populations. Like African-American and Hispanic students, Asian-Americans benefit from role models among faculty and students. Asian–American peers who are assimilated successfully into college life can provide valuable support systems to incoming Asian–American students.[35]

Since 1983 access to higher education for Asian-Americans has received intense scrutiny from the media and members of both political parties on a national level. The dedication of Asian-Americans to higher education and their rapidly increasing numbers have led to questions about admission rates at colleges and universities. At the same time, the press began calling nationwide attention to Asian-American students, first portraying them as super bright, whiz kids, or overachievers. Soon the story line took a new direction, and discrimination became the issue. In 1988 *U.S. News and World Report* investigated the freshman class at Harvard and reported that Asian-American freshmen scored some 40 points higher on the SAT than Caucasian students. At Berkeley, where Asian-Americans constitute 26 percent of the undergraduate enrollment, they are admitted at lower rates than Caucasians even though their high school grades are higher. Reporters charged that some universities, especially the more elite private schools, were purposefully limiting Asian-American enrollment.[36]

Then demographics entered the picture. Asian–Americans became not only the fastest growing segment of the U.S. population, but the fastest growing group in the college student population. As their numbers continue to increase at rates that outdistance other groups, their political influence is on the rise. Thus both conservative and liberal politicians on the national level vow that Asian-Americans will not experience admission discrimination.[37]

Colleges and universities are responding to this issue in a number of ways. Some welcome large numbers of applicants to fill the gaps left by diminishing numbers of traditional-age students. Other schools, especially elite institutions located in Asian—American population centers, declare that denying admission is justified. Although some Asian-American applicants display exemplary SAT scores and entering grade point averages, many lack the strong recommendations and broad range of interests that other students bring to a freshman class.[38]

Admissions officials also present other arguments: (1) Asian-Americans usually seek admission to academic programs with more stringent admissions criteria; therefore they compete with students of other groups who submit scores and grades higher than the mean of the applicant pool. (2) Few Asian-Americans are children of alumni, although at some private schools, this is a variable in the admissions equation that may soon lose its power as Asian-Americans attend college in record numbers and have families.[39]

Clearly the admissions question will continue to be addressed at the institutional and national level. Asian-American commitment to achievement and success through higher education is deep. Asian-Americans expect the American tradition of selection by merit to support them, especially because they have shown that once admitted, they can excel in the higher education arena.

INTERNATIONAL STUDENTS: FOUNDATIONS OF DIPLOMACY

In 1990 more than 360,000 students from other countries attended college in the United States. This 5.6 percent increase over 1989 was the largest in 7 years and represents one-third of the one million students who attend college outside their borders each year. Most international students are from Third World countries; students from Asian countries accounted for 9 percent of the increase in the international student population in 1990.[40] Although nonresident aliens received 7,700 doctoral degrees in the United States in 1988 to 1989,[41] more than half of all international students are undergraduates, and the number of freshmen are increasing.

Although international students are not numerous enough to offset the enrollment decline in the United States, they attend some institutions in significant numbers. International students compose about 8 percent of the student population in New England colleges and universities and contribute about $300 million each year to the New England economy.[42] What does this growing international presence on U.S. campuses mean for the United States? In Chapter 3, we discussed higher education as part of a new world order based on a global economy and competitiveness. The growing presence of international students on U.S. campuses suggests that the trend has profound influence at home (see Tables 4.2 and 4.3).

More than most other U.S. institutions, colleges and universities should find it natural to welcome, teach, and learn from international students, because colleges are by nature international institutions, connected by a network of knowledge spanning countries and languages. As representatives of their countries, international students are powerful contributors to the international focus of higher education. While in the United States, international students adopt many of our norms and customs and come to understand our ways of thinking and communicating. Because many international students with a U.S. education assume positions of influence in their home countries, their relationships with U.S. students can form the foundations of future worldwide diplomatic and corporate networks. [43]

In many ways the needs of international students are similar to those of U.S. students: Both are concerned about choosing the right college or university and the right major, being successful in the classroom, and developing good rapport with instructors and fellow students. Unlike their U.S. counterparts, international stu-

TABLE 4.2. Institutions Enrolling the Most
International Students (1990–1991)

Institution	Number of International Students
Miami-Dade Community College	5757
University of Southern California	3886
University of Texas, Austin	3867
Boston University	3633
University of Wisconsin, Madison	3565
University of Pennsylvania	3122
Columbia University	3077
Ohio State University (main campus)	3021
University of Illinois, Urbana-Champaign	2967
University of California, Los Angeles	2921
University of Minnesota—Twin Cities	2636
Southern Illinois University, Carbondale	2627
Texas A&M University (main campus)	2497
University of Maryland, College Park	2462
Harvard University	2409

SOURCE: *Open Doors 1990–1991* (New York: Institute of International Education, 1991).

dents must overcome the language barrier and adjust to a new culture, a new social system, and a new educational environment. Many international students come to the United States to prepare for specific careers at home and thus seek educational programs that will be relevant to professions and life-styles in their native countries.[44]

Non-Western international students bring to college aspects of their cultures that make their experiences on U.S. campuses different from those of Western students. Whereas Western students see education as just one means of achieving success, non-Western students view classroom achievement as the key to wealth and status in society. Non-Western students also perceive their instructors differently: Rather than the Western view of teachers as facilitators of learning, non-Western students see them

TABLE 4.3. International Students'
Countries of Origin (1990–1991)

Country	Number of Students
China	39,600
Japan	36,610
Taiwan	33,530
India	28,860
Republic of Korea	23,360
Canada	18,350
Malaysia	13,610
Hong Kong	12,630
Indonesia	9,520
Pakistan	7,730
United Kingdom	7,300
Thailand	7,090
Germany	7,000
Mexico	6,740
Iran	6,260

Source: *Open Doors 1990–1991* (New York: Institute of
International Education, 1991).

as revered authorities; thus in the non-Western view, responsibility for learning rests solely with the student.

Many non-Western international students display a rigorous dedication to educational excellence, and some feel significant family and peer pressure to excel.[45] When asked about the learning challenge at Yale, a student from mainland China said that

academics seemed very hard at first because of language difficulties. I read slowly, and my writing course was hard. But I am ambitious and very hardworking. Now if I go to the group lecture, I do not bother with the recitation. My mind is very active during the lecture and I remember everything the professor says. In the problem sets, I get the fine points. What is the point of review? Many times I do not need to read the text. I agree that Asian and even Asian-American students work harder than U.S. students. We are very motivated.

Both Western and non-Western international students are anxious to work in professional settings in this country, but many seek internships or other on-the-job experience without success. International students need help in designing career plans, exploring job opportunities in their majors, and interviewing for positions.[46] They also need practical work experience to succeed in the global marketplace.

STUDENTS WITH DISABILITIES: A DIFFERENTLY ABLED POPULATION

Only within the past 15 years have numbers of college students with disabilities been large enough to constitute a population with special needs. In 1977 federal legislation expanded their access to a college education when final regulations implementing the provisions of Section 504 of the Rehabilitation Act of 1973 mandated the removal of all major impediments to postsecondary education for handicapped students. To comply most colleges and universities removed physical barriers from their campuses, and many larger institutions created offices to oversee services for students with disabilities. Now curb cuts, special transportation, and elevators are available to students who need them. But the majority of students with disabilities have highly individualized needs that are more difficult to discern.[47]

From 1978 to 1985, the population of college students protected by Section 504 of the Rehabilitation Act increased from 2.6 percent to 7.7 percent,[48] and the percentage continues to grow. Although they are more numerous than ever before, students with identified disabilities still face a variety of barriers on campus. These may be attitudinal barriers, such as the opinions of faculty, staff, and peers about the abilities of students with disabilities; policy barriers, such as rules that limit access to libraries or learning centers; social barriers, such as regulations prohibiting attendants from accompanying students with disabilities to sporting events; or the more familiar architectural barriers.

For many students with disabilities the most significant barrier is being perceived as "un-able." Students with disabilities usually see themselves as "able" in ways that are different from other students, and thus they prefer a supportive college environment and information about opportunities available to them rather than offers of emotional support.[49] "Don't let anyone set limits for you," advises Gabrielle Chaput, a Brenau University student whose injuries in an automobile accident resulted in permanent disabilities. "You are the only one who can decide what you can and cannot do. My parents have contributed to my success. They let me do what I thought I could do even though I broke bones sometimes. Now I will try anything. In my high school, I set track records that still stand."

Academically college life is about the same for students with disabilities as for other students. Students with disabilities recognize the importance of college, and they are generally satisfied with their academic experiences. Like other students, they need to be involved in all aspects of college life. Although they participate in a variety of extracurricular activities, some students with disabilities find it difficult to adjust to the physical environment.[50]

Today significant numbers of students with disabilities have learning disabilities, yet this population did not seem to exist in the last generation. The concept of learning disabilities emerged about 20 years ago when doctors realized that victims of certain traumatic brain injuries could not learn as they had before they were injured. While investigating ways of educating or reeducating injury victims, researchers discovered that some children who had not been injured exhibited the same learning problems. The rights of people with learning disabilities, like those of people with physical disabilities, are protected by federal legislation. Today the population seems large because learning disabilities can be diagnosed. Approximately 14 percent of all students with identified disabilities have learning disabilities. This represents a 10-fold increase in identification since 1978.[51]

Learning disabilities interfere with an individual's ability to perceive, process, sort, store, or retrieve information. Identified through psychoeducational evaluation, students with learning disabilities usually have average to above average intelligence. Often they learn best when taught in formats that address their individual abilities rather than their disabilities. Students with learning disabilities who are highly motivated, willing to learn in new ways, and emotionally mature are good candidates for success in college.[52]

ACADEMICALLY UNDERPREPARED STUDENTS: TOO OFTEN THROUGH THE REVOLVING DOOR

The educational and counseling needs of students who enter college without adequate academic skills make them another significant component of the college student population, and about one in four college freshmen fits this profile.[53] Because the two strongest predictors of success in college appear to be scores on standardized tests and high school grade point averages,[54] underprepared students come to college with two strikes against them. They usually post low scores on such entrance tests as the SAT or the American College Testing Program examination (ACT) and have high school grade point averages below the college mean. Those who enroll only to be dismissed because of poor academic performance are said to go "through the revolving door" into and out of college.

The underprepared student population is not a new one in colleges and universities. In 1907 more than half of all students entering Harvard, Columbia, Princeton, and Yale failed to meet the usual admissions standards of their college, and remedial courses existed at 350 colleges and universities by 1915 to teach students the necessary academic skills.[55]

Now 82 percent of all institutions and 94 percent of all public institutions offer at least one basic skills course. Unlike early remedial programs, modern programs meet more than just the educational needs of the students they serve; they also address cognitive, social, and affective development.

Some educators and politicians believe that remedial education should not be offered at most colleges and universities; instead most developmental education should take place in high school. Colleges and universities should serve those who meet admissions requirements when they enter.[56] This view seems contrary to the needs of the U.S. population and to the mission of higher education, which is to provide equal educational opportunities to all citizens.[57] Today the number of students who are academically underprepared is increasing, and many of them are members of other growing population groups. They may be African-American or Hispanic students, adult students, or students with disabilities. Many come from financially disadvantaged families and/or lack basic language, writing, and mathematical skills. Some do not know how to study or have unfocused career goals. Because they do not know where they are going after college, their course work seems irrelevant to the future. To increase their investment in learning, they need the academic and career counseling that developmental education provides, since identifying interests and goals can be the first step to classroom success.

Students who are underprepared also need to expect and experience success. Many received low grades in high school and expect little more from themselves in college. Even so, mere enrollment can be a signal that they are ready to learn, and exemplary programs serve more than academic needs. They involve students in the educational process and offer routes to success in college.

WOMEN: A DIFFERENT VOICE FOR THE NEW MAJORITY

In 1985 researchers studying change in a national sample of college freshmen named the evolving role of women as the most dramatic college student trend of the last 20 years.[58] Women attend college today in record numbers and constitute more than half the college student population. They received 53 percent of the college degrees awarded in the United States in 1990, and they majored in such career-oriented fields as business administration and pre-professional studies. U.S. employers applaud these trends, because women represent an expanding source of labor; in fact women presently account for two-thirds of the increase in the labor market.[59]

As sex roles in the 1990s become more flexible than they were in the early 1980s,[60] college women, like college men, face a wide array of choices when they graduate. While in school, women need programs and services that offer flexibility and help in making informed decisions about their futures.

According to some psychologists and educators, theories about human development have not given adequate attention to the experiences and concerns of women. For example *The Seasons of A Man's Life*, a breakthrough study of adult development by Daniel Levinson and others, is based entirely on a male sample.[61] Despite its male orientation, an impressive body of research is organized around the work of Levinson and his colleagues, and some educational programs and services address their findings specifically. While calling attention to the omission of women from this and other research, Carol Gilligan argues for a new concept of adulthood that integrates the feminine voice into the developmental theory that guides educational and psychological thought.[62]

Traditionally the feminine voice has been ignored in under-graduate educational programs as well as in the research arena. In fact rather that reducing stereotypical differences between the sexes, the college culture seems to preserve them. The resulting "chilly climate" inside and outside the classroom can impede women in their personal, professional, and academic development. Amy Griswold, a junior sociology major at Chapel Hill has "not found the chilly climate at UNC. I have had a number of women professors, and people take women seriously as a group. I am a writer, and there are not as many established writers here who are women. I have become friends with men who are established writers, though."

While the male focus does not exist on all campuses, it occurs often enough to define a pattern. Female students, faculty members, and administrators receive hidden and overt messages from staff and fellow students that they are not on the same level as their male counterparts. These invisible messages often appear as normal components of our culture. As a result, women too often react by doubting their competencies and abilities. Some women are unable to resolve the conflicting aspirations about careers and traditional female responsibilities that can result.[63]

Some specific behaviors contribute to the chilly campus climate because they overlook women as fully vested campus constituents. For example, instructors call on men in class more often than women, and when women speak out in class, their contributions are often minimized. Faculty members and peers interrupt female students more often than male students, and some advisers express surprise when women set demanding career goals for themselves.

Research on these issues led psychologists to ask how women think and learn. Psychologists are interested in instructors who say that many female students are reluctant to argue a point of view in class. Findings on the "phenomenon of silence" suggest that women process information and reach conclusions differently than men. After investigating the question for 10 years, Blythe Clinchy suggests that men have a separate way of knowing[64] which embodies a detachment akin to critical thinking or the scientific method. Women, on the other hand, engage in connected knowing; that is instead of arguing, they are inclined to adopt the other person's point of view and imagine themselves in the other person's situation. Women's silence in the classroom reflects the time it takes to form this mental attachment. Clinchy suggests that separate knowing finds its voice in argument, whereas connected knowing is a narrative voice; therefore women find that sharing stories is more valuable to their learning than arguing different points of view. Beyond the "bland agreement" of the classroom, Clinchy suspects that women are learning in dynamic, collaborative ways and asks college instructors to consider this feminine point of view.[65]

Other differences between female and male college students involve career decisions. In choosing careers, many women value limitations rather than expanding horizons and explore career options in simplified, rational, purposeful, and traditional ways. They consider few alternatives, base career-related decisions on limited information supplied by immediate experiences, select career paths early in life, and continue in unvarying directions. Although men consider the same variables, they prioritize their goals differently, value achieving high career status, and choose different careers. Women often value noncareer-oriented goals and therefore choose careers that are congruent with these goals.[66]

What are the practical implications of these findings? In 1990 Janice Castro, in a special issue of *Time* magazine, looked at the work force of the twenty-first century and concluded that 20 years after a significant number of women had entered the professional ranks, few held positions beyond middle management. Since even the most accomplished professional women become discouraged when top management positions are closed to them, employers report that it easier to hire good women managers than to keep them.[67]

How can this dilemma be addressed at the college level? In a conversation about helping female student leaders better understand their position on college and university campuses, four female student body presidents spoke about their perception of female leadership in traditionally male-dominated situations.[68] One young woman noted that she is caught in a difficult time. She dreams of a still nonexistent equality and recognizes the need to network but fears that doing so carries a negative connotation. Her comments substantiate the findings of Gilligan and Clinchy: Women learn and accomplish differently, so their educational needs are different. Perhaps the connecting, collaborative perspective is just as valid in the classroom and the boardroom as the argumentative, competitive one. If colleges want to prepare the majority of their graduates to achieve their goals, the specific developmental and learning needs of women must be addressed. When this occurs, perhaps the chilly climate will warm to acknowledge the full power of the feminine point of view.

THE BENEFITS OF DIVERSITY

One aim of this book is to highlight for students and their parents, for college and university insiders, and for government and business leaders the vast opportunities that await students in U.S. college and universities. Another aim is to define creative ways of realizing these opportunities. Experiencing the diversity that defines the college student population of the 1990s is one such opportunity. Students who interact with peers from different cultures and experience different points of view are preparing to live in, and become leaders of, the future.

How is meaningful interaction accomplished? Research suggests that involvement is an answer. We support this view and investigate the advantages of involvement in the following chapters. We look at involvement in the classroom, the residence hall, and in uniquely defined activities. We suggest that many kinds of involvement are important: Interacting with faculty, with other students, with programs, and with activities can be a valuable component of college.

5 ◥ How Colleges and Universities Are Organized

There are approximately 3500 colleges and universities in the United States, with a total enrollment over 14 million. Although both colleges and universities are institutions of higher learning, they differ in mission, size, and organization. Colleges are generally smaller and less complex than universities, and most focus on the teaching mission; many award only bachelors degrees. Universities are collections of schools and colleges with a broader mission. They enroll both undergraduate and graduate students who study for bachelors, masters, and doctoral degrees. Some universities are as large as small cities, enrolling more than 40,000 students. Overall, more than half of all colleges and universities are private, but these enroll far fewer students than public institutions. States support public institutions, while private colleges are independent of state government, relying primarily on tuition, endowment or savings, and donations for support.

A NATIONAL VIEW OF HIGHER EDUCATION

In 1973 Clark Kerr developed a classification system for the Carnegie Commission that serves as a useful guide for understanding the U.S. system of higher learning. The Carnegie Commission categories, based on degrees offered, the scope of the mission, and in some cases, budget, size, and enrollment, include all colleges and universities in the United States.[1]

Research universities I and II offer a full range of baccalaureate programs; they are committed to graduate education through the doctoral degree and give high priority to research. The difference between I and II is the amount of federal support they receive and the number of Ph.D. degrees they award each year, with Research Universities I receiving more federal dollars and awarding more Ph.D. degrees.

Doctorate-granting universities I and II offer a full range of baccalaureate programs and graduate education through the doctoral degree. They award fewer Ph.D. degrees annually in fewer academic disciplines than research universities.

Comprehensive universities and colleges I and II offer baccalaureate programs and with few exceptions, graduate education through the masters degree. More than half their baccalaureate degrees are awarded in two or more occupational or professional disciplines, such as engineering or business administration.

Liberal arts colleges I are highly selective* undergraduate colleges that award more than half their baccalaureate degrees in arts and science fields, such as biological sciences, fine arts, foreign languages, literature, mathematics, physical sciences, psychology, social sciences, and interdisciplinary studies.

Liberal arts colleges II are less selective undergraduate colleges that award more than half their degrees in liberal arts fields. This category also includes a group of colleges that award less than half their degrees in liberal arts fields but with fewer than 1500 students, these are too small to be considered comprehensive.

Two-year community, junior, and technical colleges offer certificate or degree programs through the Associate of Arts level, and with few exceptions, these do not offer baccalaureate degrees.

Professional schools and other specialized institutions offer degrees

---

*An index developed by Alexander W. Astin at the University of California at Los Angeles is used to determine the selectivity of liberal arts colleges.

ranging from the bachelor's to the doctorate. At least 50 percent of the degrees awarded by these institutions are in a single specialized field. Specialized institutions include theological seminaries and other institutions offering degrees in religion, medical schools and other health professional schools, law schools not affiliated with other institutions, and schools of art, music, and design.

The number of institutions and enrollment by type of institution is presented in Table 5.1. Since 1976 overall student enrollment has increased from 11 million to 14 million. The U.S. Department of Education predicts that more than 16 million students will enroll in college by the year 2002. This projected growth is due largely to the increase, beginning in 1996, in the traditional-age college student population. The projection forecasts new periods of expansion for many institutions. Because the traditional-age population declined through the early 1990s, most institutions welcome the new challenge of planning for growth.

Although there are more private than public colleges and universities, only 22 percent of all students enroll in private institutions. However, since 1976, the rate of enrollment increase in private 4-year institutions (13 percent) has been greater than that in the public sector (6 percent), and this trend is expected to continue. Private institutions have exhibited remarkable resiliency during the period of decline. In fact during a decade of retrenchment, 484 new colleges (private and public) opened their doors; of

TABLE 5.1. Institutions of Higher Education
and Their Total Enrollment

Type of Institution	Number	Total Enrollment
Public 4-year	595	5,802,877
Public 2-year	972	4,937,663
Private 4-year	1546	2,726,255
Private 2-year	446	243,355
Total	3559	13,710,150

SOURCE: *The Chronicle of Higher Education Almanac* (26 Aug. 1992), 3.

these, 314 were community or technical 2-year colleges, 147 were specialized institutions, 16 were liberal arts colleges, and one was a new doctoral-granting institution. During this time, 167 institutions closed or merged; thus the net gain was 317.[2]

Another interesting trend, "upward drift,"[3] is the tendency for 2-year colleges to become 4-year colleges and for 4-year colleges to become universities. Institutional pride and competition for recognition account for this trend, so that as colleges obtain resources and seek prestige, they aspire to a higher status. Local communities, too, seek status, and they sometimes lobby for state-supported institutions to assume higher profiles. In the process, state budgets experience stress because upgrading means adding programs and services.

Although the number of liberal arts colleges has declined slightly, highly selective liberal arts colleges are more numerous. Some liberal arts colleges have expanded their mission to offer vocational and professional programs in business, engineering, and technology, for example; hence the orientation of many former liberal arts colleges has changed.[4] The strongest liberal arts colleges have made fewer adjustments to their curriculum to stay abreast of the market.

Although the economy has restricted growth, higher learning in the United States forms a healthy, expanding, and competitive network. Our system results from a combination of strong cultural values, market-driven ingenuity, and a dedication to diversity. As long as U.S. colleges and universities continue to achieve both excellence and diversity, our system will remain strong.

HIGHER EDUCATION AT THE STATE LEVEL

As we discussed in Chapter 1, the first colleges in the United States were private. Beginning in the late 1700s, and increasing in the nineteenth and twentieth centuries, the states assumed an important role in financing higher education. The Morrill Act of 1862, for example, allowed each state to set aside land and resources for public education of the citizens of that region. However, before World War II, only a small part of the population attended college; after World War II, the GI Bill provided tuition dollars for thousands of veterans, and by the 1950s, many middle-class citizens earned college degrees.[5]

The period of most rapid growth for state higher education was the 1960s. In addition to the older, well-established institutions, new colleges and universities emerged at this time, giving residents of many states a choice of colleges. During this time, the California system, for example, became a multitiered system unmatched by any state or country in the world. Other states followed, so that today most states fund 2-year colleges, 4-year colleges, regional universities, and flagship universities. In North Carolina, for example, a vast system of community colleges exists along with a 16-unit system of universities. Community and technical colleges, operated by a separate governing body, form the first tier of the system. Regional universities, located in Asheville, Winston-Salem, and Wilmington, for example, form the second tier. Comprehensive universities, such as Appalachian State and East Carolina, are the third tier. These regional universities offer a few graduate programs in addition to their traditionally strong baccalaureate degree programs. Fourth-tier or flagship institutions cap the system, in this case the University of North Carolina (UNC) at Chapel Hill and North Carolina State University (NC State) at Raleigh. This tier arrangement is common in most states, where local colleges prepare students for regional colleges or universities, which prepare students for state universities. In North Carolina, UNC-Chapel Hill offers strong programs in the liberal arts, law, human medicine, and other professional areas; NC State, on the other hand, is most noted for strong programs in engineering, agriculture, textiles, veterinary medicine, and other applied areas. The statewide system in North Carolina avoids duplicating programs where possible.

Statewide systems, though often complex and multilayered, are usually governed by a policy-making board that oversees the activities of the chief academic officer. Such boards and their composition vary greatly as do their ties to the governor of the state. Most academic leaders agree that governing agencies or boards should enjoy reasonable political autonomy; however, states spend a major portion of their funds for education, so the topic remains a key issue in state politics.

The chief academic officer of most statewide systems, the chancellor or president, reports directly to the governing board. The chancellor or president leads a staff of associate chancellors or vice presidents who oversee academic affairs, student affairs, business and finance, and research and development. Other specialists assist with legal affairs, computing and information technology, planning, fund raising, and faculty development.

State systems exercise varying amounts of control over individual campuses. While most major fiscal and academic decisions are made at the state level, once budgetary allocations are made, much is left to the individual campuses. In some cases, a campus-level president or chancellor of the state's flagship institution in concert with faculty governance has more political power than the systemwide chief.

Most private colleges and universities have no governmental or off-campus body to which they are responsible. Here the president, as the chief executive officer is usually called, is responsible to a board comprising individuals outside academe who volunteer their time and expertise for the good of the institution. Because private colleges and universities receive little or no state allotments, they rely on private dollars, or endowments, for survival. Many top private universities and some colleges control vast endowment funds. For example, the Harvard endowment tops $4 billion. Although this amount is exceptional, a number of private institutions have endowments of more than $1 billion. These funds are invested to ensure the futures of private institutions.

ORGANIZATION AT THE INSTITUTIONAL LEVEL

Organizational structure at the college or university level is remarkably similar in the public and private sectors and depends, for the most part, on mission, size, and level of funding. Schools or colleges, organized around academic disciplines or professions, compose universities. For example, a college of engineering faculty is educated in, and committed to, scholarship and teaching in electrical, mechanical, nuclear, and other areas of engineering. These specialties exist within departments. The chief academic officer of a school or college is a dean or director; heads or chairpersons lead departments.

At most universities, the sciences, languages, social and behavioral sciences, mathematics, and the arts are organized as separate departments within a college of arts and sciences or a college of liberal arts. Common professional areas that compose a college include agriculture, business, education, and journalism. At larger universities, colleges or schools of medicine, law, forestry, social work, architecture, pharmacy, and engineering exist as discrete units (see Table 5.2).

The highest ranking administrator at most institutions is the president or chancellor. At public institutions, this individual reports to the statewide chief (also a president or chancellor); at private institutions, the top official is responsible to a board, often called the Board of Trustees or Board of Visitors. Fund raising activities, public relations, athletics, and the general financial and political leadership of the campus occupy the time of most presidents or chancellors. Academic leadership is usually relegated to a provost or vice president for academic affairs who oversees the activities of deans and department heads as well as the library, computer center, office of instructional development or faculty development, and other significant units that support the college's or university's academic mission.

As with most contemporary organizations, specialization in academic roles is increasing. Most large universities have vice presidents of finance and business, research, service, development and alumni relations, legal affairs, computer networking, and student affairs. Subunits within these areas may also be specialized; for example, a vice president for student affairs may oversee admissions and recruitment, residence life, food services, student government, and student social organizations including

TABLE 5.2. Common Units Offering Degree Programs at Comprehensive Universities

School or College	Examples of Department/Program
Agriculture	Animal Science Food Technology
Arts and Sciences	English Mathematics Foreign Languages Natural Sciences Behavioral and Social Sciences
Business	Finance Management
Education	Teacher Education School Administration
Environmental Design	Landscape Design Historic Preservation
Engineering	Electrical Engineering Mechanical Engineering
Home Economics	Textiles Child and Family Development
Journalism	Telecommunications Advertising
Law	Criminal law Civil law
Medicine	Anatomy Physiology
Pharmacy	Administration Pharmacology
Social Work	Social Services Juvenile Corrections
Veterinary Medicine	Large-animal Medicine Pathology

sororities and fraternities. Sponsored research offices deal with grant writing, federal compliance of human subjects and animal care laws, corporate and university research and development partnerships, and patent procedures. Figure 5.1 presents the typical organizational structure in a large public university; private liberal arts colleges have a different configuration (see Figure 5.2), as do land grant universities with numerous public service agencies across the state.

Regardless of structure, the faculty is the backbone of a college or university[6] and by tradition provides strong governance at both large and small, public and private institutions. Academicians transplanted from government or industry generously concede that universities represent the last democracies worth pre-

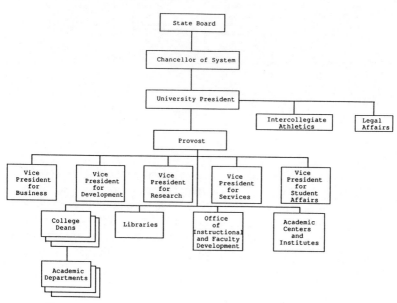

Figure 5.1. Typical Organizational Structure of a Public University.

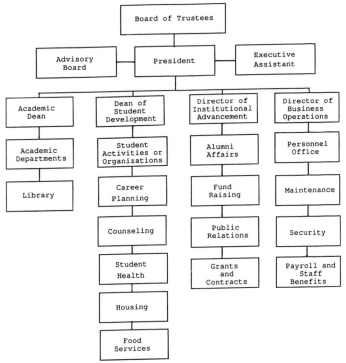

Figure 5.2. Typical Organizational Structure of a Private Liberal Arts College.

serving. Contrary to the governing structures at other levels of U.S. education, faculty governance in higher education remains strong.

In Chapter 6, we look at the people who operate our colleges and universities, examining how faculty members differ from other professionals. We follow typical career paths in academia and discuss major challenges facing the professoriate as higher education prepares to enter a new century.

6 ◣ Academic Careers: A Commitment to Learning

Who is in charge at colleges and universities? What is the faculty really like? Who are the administrators, and how did they arrive where they are? Who are the many staff people behind the scenes? Are these people who teach, conduct research, perform service, and manage administrative affairs quite different from other professionals? If so, how are they unique?

Consider the following scenarios. Dr. Jane Smith is a 26-year-old new Ph.D. beginning her first year as an assistant professor. She loves teaching and being involved with professional activities, but she already knows the pressures that lie ahead. She is one of three new assistant professors in her department, and her productivity in research will have to be outstanding to be recommended for promotion and tenure. While Dr. Smith is enthusiastic and energetic, she faces 5 or 6 crucial years. Her ability to manage her time, adjust to her new colleagues, meet the needs of students, serve effectively on committees, and secure funding for her research could determine whether or not she survives her first academic appointment.

Professor John Mendoza has just turned 45. He was recently promoted to the rank of professor and has tenure. His research record in engineering is laudable, and he is invited all over the United States and the world to give lectures on how computers and robots can perform many vital industrial tasks. All the years of working hard, publishing the results of his research, and guiding his graduate students into good careers are paying off. Professor Mendoza's biggest challenge is to balance these fine opportunities with his responsibilities to his wife, children, and aging parents.

Dorothy Chin is a staff member in student affairs. Although she does not hold a faculty appointment, she is one of several staff members at her college who play important supporting roles. Ms. Chin conducts orientation sessions for new students and coordinates residence life for students living on campus. Ms. Chin loves her work and enjoys supporting her college, but because she is not a faculty member, she wonders if she and her coworkers are fully appreciated and compensated fairly for the roles they play.

Professor Joe Hancock, a distinguished researcher and teacher, is 2 years from retirement at his university. Last year he lost his wife of 45 years; now he is withdrawn, inactive, and mildly depressed. Prior to his wife's death, he was a busy person, often accused of being a workaholic. Professor Hancock faces a period of readjustment in preparing for retirement. He needs help from his friends and his university in making this transition.

Susan Jacobson is president of a midsized public college. She was the first woman president in her state system. Located in a rapidly growing suburban area, her college is thriving. President Jacobson holds all the necessary degrees and has progressed by serving as assistant professor, associate professor, professor, and department head at a large research university. She became dean of the College of Business at a regional university before assuming her presidency.

For Dr. Jacobson, balancing the many roles of a college administrator is her on-going challenge. She must keep her faculty satisfied and spend time with various student groups, exemplifying the pledge of her college to address the unique needs of all students. She must also work with alumni and business leaders in the community and be aware of external funding opportunities. If her college is to move forward, it must gain a winning edge through a vigorous development campaign. Besides her professional duties, she has two college-age children and a husband. Dr. Jacobson has to be a skilled juggler, keeping a few dozen balls in the air at all times.

While these scenarios are fictitious, they provide a realistic glimpse into the lives of people who run colleges and universities. A closer look at faculty members and their career paths reveals certain defining characteristics.

DEFINING THE FACULTY

After analyzing the responses of more than 35,000 faculty members from 392 colleges and universities who answered questions about such topics as teaching, research, values, political orientation, and their personal lives, researchers report that faculty members across the country are satisfied with their careers, yet they feel conflict between their roles as teachers and researchers, and they say that their students are underprepared for college. Today 91 percent of all faculty members are white, 71 percent are male, and 80 percent are married. Although 90 percent name teaching as their principal activity, 28 percent report that research is their primary interest, and 13 percent are authors who have had at least five articles published in scholarly journals in the last 2 years. As to political orientation, 37 percent describe themselves as liberal; 5 percent, far left; 40 percent, moderate; and 18 percent, conservative. About two-thirds hold tenure and are satisfied or very satisfied with their jobs.

Although almost 60 percent of all faculty members view their research activities as very important, more than three-fourths believe that promoting the intellectual development of students is a high priority at their institution. Among other high-priority issues are helping students examine their personal values (47 percent), increasing the representation of minorities among students and faculty (47 percent), and developing a sense of community on campus (41 percent). Only 33 percent believe that it is easy for students to see faculty outside office hours. A mere 10 percent think good teaching is rewarded on campus.

When we investigate differences among faculty members at research universities, 4-year colleges, and 2-year institutions, other interesting trends emerge. While research is the primary interest of 28 percent of all faculty members, about half of all university faculty list research as their primary interest. Conversely less than one-fourth of all 4-year college faculty and about 5 percent of all community college professors engage in research. At these institutions, teaching is the primary responsibility, and 78 percent of all community college instructors teach more than 12 class hours a week. In the classroom, fewer differences exist: Faculty members at all types of institutions favor class discussion as a teaching method, with extensive lecturing a close second. (For a detailed discussion of teaching methods, see Chapter 7).

These statistics highlight important differences and similarities among today's professoriate. As we examine their career paths, we see that regardless of institutional type or the emphasis they eventually give to teaching and research, most faculty members prepare for their profession in comparable ways.

ENTERING THE PROFESSORIATE

Most future faculty members begin preparing for their careers by earning the masters degree, the minimum education level for college or university instructors. The doctoral degree is a standard credential, although exceptions exist in such fields as landscape design and the visual and performing arts, where a master's degree can be the terminal credential. In medicine, science, mathematics, and engineering, the doctorate is the required credential for those who wish to teach.[1]

The time required to complete the necessary degrees varies across disciplines and professional areas. Medicine, engineering, and some sciences often require postdoctoral work, such as internships, residencies, cooperative work arrangements, or fellowships before graduates can compete effectively for the best jobs in their fields. In business, social work, law, and education, it is common, even desirable, for teachers to have been practitioners before entering academe.[2] In fact in some states, instructors in teacher education programs must be certified as public school teachers and teach a minimum number of years before they can teach in a school or department of education.

Blending practical work experience with a teaching career offers many benefits to faculty members, students, and institutions. Obviously business experience makes the management professor better able to relate classroom theory to real-world practice. In other fields, such as physics, it is important for scholars to complete the Ph.D. degree and begin their research while they are attuned to the latest advances in their field. In fact young scholars often make major discoveries in mathematics, chemistry, and physics. In law, political science, and the humanities, significant contributions most often come from older scholars who have synthesized important ideas and theories over time.[3]

MAJOR RESPONSIBILITIES OF TODAY'S FACULTY

At one time, college faculty served primarily as teachers but also spent considerable time advising students, and some, with their family, even lived in student residence areas. While teaching remains a central function in some colleges today, nonteaching responsibilities may be more important at other institutions. Generally in addition to teaching, most faculty members are expected to be scholars. This involves conducting research, delivering papers at professional meetings, and writing articles or books for publication. At some institutions, the faculty must subsidize research with external grants and contracts, and promotion and tenure decisions can rest on the success of this enterprise.

In addition to teaching and research, most faculty members must also contribute to professional and institutional service activities by serving on national boards and participating in professional organizations. Numerous institutional committees also require faculty service; the Curriculum Committee, Grievance Committee, Promotion Committee, and Faculty Senate represent a few examples of opportunities for service in colleges and universities.

At land grant universities, such as the University of Wisconsin, the University of Nebraska, the University of Florida, and Texas A & M, service is one of three equally important missions of the institution.[4] Here outreach programs serve the state and service-oriented faculty members help communities become more responsive to citizens' needs, contribute to the development of small businesses, investigate new agricultural methods, or act as consultants to state government. Rather than instructing in the classroom, these faculty members further the development of state and local interests.

STAGES OF CAREER DEVELOPMENT

We have used the term professor to describe any member of the college faculty; however at most institutions, four or five levels, or ranks, exist within the professoriate, with professor being the most senior. During their professional lives, most faculty members proceed through the ranks and predictable stages of development.

After academicians complete the undergraduate and early graduate experience stage, they enter the basic training stage,[5] which usually begins with the doctoral degree research and dissertation. Afterward many graduates accept postdoctoral fellowships, internships, or other temporary assignments to obtain further training in their profession. Then comes the first regular assignment, often the first tenure-track teaching position; at this stage most faculty members have 6–7 years to become associate professors and receive tenure.[6] This "up or out" rule means that assistant professors are on probation during the first few years of employment.

When faculty members receive tenure, the probationary period is over, since in academe, tenure means job security. That is a faculty member with tenure enjoys the commitment of continued employment, barring exceptional circumstances.[7] In the early 1990s, exceptional circumstances were less exceptional than before, since financial crises led some colleges and universities to release tenured faculty whose courses or research had to be discontinued.

Standards for promotion and tenure vary among institutions. At most research universities assistant professors undergo considerable scrutiny before they become tenured associate professors. During the promotion and tenure process, departmental members review a candidate's work at the end of each academic year; in many cases, all tenured members of the department perform a periodic review. At promotion time, a candidate must assemble a comprehensive dossier containing evidence of research achievement, teaching excellence, and other scholarly activities for various review committees. The review process begins at the department level, where a candidate must obtain a majority affirmative vote from tenured peers. If the candidate is successful, the process continues at the division, school, or college level, where a five- to eight-person committee reviews the dossier and supporting letters and then votes. After this point, a universitywide committee checks for consistency and uniformity of standards, then again, votes on the candidate. The peer review process of promotion and tenure is one of the richest traditions of academe. Although deans, vice presidents, and presidents may have the ultimate authority in recommending promotion and tenure to governing boards, historically it is the faculty who set and enforce standards for performance at leading institutions. Of course exceptions exist: Promotion and tenure at some institutions depend on certain administrators deciding "when the time is right."[8]

If promotion and tenure are a rigorous process, assistant professors experience significant stress before the decision is made. One of the most ardent debates on campus concerns teaching versus research as a requirement for promotion and tenure. For the past two or three decades, publications and research grants have carried more weight than favorable students reviews about an instructor's classroom performance. Now some academic leaders are debating the meaning of effective scholarship, which may define a new era for U.S. higher education.

Once faculty members become tenured associate professors, they enter another stage in their careers. As permanent members of the guild, they can relax, consider what they are doing, and readjust career goals and objectives. Most associate professors continue to focus on their research agenda and examine where they want to make their mark. Associate professors also feel more comfortable teaching and take a larger part in deciding the future of their profession and of their institution. In *Passages: Predictable Crises of Adult Life*,[9] Gail Sheehy refers to this period as "rooting and extending" and to the midthirties to midforties as the "deadline decade." Academics experience midlife as both a time of readjustment and a time of challenge.

Most associate professors strive to become professors (or in slang terminology, "full professors") within 4–7 years of receiving tenure. At research universities with rigorous promotion systems, professors are expected to become nationally, even internationally, recognized scholars in their fields. The most talented and thoughtful manage this while finding a balance between teaching and research and contributing to the development of their younger colleagues. Not all associate professors advance to professor. The terms "terminal associate professor" or "delayed promotion" describe the faculty member who becomes less active in research or moves at midcareer into an administrative position.

As professors most faculty members enter a stage of full maturity. Most succeed in sustaining an interest in their work, or they enter a period of resignation. Some focus on continued advancement, for although professor is normally the highest faculty rank, other opportunities exist: department head, dean, vice president, or even president. Some faculty members become research professors, university professors, or move into special endowed chairs, such as the Kennedy Professor of Political Science or the Sandra Day O'Connor Professor of Law. Donors fund such chaired professorships, which often carry salary enhancements and other benefits. These professorships are important to universities because they attract and retain prestigious faculty with salaries that tuition, endowment, and state allocations could not support.

WHAT MAKES FACULTY DIFFERENT

College professors are an interesting lot. They are intelligent and among the best educated members of our society. Of course many stereotypes abound, including the one about the professor who met a colleague at noon, spoke with the friend, then asked, "What way was I headed when we met?" When the friend pointed out the direction, the professor replied, "Good, that means I've had lunch."

Because of their diversity, even eccentricity, faculty members often fascinate outsiders. What sets apart this group from other professionals? First college faculty value autonomy.[10] They prefer to pursue ideas; they are self-guided and intrinsically motivated. Second college professors enjoy learning and prefer intellectual challenge to routine agendas.

Despite the relaxed image some faculty members project, professors are among the hardest working of all professionals, averaging close to 50 hours of work per week.[11] Professors desire and require mental stimulation, and many are among the most creative members of society. Despite increasingly unfavorable working conditions, most professors like their work and would not choose to change if given the opportunity. Although most faculty members are self-directed and autonomous, they appreciate support from colleagues and families, and they enjoy interacting with students. Professors are basically altruistic; in fact one of the enduring characteristics of outstanding teachers at all levels is a strong motivation to help others and contribute something of value to society. The most stimulating teachers believe in the

After two decades, I remain cognizant of the awesome responsibility I have accepted as my life's personal challenge and greatest privilege: being a teacher. Fully aware of my commitment to society, I approach my daily work knowing that the world is a precarious place for youngsters who are in the process of becoming—becoming the best they can be given the circumstances of their lives.

It is my belief that one of the most critical variables affecting achievement is the quality of the interpersonal relationship between teachers and learners. Intellectual growth is dependent upon the vibrancy of opportunities for sharing ideas and attitudes. Empowering students to feel capable and productive, keeping their curiosity alive, and encouraging dialogue are some of the keys I rely on to open the doors to their success.

Focusing on our "world in transition" on the eve of the 21st century, there are many challenges society must face in order to improve the quality of life. At this historic moment, teaching and relating to students have become more important than ever as students increasingly seek wisdom and guidance: to learn from the past, understand the present, and envision the future. With trust and mutual respect, students can venture forth with confidence in search of their futures and a brighter tomorrow for all with whom we share our global village.

Sheryl L. Santos, professor, Arizona State University

human potential and are idealistic enough to try to make a difference in the life of another person.[12]

Freedom of thought and deed is another long-held academic tradition. While most institutions are rather conservative, faculty members in the arts and sciences tend to be liberal individuals.[13] Over the years scientists, humanists, and other scholars have been the first to speak out on important issues. Academicians abhor rhetoric, and most are skilled at critical analysis; after all a doctoral candidate must learn to evaluate both process and product, hopefully in positive and constructive ways.

Finally most faculty members are less materialistic than other people: Professors know they will never be rich and they knew this before entering academic life (see Table 6.1 for average salaries of professors in various fields). Some members of the academy can be quite entrepreneurial, and most value recognition. The climb to the top of their field motivates them more than money. In social circles college people seldom talk about their investments, clothes, or cars. Although some academicians speak tiringly, even inces-

TABLE 6.1. Average Faculty Salaries in Selected Fields at Public and Private Institutions (1991–1992)[a]

Field	Public	Private
Accounting	$50,714	$42,009
Anthropology	43,665	43,590
Business and management	50,443	51,647
Chemistry	45,073	43,910
Communications	38,084	35,380
Computer and information science	47,345	43,504
Economics	47,491	48,905
Education	41,207	37,986
Engineering	50,158	59,027
Foreign languages	38,889	38,412
History	43,619	41,724
Life sciences	43,364	41,266
Mathematics	41,163	41,184
Nursing	36,029	33,489
Philosophy and religion	43,281	39,640
Physics	47,095	48,466
Political science	43,009	42,961
Psychology	44,147	41,238
Sociology	42,638	39,805
Teacher education, general programs	40,525	34,758
Visual and performing arts	38,491	37,006

SOURCE: College and University Personnel Association, Washington, DC.

[a]Data are based on reports from 290 public institutions that are members of the American Association of State Colleges and Universities and from 517 private colleges and universities.

santly, about their work, ideas, not the routine happenings of the day, tend to dominate their conversation.[14]

SUPPORT STAFF

Though professors and administrators are visible, the modern college or university depends on a multitude of nonfaculty personnel for important support. From the day students enter college until they become alumni, a cadre of student affairs personnel serve their extracurricular, residence life, and career-planning needs. Many of these nonfaculty personnel are specialists with doctoral degrees, and the same is true for the staff of libraries, computer centers, research offices, and continuing education centers.

Staff, unlike faculty, does not work in an "up or out" system of promotion and tenure. Although staff members do not experience the same "publish or perish" pressures of faculty, they are also not rewarded with promotion and tenure. While faculty members can take advantage of today's market-driven society by accepting the offer of the highest bidder, staff members have less flexibility. Some are classified personnel with fixed salaries based on an institutionwide compensation schedule. Currently many institutions are working to improve the status and reward of these vital contributors.

CHALLENGES FACING FACULTY AND ADMINISTRATORS

At one time, higher education insiders needed to read only *The Chronicle of Higher Education* to learn of the many issues facing faculty and administrators on U.S. campuses. Today we find such issues discussed in the popular press, so that many outsiders are well-versed on external pressures stemming from national reviews of U.S. education, public calls for accountability and assessment, the economic crisis, and the political arena. Internal pressures are no less troubling to academics: Factions debate promotion and tenure policy; staff members actively seek the kind of respect faculty enjoy; and questions about diversity, equity, and gender bias engage students in debates ranging from lively to heated. As many fields face faculty shortages in a market-driven society, salary compression will fuel increasing competition among major institutions for star faculty.

Expected Faculty Shortages

Projections suggest that substantial shortages of faculty with doctorates will begin in the mid-1990s and continue through 2010. Three factors are responsible for these shortages. First new faculty must replace the many professors who are reaching retirement age. Second although the number of doctorates granted in the United States remains somewhat constant, nonacademic careers for Ph.D.s are becoming quite numerous and attractive. Also more recipients of doctoral degrees are foreign residents who may return to their home countries after graduation, so universities will have a smaller number of Ph.D.s from which to choose. And third in 1996, the number of college students is expected to increase and continue to do so at least through 2002. This new projection, based on 1990 census data, infers that the academy will need more instructors.[15]

Teaching versus Research

One of today's most intense debates concerns balancing the priorities of teaching and research. In Chapter 2, we discussed Boyer's study of how colleges and universities value the work of faculty members. In *Scholarship Reconsidered*, Boyer proposes that instead of placing undue value on research as traditionally defined, institutions should expand their reward systems to consider the contributions of four distinct types of scholarship: discovery, integration, application, and teaching. Soon after Boyer's

There are a number of reasons why it will be difficult to bring change to the balance of priorities in the university. First, the university is not solely in control. Faculty get their rewards from two communities, the local university community and the professional community, and it is in their standing in this external community that the university itself judges faculty merit. Any university that elects to become independent of it risks a loss of competitive advantage in the academic marketplace. Who will take the first step?

Second, resources are limited, and most universities cannot alleviate the conflict between research and other aspects of scholarship by providing more faculty to share the load. Because we depend on sponsored research funding, universities themselves are caught in a vicious research and publication spiral that is driven by both the need for money and the dominant value system of academe. Where does cause leave off and effect begin?

Third, we want the faculty to be both productive and excellent, and it is difficult to measure the comparable worth of the very different activities that lead to productivity and to excellence. Human societies, including academics, often tend to be exclusive, hierarchical, and elite rather than inclusive and open. It is difficult for any institution to establish its own standard of excellence when the basis for it is not recognized by the larger academic community.

Fourth, there is the practical matter of the academic marketplace. Given the forthcoming Ph.D. shortage, the most promising scholars are apt to go to those institutions that offer them the greatest opportunity, not for teaching, but for research.

Finally, there is the problem of the education of the future professoriate. If not taught to resent teaching and disdain practical application, Ph.D. graduates are certainly not often taught how to teach or to value teaching positively. So prevailing professional priorities continue to prevail, and any individual who attempts to march to a different drummer does so at considerable personal and professional costs.

Having noted these difficulties, let me note also that some conditions work in favor of redressing the imbalance. Most faculty like to teach, have an intrinsically broad view of what comprises scholarship and intellectual creativity, and wish to see the imbalance redressed. Moreover, public opinion, the tuition rebellion, and the fact that students can and will "vote with their feet" implies that something must be done to restore education to a central position in the landscape of scholarship.

Billy E. Frye, provost, Emory University from his response to Boyer's *Scholarship Reconsidered*, at the Speech Communication Conference, Atlanta (2 Nov. 1991)

book appeared, the administration of The University of Georgia, in a bold move that signaled a new validation of the faculty's teaching role, organized a symposium to address the issues Boyer raised. At a 2-day retreat, a diverse group of faculty came together to discuss teaching and research. At that time, Professor Jack Schuster of the Claremont Graduate School raised several critical questions—how do teaching and research complement each other? How do they compete? Is research a university's central mission? If so, should it be? What about teaching? The majority of the faculty members present believed that university professors should be scholars, not merely researchers; they should both teach and conduct research.

Today faculty members and administrators across the country are examining reward systems and reconfiguring academic priorities. Many academicians agree that the concept of scholarship, as Boyer posits it, should be broadened, so that organizing and communicating knowledge are valued as much as discovery or traditional research. Learning should be the prime activity of a university. Although such discussions are far from reaching points of closure, faculty are reflecting on their profession and clarifying their values and goals.

The Need for Faculty Renewal

Any profession, particularly one that relies on human capital, must allow for such reflection, if not, "burnout" or "rustout" can occur. In more positive terms, renewal should be an integral, ongoing part of any human enterprise, and higher education is no exception. To be sure, high-quality teaching, research, and service require substantial amounts of emotional and physical energy. Considering the stresses under which professionals work and their decreased mobility due to economic constraints, many academicians may have to renew their outlooks on professional and personal issues.[16]

Howard Bowen, former president of the University of Illinois, and Jack Schuster[17] sounded an alarm in 1985 when they announced that the quality of the academic work place is deteriorating. According to Bowen and Schuster, frustration, low morale, detachment, and poor working conditions contribute to decline in the profession.[18] Faculty exist in crowded offices, stretch inadequate travel and library budgets, conduct research with outmoded equipment, and have little clerical support. As campus values (and criteria for rewards) change, faculty members hired only to be effective teachers find that promotion and tenure depend on scholarly productivity. The same faculty members are also expected to revitalize the undergraduate curriculum, instruct poorly prepared students, and answer to those who chastise them for permitting academic standards to slide. The expectation that faculty can solve current problems in higher education with the limited available resources creates uncertainty and encourages withdrawal of the faculty.[19]

External pressures affect the faculty also. Pressure to placate students and escalating political demands for public accountability undermine the faculty's ability to control its agenda or its destiny. Consequently, a significant number of faculty members experiences problems with job satisfaction and professional productivity.[20]

To compound the problem, faculty salaries have decreased over the past decade and a half. Though there was a modest recovery during the 1980s (averaging 1.9 percent per year above inflation), faculty members on the average lost about 8 percent of their earning power from 1971 to 1991 measured in real 1991 dollars (see Table 6.2 for recent salary gains).[21] This record compares

TABLE 6.2. Average Faculty Salaries By Rank (1991–1992)

	Public		Private	
Rank	Salary	Increase (%)	Salary	Increase (%)
Professor	$57,370	2.8	$66,060	4.6
Associate professor	43,420	2.8	45,570	4.7
Assistant professor	36,330	3.2	37,820	4.8
Instructor	27,180	3.6	28,470	4.6

SOURCE: American Association of University Professors.

unfavorably with every other major occupational group in the nonagricultural sector over the same span of time. However, academicians who wish to build new careers cannot find more desirable opportunities in their field, because the robust academic labor market in the 1950s and 1960s has become a strong buyer's market that is likely to persist well into the 1990s.

Despite a deteriorating work environment, most faculty members exhibit unwavering dedication to their calling. Nevertheless we must look for more effective ways of encouraging faculty commitment and renewing their vigor.[22]

A NEW MESSAGE

While conditions sound grim, a double-barreled force is addressing at least some of these challenges. First many highly respected college and university presidents recognize the seriousness of the situation and have begun speaking out on issues related to teaching and faculty development. Second offices responsible for instructional improvement and faculty development are receiving visible support.[23]

In the 1970s, the first generation of instructional and faculty development offices emerged, but many closed by the end of the decade because their funds—"soft money" from external funding agencies for faculty retrenchment and the new-found notion that support services may be as beneficial for faculty as they are for students—were withdrawn.

Since the mid-1980s, a second generation of offices has joined the few, namely, those at Syracuse University and the University of Nebraska at Lincoln, that have operated for over two decades. Successful second-generation endeavors now exist at the University of Washington, the University of Texas, Penn State, Texas A & M, the University of Tennessee, Georgia Tech, the University of Oklahoma, UCLA, and The University of Georgia. At many smaller institutions, where teaching has always been taken seriously, activities of these kinds are the direct responsibility of the president, academic vice president, or dean of the faculty. Thus teaching and support services for faculty now receive main-line attention.

In Chapter 7 we examine how faculty teach and what some institutions are doing to improve instruction. In many colleges and universities special services enhance the feeling of community and maintain a sense of vitality among faculty.

7 ◥ How Professors Teach

Consider this portrayal of Professor Woodrow Wilson as a faculty member at Princeton University during the early years of the twentieth century[1]:

> Professor Wilson habitually stood during his lectures. Speaking from a mere skeleton of notes, he hammered in his teachings with an up-and-down, full-armed gesture. Thus he was a perpendicular lecturer, his talking nose and his oscillating Adam's Apple moving up and down with speech, along with his pump-handle gestures. He gestured as if operating the handle of a spray pump. He was there to spray students with a shower of knowledge, his superior mind acting downward upon the mass—a Scotch Covenanter bent upon describing how man acts politically, hammering information into reluctant minds. He was essentially the lecturer rather than the teacher.

Dr. C. Roland Christensen, a university professor at Harvard, teaches by the case method[2]: Instead of delivering lectures, he assigns cases based on situations that involve important concepts in business administration. Dr. Christensen requires students to prepare diligently for class and demonstrate their understanding of what they have read.

In Dr. Christensen's classes, students sit in assigned seats, and he quickly learns every student's name. Timid students are interspersed with more aggressive students, and class leaders occupy "power positions" throughout the room. Dr. Christensen plays the role of questioner, listener, discussion moderator, and evaluator. A large portion of a student's grade is based on Dr. Christensen's evaluation of the quality of thinking displayed in discussions. Dr. Christensen is a warm, sensitive person who exudes empathy and understanding. His personality engages both the minds and hearts of students and colleagues as he goes about his teaching in a way quite different from traditional approaches.

From this account, we see that the role of the college professor has changed. Earlier professors were fountains of knowledge who spent most of their time disseminating knowledge to students. In fact before the printing press was invented, the professor often had the only copy of the textbook; thus students made copious notes so that they, too, would have knowledge. After books became available, college professors still emphasized the important segments of each chapter and checked to see that students had completed their reading assignments. As late as 1950, instructors held weekly class recitations during which they embarrassed students who could not recount the day's lesson.

While some college classrooms still resemble those of a century or more ago, many changes are evident, as today's instructor draws from resources that were not available a few years ago. For example an instructor can turn on a microcomputer and projection system and present video, sound, graphics, or other forms of information directly to one or more classrooms, with printed materials reinforcing such multimedia presentations. Students follow up by attending discussion sessions or engaging in individualized learning activities on their own or in computerized learning centers. In short, modern instructors and students work together to meet course objectives by using a variety of tools and methods.

METHODS OF REACHING STUDENTS

Three broad categories define the teaching processes most used: teacher-centered methods, interactive methods, and individualized methods. In practice, these methods overlap as dynamic instructors engage students in learning on a daily basis. Recent research confirms the importance of the teaching method and highlights the critical role faculty plays in student learning. Method, it seems, is more important than content, suggesting that faculty members should think carefully not only about what they teach, but how they teach.[3]

Teacher-Centered Methods

The lecture or modified lecture is the most common method of college teaching today. With this method, the teacher or lecturer is the center of attention, and information flows from the instructor to the student. Students sometimes jokingly charge that during a lecture, information passes from the instructor's notebook to the student's notebook without going through either head. While it is easy to criticize the lecture method, it remains an efficient and comfortable way for many instructors to teach and for many students to learn.

Lectures can be completely teacher oriented, with little or no involvement from students, as in classes of 300, 500, or 1000 students, where most instructors find it difficult to lead a discussion or answer students' questions. An instructor can enhance a lecture with microphones; special lighting; electronic chalkboards; overhead, slide, or film projectors; or videotape players. New microcomputers and liquid crystal display (LCD) projectors allow instructors to present anything that is available on videotape, laser disk, computer software, or cable television. In effect today's lecturer can bring the outside world into the classroom.

Unlike other methods of instruction, with a teacher-centered approach, information flows from the instructor to the students.

Content → Teacher → Students

In a formal lecture, information flow is usually one-way only, while in a less formal setting, a small amount of information may flow back to the instructor from the students. Many highly skilled instructors of large classes use questions to motivate, emphasize, summarize, or provide feedback to students.

Regardless of how a professor uses the teacher-centered approach, students prefer instructors who are friendly and open with students; communicate the day's objectives at the beginning of class; speak clearly and loudly; proceed in a well-organized, timely manner; use easy-to-read visual materials; demonstrate their points with large objects; distribute well-constructed materials; establish eye contact and change positions occasionally; and use humor in the classroom. In other words, students prefer to be involved in the learning process, and they appreciate methods that engage their attention.

Interactive Methods

Lecture classes focus on the teacher; in contrast interactive teaching methods focus on students. The following diagram depicts an interactive classroom session.

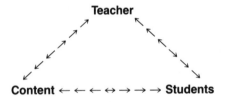

The interactive method offers several advantages. First student involvement is enhanced, taking advantage of research showing that students learn more when they actively participate in the learning process and assume responsibility for learning.[4] Classroom interaction also stimulates and motivates students. Rigorous discussion on topics of current interest, for example, brings the subject alive and provides opportunities for growth. While students may sit passively in a lecture class, they are forced to assume active roles in a discussion.

Numerous techniques facilitate classroom interaction, such as instructors who ask questions and allow students to respond. Instructors who allow students to react to other students' comments open the door to further interaction; in fact highly skilled instructors often slip into the background to further student interchange.[5]

Many other techniques encourage specific forms of interaction. Small groups of students can probe an issue at length through brainstorming, a problem-solving technique that invites uninhibited ideas in a creative and nonjudgmental environment. Buzz groups offer similar advantages for medium-to-large-sized classes. Debate, a formal, structured form of interaction, also fosters student participation.

Some instructors use games to introduce students to the concept of role playing and to stimulate cooperative learning (that is, students learning as a team). In role playing, another small-group method, participants discuss a topic surrounded by a larger circle of listeners. When the roles are reversed, the listeners observe and reflect.

Good teachers assist discovery. They introduce students to questions and then guide them through a series of investigations, so that the excitement of real-life problem solving enters the classroom. Problem-solving techniques include colloquia, symposia, forums, panel discussions, seminars, and workshops. With these formats, groups come together with experts to learn about new ideas or discuss new solutions to problems. The hallmarks of these methods are high levels of student participation.

Another problem-solving technique involves accessing information. In the real world, people have to know where to obtain information and how to condense it. Students who learn how to locate pertinent material, analyze and summarize data, then draw meaningful conclusions will be prepared for the demands of the work place.

The case method has proven effective for learning business concepts and for building the skills necessary to succeed in a business environment. Every night students have two to three cases, each of which requires several hours of preparation. A case describes a business situation tailored to the subject of the class and raises issues for the student to analyze. Most students belong to a study group of three to four students with diverse backgrounds. If students have a weak background in a particular subject the other students can help them get up to speed on the concepts. In addition, the study group is a very low risk environment in which to test ideas and debate key case issues.

The professor calls on one student to "open" the case. The professor then calls on students to enter the discussion, building on the comments of the other students. Oftentimes, students will have to defend their point of view to the professor or to another student, which helps the students develop their abilities to think quickly and speak confidently.

In the case method, the professor acts as a discussion facilitator, guiding the discussion through questions. The diversity of students in the classroom, in terms of nationality, educational background, and work experience, create the rich and challenging learning environment.

Elizabeth Anderson, graduate student, Harvard University

Individualized Methods

A third teaching method, the most student-centered approach, is individualized instruction, where students become directly involved with the material to be learned and move at their own pace. Personal computers enhance individualized instruction, so that instead of reading a book or going through a series of guided activities, students interact with the course material. For example, through computer-assisted instruction (CAI) veterinary medicine students can see a diseased animal and diagnose the disease through a series of branching exercises. Individualized instruction not only allows students to proceed at their own pace, it allows them to develop problem-solving skills as they learn.

Individualized instruction is not necessarily a solitary undertaking. In many engineering schools, for example, students complete projects cooperatively. When working in groups, they divide assignments into small tasks, with individuals taking responsibility for different segments. Later they put the pieces together, and a new entity emerges from the individual efforts. The mathematics department at the University of California at Berkeley has developed a highly successful individualized program that assists students from diverse cultural backgrounds learn mathematics.[6] Helping students learn in ways that match their backgrounds, needs, and preferred style of learning has proven to be a relevant teaching method.

Distance learning is another learning method. This new form of individualized learning delivers instruction from the point of origin to students at a different location, for example, a dormitory room or a home. Through distance-learning techniques, the University of the Mind and the British Open University offer complete degree programs to students who need never leave home.

Still other teaching methods give students opportunities to learn outside the classroom and away from the campus. For example many majors now require students to complete internships or practica for on-the-job experience. Such programs are often preceded by field trips for direct observation or hands-on learning. Current research on involvement confirms that students learn and retain more when they are involved. Thus involving students in academic pursuits is a recommended practice for all instructors, regardless of the methods they employ.

PRINCIPLES OF GOOD PRACTICE

In 1986 the American Association for Higher Education (AAHE), the Education Commission of the States (ECS), and the Johnson Foundation initiated a project that resulted in specific recommendations for undergraduate instructors.[7] Since the recommendations appeared in 1987, more than 100,000 people from the United States, Canada, and the United Kingdom have received copies of the "Seven Principles for Good Practice in Undergraduate Education." The first principle encourages student–faculty contact. Researchers know that frequent interaction between faculty and students in and out of the classroom motivates students to become involved. Faculty concern enhances students' intellectual commitment and encourages them to think about their own values and future plans (see Chapter 9 for more discussion of student–faculty contact).

Since team effort is more effective in learning than solo attempts, the second principle encourages students to cooperate with one another. Working with others enhances involvement, and sharing ideas and responding to the reactions of others improve thinking and deepens understanding.

The third principle of good practice encourages active learning. Learning is not a spectator sport; sitting in classes listening to teachers, memorizing prepackaged assignments, and spitting out answers are not the most effective ways of acquiring knowledge. Students need to discuss what they are learning, write about it, relate it to past experiences, and apply it to their daily lives. They must make what they learn part of themselves.

Being aware of what they know and do not know focuses student; thus the fourth principle is to give prompt feedback to students on performance. Once students have assessed their current knowledge and competence, they need frequent opportunities to perform and suggestions for improvement.

The fifth principle emphasizes actual time devoted to a task. Allocating time wisely results in effective learning for students and effective teaching for faculty. One of the most important things any college student can learn is how to manage time wisely and how to minimize behaviors that result in wasting time.

Communicating high expectations is the sixth principle of good practice. High expectations are important for everyone, since they become a self-fulfilling prophecy.

The last principle concerns respect for diverse talents and ways of learning. People bring different talents and styles of learning to college. Brilliant students in the seminar room may be all thumbs in the lab or art studio. Students skilled at hands-on application may not do well with theory. Once students have discovered their own particular talent and way of learning, instructors can encourage them to grow by learning in ways that do not come easily. In 1986 when this principle was first established, the college student population was less diverse than it is today. Today's reality makes respect for diverse talents and needs more important than ever before.

PROGRAMS TO ENCOURAGE BETTER TEACHING

The typical college professor is a product of over 20 years of formal education. Most earn the baccalaureate degree, the master's degree, and the doctorate. In mathematics, medicine, and the sciences, graduate students may bypass the master's degree and go directly to the doctoral level. In a few areas, such as environmental design and some of the performing arts, the terminal credential is the master's degree. Regardless of degree, the typical college professor is not taught how to teach; fortunately research gives clues about effective teaching techniques, and many professors are interested in mastering them.

Across the country, programs for instructional or faculty development help faculty develop skills, gain access to instructional resources, and foster a supportive climate for teaching. Research on stages of personal and career development reveals faculty needs that emerge at predictable times during an academic career; for example new instructors benefit from orientation programs, and instructional assistance. The University of Texas offers a week-long seminar for incoming faculty that discusses how to design a new course and lead discussions and how to construct tests. Programs at other universities deal not only with teaching topics but also introduce new faculty to the history, culture, and

During the 1970s and 1980s, changes in the backgrounds and preparations of students, in the development of life-style and employment patterns, in high school curricula and instructional methods, in college and university priorities, and in demands on faculty time created an enormous gap between faculty instruction and student learning. The problems that resulted were little recognized then and are only beginning to be addressed now. Fifty percent or more of our students either drop out or flunk out—most after the freshman year.

These are some of the reasons why there is a new agenda for reforms in higher education, an agenda that is based on an increased—and expanding—awareness of what truly works in the classroom. It has influenced policy and practice at campuses nationwide and has begun to alter the look and feel of the freshman classroom. Some high points of the new agenda include bridging the gap between high school and college, assisting faculty in understanding how students learn, training teaching assistants, promoting the seven "principles of good practice," and assessing student learning.

These few examples force us all to realize that we must respond to the challenge that today's undergraduates present to us, that effective teaching is far more complex, difficult, and demanding than usually acknowledged by the public or even within higher education.

Diane W. Strommer, dean of University College and Special Academics Programs, University of Rhode Island and coauthor with Bette L. Erickson of *Teaching College Freshmen*

resources of the institution. At the University of Kentucky, the chancellor meets with new faculty at the end of their first year to address needs for change in campus practices.[8] Some colleges and universities arrange for new faculty members to carry lighter working loads the first semester so they can spend time planning their teaching and research assignments.

Some institutions make grant funds available to faculty to support scholarship, attending professional meetings, or visiting other institutions to promote professional growth. To qualify for support, faculty members submit proposals for review by other faculty and administration. Committee recommendations for funding then go to an academic or research vice president for final approval. Instructional improvement grants not only stimulate ideas from faculty but affirm the importance of good teaching.[9]

Faculty development programs also offer seminars on specific areas of importance to faculty; for example most faculty members find testing and evaluation a difficult part of teaching and welcome information on this topic. Other subjects of interest concern instructional technology, dealing effectively with students, absenteeism, academic dishonesty, or other disruptions that have important institutional or legal implications. Some faculty use training tapes to learn about the challenges associated with teaching.

Faculty members also benefit from topics concerning personal growth, such as financial planning, stress management, time management, and balancing family with work. About 10 years ago, a faculty group at The University of Georgia planned and conducted a conference on professional and personal renewal. Three on-campus conferences were so popular that the university's Office of Instructional Development now offers national conferences on the topic. The success of these conferences underscores the need for today's faculty to continue learning.[10]

Students enrolled in research universities frequently meet members of another student population—graduate teaching assistants (GTAs) in the classroom. Some GTAs are full-scale instructors with all the rights and responsibilities of regular faculty members, while others work as laboratory assistants, graders, proctors, or discussion leaders.

Some GTAs are former high school or college teachers, but others have never taught. The GTAs may be older students, returning to graduate school after years of work or parenting, or recent degree recipients who enter graduate programs directly after college. Many GTAs are international students who have only recently come to the United States for postgraduate study. Most GTAs are well versed in their fields because they study the latest research as part of their own curriculum.

In most universities, GTAs represent a substantial portion of the instructional work force, and as new teachers they need assistance, support, and supervision. College instruction receives attention today because students and parents expect high-quality teaching and institutions wish to prepare future college teachers; thus many universities help GTAs become effective instructors through a variety of programs and credit-bearing courses. Such programs develop the GTA's confidence in the ability to design a course syllabus, conduct class discussions, construct a good exam, and handle classroom situations.

International GTAs assigned instructional responsibilities that require a high level of language and cultural expertise often take special courses to learn how to communicate properly in the classroom and to interact effectively with students. Cultural aspects are as important as language factors.

A LOOK TO THE FUTURE

To maximize the learning experience for students, colleges and universities must identify and meet the needs of the teaching faculty, and today well over a thousand institutions promote instructional and faculty development through centralized units devoted to these issues. Never has so much attention been paid to redressing the balance between teaching and research and never have institutions been so concerned about human capital and its management. No longer can college professors rest solely on their academic credentials. We suspect that future professors will be trained in such areas as interpersonal communication, instructional technology, legal issues, and evaluation techniques.

Who decides what to teach and how do they go about it? Chapter 8 examines the social forces and academic factors that influence curriculum development, or what is taught.

8 ◥ Curriculum of the New Millennium

In 1860 Herbert Spencer, a noted British sociologist, philosopher, and scientist, wrote an essay titled "What Knowledge Is of Most Worth?" Spencer set forth a hierarchy of activities he thought important. These activities pertain to self-preservation, securing the necessities of life, rearing and disciplining offspring, maintaining proper social and political relations, and gratifying tastes and feelings.[1]

How would Spencer answer the question if he viewed today's society? Perhaps he would begin by asking students why they go to college. While motivation varies, most students agree that college helps people realize their full potential. There are of course notable exceptions: Many artists, skilled technicians, actors, and professional athletes hone their marketable skills without his or her education. But for others, a college education has become, much like the high school diploma of a half-century ago, a basic expectation and minimum credential.

In 1992 Ernest Boyer addressed a question similar to Spencer's. Before giving advice about curriculum reform for the new century, Boyer reflected on the themes of higher education during the past four decades. In the 1950s, the decade of optimism, robust expansion took precedence over introspection about undergraduate learning, while in the 1960s confrontation was the order of the day. Boyer suggests that universities were most useful in the 1960s, when campuses across the country became forums where opposing views were presented with some degree of rationality, thus avoiding confrontation and rioting.[2]

In the 1970s, a decade of depression, colleges and universities existed without a sense of purpose, but in the 1980s, the academy assumed a defensive stance. Harsh, unrelenting critics, some of whom we discussed in Chapter 2, brought attention to problems in undergraduate education without suggesting viable solutions.

Boyer sees a more positive trend emerging in the 1990s, and he declares that the last years of the millennium will be the decade of the undergraduate. As the academy rediscovers its obligation to students, the commonalities of human beings, not their differences, will serve as a framework for education. Boyer's intriguing ideas may herald a new, more creative and cooperative approach to the curriculum, but before his proposals or any others become part of what is taught, certain processes must occur.

DERIVING THE GOALS OF INSTRUCTION

Though Boyer's ideas, like those of Herbert Spencer, are valuable, they are unlikely to become part of the curriculum without receiving a great deal of thought and discussion on campuses across the country. While academicians rarely engage in the process in a formal way, they use rational mechanisms to determine curriculum goals, which in turn influence what is taught and how it is taught.

To be meaningful, the nature of society, the nature of the learner, and the nature of the discipline should guide the development of the curriculum.[3] Because our society is open and flexible, we teach in an environment of inquiry and discovery where independent thinking is the natural approach. In fact this approach is so natural that we hardly recognize that it is inherent in most materials developed for use in schools. However when other countries adopt U.S. textbooks and curriculum materials, unforeseen problems may result. For example in countries where democracy and human rights are not valued, some view teaching young people to think for themselves as a liability rather than an asset.

At least until recently, our economic health has set apart the United States from other societies. Through capitalism we have become, by worldwide standards, a wealthy nation, but capitalism also has influenced the nature of the learner. Our educational system produces competitive individuals. Children in elementary schools learn to value doing well, and nonconformers are labeled as failures. Although precollege educators promote cooperation over competition, children compete for grades, honors, and other awards. Most students entering college are unfamiliar with another approach.

William Perry of Harvard University studies how students mature intellectually during their college years.[4] Perry sees most 18-year-old freshman as dualistic thinkers who consider alternatives in terms of right versus wrong or black versus white. Students at this level want instructors to supply answers, and students tend to compartmentalize knowledge into clear-cut categories: "If it's this, then it can't be that." As people progress intellectually and socially, they move toward what Perry calls relativism, and relativistic thinkers see the gray between the black and white. For example, while a dualistic thinker may view war as clearly right or wrong, the relativistic thinker looks at a variety of factors and may conclude that war is neither right nor wrong. A college education, at least in part, should nurture intellectual development toward a more relativistic way of thinking and solving problems.

Although Perry's ideas about how young adults perceive the world are important, they do not help instructors understand students who are older than traditional age, with families, careers, or even plans to retire. These students, sometimes older than their teachers, bring new maturity, experience, and motivation to the campus, so that what is taught and how it is taught must be reconsidered.

Educational researcher Rosalind Driver of Australia proposes that instead of entering the classroom as empty vessels, students are already partially filled.[5] What the partially filled vessels contain is important because as we have known for years, people learn based on what they already know. As a constructionist, Driver believes that learners put together or "construct" knowledge in various ways.

Driver's ideas can help instructors whose students differ not only in age but in many other ways. Although some college students are 18 years old and undecided about their futures, others know who they are and what they want. The desire to see students well-equipped to enter the job market has fostered debate at some institutions on how to combine a liberal arts education with professional training.[6] Many academicians fear that courses designed to enhance the student's ability to compete in the job market are replacing basic courses in the humanities, sciences, and the arts. On most campuses, educators are already struggling to balance the core curriculum with courses in the student's major.

The third component of curriculum design, the nature of the subject matter, concerns subject-related knowledge and the processes used to generate that knowledge in various disciplines. In most disciplines, both knowledge and process are bound together in terminology and tradition particular to that field.

The structure of science and mathematics and the processes by which they are taught and learned differ from approaches to mastering a language or understanding an art form, for example. Therefore decisions about what to teach and how to teach must be based on the nature of the discipline.

DESIGNING THE CURRICULUM

Investigating the principles of curriculum development is easier than learning how educators design and implement the curriculum. Figure 8.1 illustrates the complex interrelationship of factors that must be considered in curriculum design. However

My ambition is to help create the model of a modern, technological university. In so doing, we will help define what is meant by any great university in the 21st century.

Why should any state aspire to have a great university, and why a great technological university? The answer is straightforward. Increasingly, technology is becoming a driving force for our society. Focusing only on economic impacts, it is clear that no significant technology-based regional or national economic center exists without the presence, participation, and preeminence of great universities. Great cities, great universities, and great regions fuel and sustain each other. Great research universities attract human capital, produce knowledge and new technology through research, and create new human capital through education.

Technological universities are well positioned to define what is meant by an educated person in the twenty-first century. I believe any technological institution is better positioned than are traditional liberal arts institutions to redefine what we mean by an educated person in an increasingly technological world. Adding nontechnical dimensions to a technical education is much easier than adding engineering, science, and technology to a traditional liberal arts institution. Not only is it easier intellectually and organizationally, it is far more feasible financially. To some, it may seem that I am advocating an engineering and science "takeover" of the liberal arts. Not at all, but I am advocating making technology one of the liberal arts of the twenty-first century. If this proposal seems audacious, remember that the seven "liberal arts" in the Middle Ages—the trivium and the quadrivium—were grammar, rhetoric, and logic; music, astronomy, geometry, and arithmetic.

John P. Crecine, president, Georgia Institute of Technology

some common influences are at work: At medium- and small-sized institutions the president and academic vice president are key players, while at larger institutions, faculty from colleges, schools, and academic departments within the university are responsible for curriculum design. However whether large or small, most institutions have curriculum committees composed of

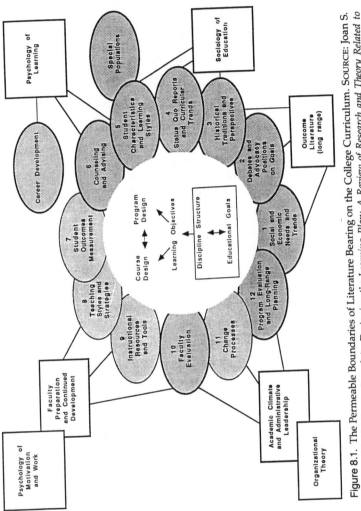

Figure 8.1. The Permeable Boundaries of Literature Bearing on the College Curriculum. SOURCE: Joan S. Stark and Malcolm A. Lowther, *Designing the Learning Plan: A Review of Research and Theory Related to College Curricula* (Ann Arbor, MI: The University of Michigan, 1986), 7.

faculty members who examine proposals for new courses, review old courses, and institute changes in the basic curriculum. In state institutions, the central administration must usually authorize the adding or deleting degree programs, normally with the approval of a governing body, such as a board of regents.

Many external factors influence the curriculum, for example areas of study leading to jobs that are plentiful usually experience enrollment increases, and more students lead to more faculty and to new course offerings. In recent years, business, computer science, and biotechnology have been high-growth fields, so that liberal arts colleges now offer business programs to attract students. Alternatively enrollments in some of the basic liberal arts areas have declined: Mathematics, history, philosophy, and some areas of foreign language are examples, although there is evidence that 1980s' enrollment trends may be reversed in the 1990s.[7]

The professions they serve influence the curricula of professional schools; for example, since medical practitioners must be skilled problem solvers, many courses in medical school have a problem-based format. Because modern agricultural professions require students with technological skills that were not necessary in the past, and journalism students face new challenges in management and ethics, curriculum in these fields have been modified.[8]

Unfortunately most university faculties do not engage in systematic institutionwide curriculum planning processes, and course offerings at universities are so numerous and varied that it may be impossible to determine what courses of study typical undergraduates complete. College faculties, on the other hand, periodically step back to take a fresh look at the curriculum. Since the 1970s, faculty at Alverno College, a liberal arts college for women, has sought to develop in all courses certain skills and values they believe every student should possess; these include communication, analytical reasoning, problem solving, decision making, social interaction; and environmental responsibility, involvement in the contemporary world, and aesthetic response.[9]

The Alverno faculty has conducted extensive research to evaluate the curriculum, and having found that students can learn complex skills, the faculty has incorporated eight major abilities in each individual courses. Instructors then use the course material to help students master these skills. Students have consistently demonstrated performance across settings and disciplines.

In addition to learning complex improvement skills, Alverno students work toward become self-sustaining learners. Students describe learning as the process of experiencing, reflecting, forming new concepts, and testing their judgment and abilities on real issues. Students describe relating abilities to each other, taking responsibility for learning, and using different ways of learning. Alverno students also identify curriculum elements that validate the usefulness of learning.

In addition to course-related abilities, students show improvement in leadership motivation, self-definition, and personal maturity. Both older and younger students change their ways of thinking, with intellectual development occurring in a less linear fashion. Traditional-age students move from using concrete thinking more than abstract and from using reflective observing more than active experimenting toward more balanced positions combining these styles.

Alverno alumnae stress the importance of both intellectual and interpersonal abilities at work, as do other practicing professionals. Alumnae continue as self-sustaining learners and experience a sense of competence in their lives.

An integral part of the Alverno process is assessment, or evaluating the outcome of learning, and such assessment procedures are becoming routine on many college and university campuses. At Furman University for example, course results are assessed empirically, and faculty committees use the findings to make relevant changes in the curriculum. In some state systems, assessment is required by law.

At other institutions, curriculum evaluation takes place through less formal, more qualitative procedures. At Emory University for example, colleagues from peer universities are invited to review the academic departments and recommend change. Many educators prefer a less structured approach to assessment;

The first challenge of assessment is that of assuring that the assessment measures are appropriate to the institution where it will be used. The assessment program must be derived from the purpose of the institution and from a clear statement of the educational goals of the college or university expressed in terms of expected student achievement. Without explicit goals and objectives, satisfactory measurement is not possible.

Also, the assessment program should be multifaceted and examine the total student development process as opposed to focusing on any one aspect or any one measure. It should incorporate data in areas such as achievement test scores, opinion surveys, exit interviews, peer reviews, and postgraduation performance indicators. Within the academic program emphasis should be placed on individual course evaluation, evaluation of the academic major, and evaluation of the general education program. All assessment activities should be provided the necessary support services by the institution's administrative structure.

Finally, the greatest challenge of all is to assess continually the assessment function itself. The program for assessment established by each institution should be a part of a larger, well-conceived, and clearly articulated planning/evaluation process and should not become an end in itself. In any program of assessment there lurks the very real danger that assessment will take on a life of its own and thereby undermine the very outcomes that it is intended to measure.

Philip Winstead, coordinator of Institutional Planning and Research and professor of education, Furman University

in their view, the most positive outcomes of higher education cannot be quantified.

Regardless of the goals of a specific curriculum, an adequate outcome includes experience in various disciplines, cultures, and value systems; experience with the student's cultural heritage; and experience with current problems, both in relation to traditional approaches and to newly developed approaches. Other important objectives encompass living and working in a community, including collective academic and social activities; independent study of an area the learner defines or helps to define; practice in oral and written communication; continual contact with faculty members; continual evaluation, including self-evaluation; involvement in personal and impersonal, long-term and short-term learning situations; personal development; and creative activities and play.[10] Incorporating these goals into each student's curriculum represents an important challenge for college and university faculty.

DEVELOPING A CORE CURRICULUM

Most institutions require students to complete a core or general education curriculum before graduation. At public colleges and universities, the core curriculum is usually mandated by the systemwide governing body; at independent institutions, the faculty determines general education requirements. Most core curricula include basic courses in science, mathematics, English, foreign language, social and behavioral sciences, art, humanities, physical education, and elective areas. Core courses vary depending on the degree sought; for example students enrolled in agriculture or engineering may not have foreign language requirements, but they may be required to take additional mathematics or computer science courses. Required core courses for the bachelor of science and bachelor of arts degree programs are usually different.

The State University of New York at Albany requires all students to complete six credits in each of six categories: mathematics, natural sciences, social sciences, literature and fine arts, world cultures, and values. These basic requirements are similar to most other core curricula across the country.

At Antioch College, a small, progressive liberal arts college in Ohio, students participate in designing the curriculum. Other colleges and universities offer creative and innovative approaches to curriculum design with varying results.

In the 1920s, President Arthur Morgan envisioned Antioch College as "a laboratory of democracy." In addition to initiating the work-study program in which students alternate between experience in the world of work and classroom study throughout their years at the college, Morgan established the Administrative Council (Adcil), which includes not only faculty and administrators, but student members as well. It was President Algo Henderson who built upon Morgan's democratic vision and made students fully enfranchised members of Adcil. As such, students participate in the shaping of basic institutional policies and decisions regarding the tenure and promotion of faculty. Students on Adcil also participate in the development and approval of the annual budget, the appointment of senior administrators, and the approval of the membership on the college's key committees.

While the faculty takes primary responsibility for planning the educational program of the college, students serve on the selection committees for every faculty member appointed and participate on committees shaping the content of the curriculum.

As dean of the faculty, I sit with students on the college's Administrative Council that meets for protracted periods every week. The debates are often long, arduous, and, sometimes, tedious. But the education in democratic process that takes place in those meetings is invaluable for all of us and, I am confident, will make a difference in the lives of the participating students and the communities to which they give themselves in the future.

R. Eugene Rice, vice president and dean of the faculty, Antioch College

CONTEMPORARY CURRICULUM ISSUES

In the 1990s scholars and researchers discuss, and sometimes debate, controversial trends and issues related to the curriculum. Such topics as abortion, creationism, evolution, pluralism, and ethics are always difficult to treat, and thoughtful instructors respect the rights of all students, guard against indoctrination, and present topics in a reasonable and professional manner.

According to many scholars, the curriculum is on the brink of profound change much like the change that led to modern science becoming an accepted area of study. In the early 1800s, students demanded courses in the physical sciences, but professors labeled them too professional and opposed replacing elements of the classical curriculum with chemistry and physics. When such courses were adopted, some faculties relegated them to separate schools. Before long however, other disciplines began borrowing the methods of science,[11] indicating that as courses of study, the sciences had arrived.

Today an equally profound movement is underway, as multiculturalism, a broad term describing programs designed to acknowledge the pluralism of society, is becoming widespread throughout higher education. For example, more than one-third of all schools have a multicultural general education requirement, more than half have added multicultural elements to departmental course offerings, and more than 60 percent have multicultural recruitment and retention programs.[12] In the past the viewpoints of certain ethnic groups and women were not addressed in course offerings, textbooks, or classroom discussions. (For a discussion of how women learn, see Chapter 4.) Only recently have there been serious attempts to present balanced views on topics involving gender, social equity, and equal opportunity. Future college curricula will encompass pluralistic and international views.

Other curriculum issues are more closely tied to particular disciplines; currently for example, humanities scholars debate the centrality of Western civilization. Should Western views continue to form the cornerstones of required literature, history, and philosophy courses? Should ideas from Asian, African, and native American cultures join or replace them? The concept of internationalization creates other debates.

These questions and others concern political correctness, an issue that some view as the big news on campus in the 1990s.[13]

During the 1980s, William Bennett, first as Director of the National Endowment for the Humanities and later as President Reagan's Secretary of Education, accused multiculturalists and feminists engaged in establishing a globally oriented curriculum of undermining traditional American values: They were failing to instill in students a pride in the West, which had set "the moral, political, economic and social standards for the rest of the world." For Bennett and other neoconservatives, the critique of Western ideology the "leftists" were developing, in their analysis of Western imperialism, racism, and patriarchy, was unpatriotic.

The neoconservative resistance to the transformation of the curriculum is actually a resistance to a new way of thinking that I call *cultural holism*. Cultural holism is a vision of the human world as a dynamic, complex, open system of interdependent cultures, none of which enjoys any absolute superiority to any other, all of which evolve in relation to each other and to their nonhuman environment. The cultural holists' perspective is like that of ecologists, for whom nature is an ecosystem whose well-being is affected by the interaction of its diverse constituents. Understanding humankind as a global cultural system, cultural holists view an assumption of national or cultural superiority as unconducive to world peace, just as they view racism and sexism as unconducive to social harmony. Their interest in the "whole" of society leads inevitably to an analysis of ideology, the analysis that the neoconservatives find dangerous to the West's long-standing identity.

In the United States, cultural holism is gradually supplanting the dualistic, atomistic, and hierarchical conceptual model—inherited form Plato and Aristotle and expressed in imperialism, racism, and patriarchy—which underpins our present social order. Because a new conceptual model will eventually bring about a new social order, we should not be surprised that cultural holism is generating vehement opposition not only from traditionalists within the academy but also from conservative politicians.

Betty Jean Craige, professor of comparative literature, The University of Georgia

Those of a more liberal persuasion contend that political correctness is a term (and a tactic) used by conservatives to suppress topics that go beyond traditional boundaries. Joan Wallach Scott, for example, warns academics to be alarmed by the conservative agenda, which would deny us our most valuable activities: thinking hard and teaching others to do so.[14] Regardless of one's views, it is clear that universities are, and should continue to be, places where differences flourish. Classrooms are open forums where critical thinking should receive the highest priority. This distinguishing characteristic of U.S. higher education is a foundation for all courses of study, and as such it should be reflected in today's curriculum.

BEYOND DIFFERENCES TO SHARED EXPERIENCES

In reflecting on higher education since 1950, Boyer is encouraged by the vigorous and widespread conversations, and sometimes debates, that accompany the redefinition of the curriculum. As we enter the new millennium, a healthy examination of what is taught and what is learned is in order, and research shows that instructors and students are serious about exploring the differences we bring to the campus, classroom, and society. But our emphasis on difference alone concerns Boyer, who urges curriculum planners to use human commonalities to build a new framework for learning.

According to Boyer, as humans we share at least eight experiences: the life cycle; communication; aesthetic response to our world; such life-shaping institutions as family, school, and political processes; the ability to recall the past and anticipate the future; a connection to the natural world; ties to productivity and consumption; and a search for deeper meaning to life. If these experiences connect human beings at the most basic level, perhaps they, and not the disciplines as we conceive them today, should undergird teaching and learning.[15] We find Boyer's thoughts provocative and agree that the sometimes boisterous discussions about teaching and learning truly are the good news of the 1990s. Widespread commitment to new ideas and the search for more meaningful ways of understanding our culture, and a commitment to solid and collaborative processes developed over time, will result in a continually evolving, relevant, and profound concept of learning.

9   New Paths to Learning

Why do some students succeed in college while others do not? College and university administrators, professors, parents, and students are interested in answers to this question, and today answers are available. As we approach the new millennium, definite patterns describe the outcomes of college for students. Rather than occurring in isolated areas of a student's life, new findings suggest that changes during college occur in integrated ways. Study after study shows that students involved in curricular and extracurricular endeavors remain in college longer and are more satisfied with college than other students. The type of institution seems to have less influence on achievement and other long-term benefits from college than other more controllable variables. For example, completing required courses in a general education core appears to increase a student's critical thinking skills, and certain types of involvement in college life seem to influence success more than others.

These issues are important to educators who care about effectiveness and strive to make a positive difference in a student's life. At some schools, a more institution-oriented reason is survival in a time of both declining enrollment and funding. Since it is expensive to recruit students only to have them drop out, colleges and universities need to know what can be done to increase the likelihood that students will persist and succeed in college.[1]

In Chapter 9, we examine the findings of four researchers who study students behavior and performance: Alexander Astin of UCLA, Ernest Pascarella of the University of Chicago, Patrick Terenzini of Penn State University, and Vincent Tinto of Syracuse University. Taken as a whole, their work is changing the way colleges make decisions about educational programs.

In the context of their work, we also examine three out-of-class efforts to help students succeed: programs designed to enhance the quality of the freshman year, academic advising, and on-campus residential arrangements. These programs offer opportunities for meaningful contact with others on campus, involve students in learning, and encourage them to plan for the future. Ultimately, they offer new paths of learning to students who want to maximize the positive aspects of college.

ASTIN: COOPERATION IS THE KEY

Each fall more than 275,000 freshmen at 600 colleges and universities participate in the nation's largest and longest running empirical study of higher education, the American Council on Education (ACE)—University of California at Los Angeles (UCLA) Cooperative Institutional Research Program (CIRP). The CIRP founding director, Alexander Astin, organized the research team that investigates who freshmen are, what they think, and what they expect to do after college. In 1991 Astin synthesized freshman trends of 25 years. Some conclusions are startling, while others are expected benchmarks of our society.[2] For example, today's freshmen are not so well prepared for college as freshmen in 1966, a trend that may be attributed to students completing less rigorous courses of study today than in the 1960s. Rather than expecting to concentrate only on college-level work, freshmen expect to be tutored or improve reading skills in college. They are less likely than their predecessors to argue issues with professors, borrow books and journals from the library, or visit a professor's home. Conversely more freshmen asked for advice after class and belonged to scholastic honor societies in high school.

Despite the decline in preparation, more of today's freshmen have positive views about their intellectual abilities. They are less likely however to enroll in science courses. During the past 7 years, the number of students taking recommended levels of science and math courses has declined by about 10 percent. This trend is puzzling in view of responses about educational and career plans. Record numbers of freshmen entering college in 1990 planned to seek graduate degrees. While the number of male freshmen planning to go to graduate school has remained somewhat constant, women's interest has increased sharply. Both men and women show less interest in business school than did students only a few years ago, while interest in a career in education is on the rebound.

Considering the implications of these trends, Astin concludes that educational excellence depends on an institution's ability to influence the development of students' talents and abilities. Astin's view is not inconsistent with that of Rosabeth Moss Kanter, Harvard Business School professor, who advises business leaders to cooperate with one another. Astin and Kanter espouse a society built on cooperation rather than competition.

Astin expands his views in *What Matters in College: Four Critical Years Revisited*, a work based on a study of more than 20,000 students, 25,000 faculty members, and 200 institutions. Astin has long attributed educational effectiveness to an institution's ability to involve students in campus academic and social life. Astin's new study underscores the importance of an environment that encourages students to be involved. Astin concludes that a student's peer group is the single most important environmental influence and advises colleges and universities to strengthen learning and personal development by using peer groups imaginatively.[3]

TINTO: WHY STUDENTS STAY OR LEAVE

Like Astin, Vincent Tinto of Syracuse University is a researcher who has been asking questions about college students since the 1970s. His book, *Leaving College: Rethinking the Causes and Cures of Student Attrition*, focuses on persistence, or why some students remain in school when others withdraw. Tinto notes that more students leave a school prior to graduating than stay. In 1987 Tinto predicted that over 1.6 million of the 2.6 million students enrolling in college for the first time in 1986 would withdraw from the institution without receiving a degree; of these, 1.2 million would leave higher education altogether. Tinto's prediction is a discouraging commentary on U.S. higher education.[4]

As a sociologist, Tinto's views differ from those of many college and university officials who focus on full classrooms and residence halls. For Tinto mere enrollment is not the long-term objective of retention efforts; rather concern for a student's intellectual and social growth should guide institutional action, so that students naturally remain in school.[5]

To confront the dropout problem, Tinto recommends that each college and university define an educational mission, adopt goals to support the mission, and develop a course of action to support their goals. "Why students are admitted to the institution" is the first appropriate question, and "how can they be retained" follows. Answers to these questions should serve as guides in designing relevant and stimulating settings in which students can learn.[6]

Before examining ways of retaining students, Tinto looks at college students themselves. He envisions a student's career as a process of becoming incorporated into the college community. This process, or passage, is easier for some students than for others. The first step involves separation from the past communities—family, high school, and hometown. When students find the college community very different from their accustomed environment, separation can be quite challenging. Students who accept these differences and willingly leave their former community are often the most successful in college.

The second stage in passage, transition, can accompany or follow separation. During transition students are both leaving their former communities and adopting the new college community. Again students who find the college environment quite different from home and high school face difficulty. As a result, some withdraw from college during their first year because they cannot withstand the stresses of transition. Researchers note convincing statistics: Students' chances of remaining in college improve considerably if they complete their freshman year. The most critical period appears to be the first 6 weeks; Of the freshman who drop out of college, half leave during the first 6 weeks.[7] Although separation from the high school community and transition to college are stressful, these processes need not lead to departure.[8]

The final stage in passage is incorporation into the collegiate society, or "fitting in." Students who have regular contact with faculty members outside the classroom, develop meaningful relationships with peers and peer organizations, or become involved in some aspect of college fit in more easily than others. The former invest in their new communities and move through the transition process to become full-fledged members of the college society.[9]

Like Astin, Tinto urges students to involve themselves in both curricular and extracurricular activities, and he supports institutional action that encourages faculty–student interaction.[10] But Tinto warns that actions aimed only at keeping students in school may fail. Effective programs offer students valuable educational experiences, not mere enrollment. What are some of these programs? While programs aimed at incoming freshmen are critical, efforts cannot stop there. Freshman-year offerings, academic advising, and opportunities to live on campus are a few of many organized efforts Tinto recommends. The secret to success in college lies in the degree to which the college community engages students on many levels. Involvement, and the two-way commitment it reflects, is the primary source of students' dedication to their own learning.[11]

PASCARELLA AND TERENZINI:
DOES COLLEGE MAKE A DIFFERENCE?

In 1991 Ernest Pascarella of the University of Chicago and Patrick Terenzini of Penn State University published a review based on 20 years of research on college students. In *How College Affects Students: Findings and Insights from Twenty Years of Research*, they draw conclusions from more than 2600 studies involving all components of college and university life. Pascarella and Terenzini ask a number of questions: Does college make a difference? What can be done to influence positive student change?[12] Their almost 1000-page investigation is a new handbook for the profession.

Pascarella and Terenzini conclude that (1) the college years are a time of change on a broad front: Students grow in factual knowledge and develop general cognitive and intellectual skills, values, and attitudinal, psychological, and moral dimensions. (2) Students develop in integrated and mutually reinforcing ways. (3) The enduring effects of college are important not only for individuals who attend but for their children as well. (4) Attending college is a dynamic affair, and its benefits are directly related to the extent to which individual students take advantage of everything the institution has to offer.[13]

As for differences among colleges and universities, Pascarella and Terenzini conclude that institutions "are not all that different." Nonelite schools compete successfully with top schools in significant areas. Bulging libraries and hand-picked student bodies tell little about the quality of the educational result.[14]

What advice do Pascarella and Terenzini offer students who are choosing a college? First select a high-quality institution—one offering a strong core curriculum of general requirements, excellent teaching, and frequent interaction between students and faculty members outside the classroom. Then learn about the school's resources and tailor its offerings to meet your needs. By taking advantage of even a few of most colleges' or universities' numerous resources, students can reap the educational rewards these researchers describe.

FRESHMAN YEAR: IMPORTANT NEW BEGINNINGS

When freshmen arrive on campus, they make decisions that determine the framework of their future life. Unfortunately "How to Make Informed Choices" is not a course in the high school curriculum, and most 18-year-olds come to college with little experience in decision making. Many unsuccessful freshmen find that poor choices contribute to their difficulties, while others make no choices. They are swept along by the flow of campus life without choosing intentionally to fail or to succeed.

In the early 1970s, some educators especially attuned to the needs of students recognized the freshman dilemma: High school graduates who do not know how to be successful college students need to learn appropriate skills early in their college careers. Freshmen need to fit into the college environment, build meaningful relationships with advisers, register for classes, take tests, and plan majors. They need to know how to study, manage their time, and take advantage of their college's or university's resources. John Gardner of the University of South Carolina understands the needs of freshmen, and he has dedicated himself to helping them. His personal energy and enthusiasm have resulted in an international movement, known as the Freshman Year Experience, to enhance the quality of the freshman year.

Although Gardner was the first person to make freshman needs a national issue, others before him had acknowledged the special circumstances of first-year college students. Before 1900 officials at Johns Hopkins and Harvard established systems of

The Freshman Year Experience is an effort involving a partnership of college and university faculty, academic administrators, and student affairs administrators to make first year men and women a much, much higher priority in our institutions. The focus has been to improve instruction in and out of class, support, advising, counseling, tutoring, orientation, student activities, residence hall accommodations, and every aspect of student life for college freshman. The overall objective of this movement has been to increase success of first year students, their retention rates from first to second year and beyond, and ultimately their graduation rates. It is a consensus of higher educators from developing and developed nations that the future of their societies, the quality of their national lives, the vitality of their economics, the ability to meet work force needs for quality graduates, all depends ultimately on greater emphasis being placed on the first year of the college and university experience.

But the freshman year experience is more than anything else an initiative to redefine freshman success. This argues that institutions must make students not only academically competent but simultaneously provide them with rewarding interpersonal relationships which support growth and learning; an enhanced personal identity and self-esteem; an introduction to a lifelong process of career planning; education that takes a holistic perspective and attempts to teach and support students in terms of their intellectual, moral, spiritual, and physical well being; and finally, help first year college students begin to develop an integrated philosophy of life.

John N. Gardner, director, University 101 and the National Resource Center for the Freshman-Year Experience, University of South Carolina and coauthor with M. Lee Upcraft of *The Freshman Year Experience* (San Francisco: Jossey-Bass, 1989) faculty advisers for freshmen, and in 1925, Emory University instituted Freshman Week to acquaint new students with various phases of college life. By 1930 one in three colleges and universities offered organized freshman courses, and nine out of 10 students were required to enroll.[15]

This trend soon changed. By the late 1930s, faculty members opposed granting credit to students for learning how to adjust to life situations; thus most courses were discontinued, and by 1960 they were nearly obsolete. Then Gardner brought the needs of freshmen to the forefront. He began his movement by recommending that freshmen come together in seminars to learn how to be successful college students.

Definitions of Success

According to Lee Upcraft and John Gardner, authors of *The Freshman Year Experience: Helping Students Survive and Succeed in College*, freshmen enter college to prepare for careers, but soon find that more is in store for them. Before they can learn, they need to learn how to learn, think critically, and take responsibility for planning their educations. Freshmen also need the support and encouragement of their peers. Most students discover people from different ethnic backgrounds and cultures, of different sexual orientations, with different abilities and life experiences.[16] Well-designed freshman programs can help college freshmen develop the skills they need to establish good relationships with others who are different from themselves.

For Neva Daley, freshmen counselors who were also undergraduate students helped make the first semester at Yale successful:

> I have a freshman counselor, an ethnic counselor, an academic adviser, and a residential dean. They make sure my objectives are strong. I came here knowing I would major in premed, but my counselors got me into the right science courses. My ethnic counselor is another African-American student and a premed

> major. She was a real friend when I first came here and I was
> alone. Now I don't need her as much.

Successful freshmen begin early to think about careers and life-styles as they develop identities as college students.[17] Quite naturally many freshmen enter college undecided about majors and careers. They are in college to discover their futures, not proceed from the beginning according to a well-ordered plan. Although many colleges encourage freshmen to list a major, being undecided can be an advantage if students seek information and make informed choices about majors and careers, undertakings that are central to most freshman programs.

In addition to addressing academic and intellectual needs, good freshman programs consider students' health and safety while on campus. New students experience changes that affect their physical health and safety or their emotional well-being,[18] but freshman programs can help them learn to establish and maintain healthy, well-managed, and secure life-styles.

While freshman courses follow a variety of formats, most reflect an institutionwide commitment to helping freshmen become fully vested members of the college community. Courses may be extensions of orientation or actual academic seminars, and participation may be required or optional. Common themes concern transition from high school to college, the value of a college education, study and time management skills, understanding the curriculum, and investigating majors and careers. More comprehensive courses offer instruction in critical thinking or teach students how to identify and best use their preferred learning styles, while others incorporate academic advising, registration, and personal development.

Today an equal number of public and private 4-year and 2-year institutions offer freshman programs, including 70 percent of the institutions enrolling more than one thousand students; about 43 percent require all freshmen to participate.[19] Regardless of format, the freshman seminar attempts to foster positive attitudes toward all aspects of college.

Why Do Freshman Programs Work?

According to Tinto, successful students make the transition from high school to college and become full-fledged members of the campus community, though not always with ease. If college is quite different from high school, adjustment can be difficult. To complicate matters, freshmen arrive on campus with well-defined expectations of college life. Having survived the stressful admissions process, they expect to meet the perfect roommate, move into the perfect residence area, register for the classes of their choice taught between 10:00 A.M. and 2:00 P.M., and sail through sorority or fraternity rush. Reality disappoints many freshmen and devastates a few if adjusting to sharing a small room with another person, considering the habits and needs of many neighbors, matching academic plans to vacancies in classes, and competing in new social systems proves difficult. Many freshman find an outlet by discussing these problems in freshman programs with a small group of peers who share their concerns.

On large campuses, freshman programs may be lifelines for students who must learn how to register for classes; use the library; establish rapport with professors; and avail themselves of such out-of-class learning opportunities as residence living, academic advisers, health and wellness programs, career and personal counseling, and courses on study skills and time management. While content is important, the process of the freshman seminar is essential. Successful educational programs have an equal ratio of students to opportunities for involvement on campus. It is difficult to become involved if the environment is too large for the number of people who want to participate.[20] On the other hand, if the environment is too small, too few opportunities exist.

Although parents and faculty members may assume that freshmen focus primarily on personal and social issues, freshmen list academic and career planning concerns as the most important issues they face. Even during orientation, they think about getting good grades and investigating careers. Accordingly freshman programs are natural vehicles to engage new students fully in all aspects of college. When freshmen find a "fit" both academically and socially, they are likely to remain in college and be successful learners. A full-time mother who returned to college to become a psychologist and attorney found the student success course at her community college invaluable. "The course helped me get back into my studies and get acquainted with the college. We had a separate orientation, but my section of the success course for adult students only was more helpful. We shared our problems and learned from each other. It was great."

ACADEMIC ADVISING: MORE THAN WHAT TO TAKE WHEN

Like instructors of freshman seminar courses, academic advisers have the good fortune to build relationships with students around a shared interest—the student's future. Whether faculty members, peers, or professionals charged solely with advising students, academic advisers are official representatives of the institution who help students plan their courses of study. Ideally advisers take the long view and first help students identify their academic and career goals, then they help students plan educational programs congruent with these goals.

Unlike most other campus officials, academic advisers are concerned about an area of student life that students consider important—academic matters and planning for careers.[21] Therefore both advisers and students should value the relationship, but too often, this is not the case. When Carnegie Foundation for the Advancement of Teaching researchers asked 4500 college students about their teaching and learning experiences, more than half replied that they never seek advice on financial, personal, or vocational matters, and one in four say that no faculty member ever takes a personal interest in a student's academic progress. In general university students tend to give advising services lower ratings than do students at smaller, liberal arts colleges. Ernest Boyer, president of the Carnegie Foundation, attributes this finding to the fact that faculty members on small campuses usually are more involved with students than are university faculty members. Astin agrees with the findings of the Carnegie Foundation: Undergraduates are likely to be dissatisfied with advising. This concerns him because he views advising as the primary tool for involving students in their education.[22]

The Advising Relationship

Advising services have evolved as U.S. higher education has matured. The first college students did not need advisers because they had no choice about their courses of study. Then in the late 1800s, colleges introduced electives, which allowed students to choose some courses in the curriculum. Faculty members assumed the task of helping students decide about courses, and soon academic advisers were a popular on-campus addition.

In the years between World War I and the Great Depression, some colleges evolved into universities, the research mission assumed primary importance, and many faculty members became researchers, not undergraduate instructors. As specialists these faculty members no longer had time to counsel students about their futures. At the same time the student body also changed, becoming more numerous, more diverse, and more independent. Students complained about advising services, but institutions, having more applicants than they could accommodate, ignored the problem.

By 1970 a shrinking pool of high school graduates and growing numbers of college dropouts signaled a need for change. Advising was no longer effective. Students who needed advisers avoided them; and advisers did nothing to rectify the situation, paying scant attention to a chore of low importance in the reward system of higher education.

Also by 1970 theoretical developments had led to new academic advising concepts. Through most of the 1960s, college students were considered children, and institutions of higher learning replaced their parents (*in loco parentis*), imposing strict rules of behavior. But student activism and new theories of psychological and social development changed the thinking about undergraduates, who gradually came to be viewed as developing young adults.

Among others, Arthur Chickering's psychosocial theory influenced new concepts of student development. According to Chickering, individuals grow and change throughout life. The college years are a time of considerable growth during which young adults have seven specific tasks to accomplish: developing competence in intellectual, social, and physical areas; learning to manage their emotions; recognizing their independence; establishing identity by integrating their experiences; increasing their tolerance of differences in others; developing purpose by clarifying their interests, options, and preferences; and developing integrity or sets of values to guide their actions.[23] Chickering's vectors are the core for educational programs designed specifically to help college students achieve competence in the seven areas.

In 1972 Burns Crookston set forth his concept of developmental advising as a route to meaningful out-of-class relationships for students and faculty members, not just a schedule-building activity. Rather than passive recipients of advice, students are full partners in the new process of developmental advising. Crookston encouraged advisers to teach students to assume responsibility for their education.[24]

The heart of developmental advising is the adviser–student relationship, and the heart of the relationship is shared responsibility.[25] When advisers view students as maturing individuals capable of learning from the educational planning process, they discuss important questions with students—What do you want to do with your life? What do you want from college—before worrying about class schedules and registration procedures. When students understand that advising is a forum in which to investigate the relevance of college, plan in an organized manner, and make informed decisions, they seek their advisers for more than signatures on forms. Admittedly developmental advising requires more time than traditional advising, especially on the part of the student, who seeks answers and gradually assumes responsibility for planning the future as questions about careers, majors, and courses arise.[26]

Students who list learning to solve problems and set goals as important components of advising prefer advisers who allow them to make their own decisions, become acquainted with them beyond their test scores and grades, and know about all aspects of the institution. Although students want personal relationships with advisers, they prefer to discuss academic and career matters—not issues concerning families or peers.[27] Developmental advisers emphasize issues that concern attitudes and experiences related to programs and opportunities offered by a college or university and are quick to refer students to campus and community resources when needed.[28]

Unlike freshman-year programs, the concept of developmental advising is more discussed than implemented. The Third National Survey of Academic Advising, conducted by ACT, revealed a disappointing picture of advising on most campuses. Although experts recommend that advisers (1) serve because they choose to do so, (2) receive specific training, (3) accomplish well-defined objectives, and (4) be evaluated and rewarded for their service, in practice advisers on many campuses are neither trained, evaluated, nor rewarded. Even though frequent contact with advisers can influence a student's perceptions about college, many advising programs do not promote meaningful advising relationships.[29]

LIVING AND LEARNING: A NATURAL PARTNERSHIP

College becomes more than a classroom for about two-thirds of all freshmen each fall—it becomes home; in fact about 70 percent of all first-year men and 65 percent of all first-year women lived in college housing.[30] Most freshmen live away from their parents and siblings for the first time when they move into residence halls; they also begin an important part of the college learning experience.

Research shows that students who live on campus earn higher grade point averages, express more satisfaction with their college experiences, and are more likely to graduate than are commuting students. They participate in extracurricular, athletic, and social activities more often and are more likely to become campus leaders.[31] Students who live on campus also share many important experiences, such as working toward independence, making friends, and mastering a new environment, with their peers.

The Collegiate Way of Life

While peer relationships are important to students, they are not the only relationships affected by living on campus. Studies show that residential students find the quality and quantity of time they spend informally with faculty more satisfying than commuting students.[32] These findings reflect an important part of U.S. higher education—the collegiate way[33] of life—the belief that college is more than curriculum, library, faculty, and students. Early proponents of the collegiate way recognized that students who lived together could support one another, while extracurricular activities and daily contact with faculty members in informal settings would help students adjust to college. In 1870 President Noah Porter of Yale applauded the benefits of the collegiate way—"idlers" sometimes matured, even if they accomplished nothing in the classroom.[34]

Roommate Matching: An Important Process

Roommate assignment is perhaps the most important decision a college makes for an entering freshman, because the decision can affect the quality of life for two students for one year and may determine whether they stay or leave. Roommates may challenge each other's self-confidence, encourage tolerance, and affect study habits. For example when high achievers room with lower achieving students, the grades of the latter usually improve, while roommates who are highly dissatisfied with one another earn significantly lower grades than roommates who are well matched.[35]

One student at a public research university would agree. "My first roommate was a problem, but we lived in a small room. There was little space and lots of noise. I am sure my alarm rang in her ear, because hers rang in mine. I think it would have been hard to get along with anyone in that space. I prefer living in an apartment. I can study much better here."

Because roommate and other residence hall relationships are so important, some colleges and universities invest considerable time and resources in programs that increase students' satisfaction with the residential environment. Roommates paired on the basis of academic interest or ability or by their own choosing are usually more compatible than randomly matched roommates.[36] Student-centered colleges and universities take advantage of roommate-matching opportunities to construct well-suited living arrangements for students that may contribute to successful academic experiences.

New Options for Living and Learning

Some newer learning plans in residence areas take maximum advantage of Astin's findings on student involvement. Under such learning plans, students choose unique living situations organized around planned routes to learning that promote interaction among motivated students and faculty members.[37] Two of these innovations, living–learning centers and academic theme houses, offer students opportunities to live with others who share their academic interests or desire to learn.

Academic theme houses bring together students with similar interests, such as science, languages, engineering, theater, creative writing, or the arts. Residents may speak a foreign language exclusively or attend lectures arranged for them specifically. Living–learning centers, another residential alternative, provide intense and stimulating learning experiences for all residents. The centers house students as well as classrooms, learning labs, faculty offices, and computer centers. Here faculty members become part of the environment by teaching courses or seminars in residence areas. Ideally academic theme houses and living–learning centers offer university students the advantages of a small college on an large campus, thereby creating an academic community of manageable size in which students can expand their intellectual lives.

Such formalized concepts of living and learning are working. Theme house residents spend more time in formal study groups and less time watching television; they show a greater appreciation of the arts, participate more frequently in class discussions, and report more satisfaction with their general education courses and their peer relationships than students who live in regular residence areas. Like theme house residents, residents in living–learning centers are more satisfied with their academic experiences, spend less time watching television, and are more likely to remain in college than students who live in heterogeneous residence areas. Freshmen in living–learning centers find time to explore career options and develop an appreciation of the arts. Although they surpass other students in academic and social development, they report less progress in learning to manage their time effectively.[38] Perhaps they are less compelled to practice time management skills because they live and learn in more focused environments. Like students who participate in organized freshman-year programs or developmental academic advising, students who choose to live and learn in unique environments are taking advantage of special opportunities offered by their institution.

WELLNESS AND SECURITY:
TWENTY-FIRST-CENTURY ISSUES

Maria King arrived on campus full of excitement and anticipation. Her first day of college had arrived, and she could not wait to get to campus, move into her dorm, and become one of 4000 new freshmen at the flagship university in her midwestern state. Although Maria could have roomed with one of her high school classmates, she did not; she wanted a real university experience of which a potluck roommate is part. Maria was dismayed to learn that her roommate was not a fellow freshman, but a junior. She was a little apprehensive to learn that she was one of only two freshmen on a hall of juniors who had lived together the year before, and she was terrified when her roommate's boyfriend arrived to share the small cubicle and community bath.

After 3 days of being locked out of her room, embarrassed by the couple, and afraid that she would find herself alone with her roommate's boyfriend, she asked for a new assignment. In desperation Maria slept on the floor in a neighboring dorm for 10 nights, since only after the regulation waiting period would the housing office grant her request to move. Although she was not physically harmed, the experience changed her view of college. She felt that the university was more interested in protecting her roommate's right to live as she chose than in providing Maria with a safe, educationally sound living environment, not to mention protecting her from harassment and possible abuse. "Every freshman needs someone to be lost with," said Maria. "I was not expecting my roommate to become my best friend, but I did not think I should have to be afraid to go to my room at night."

Roommate abuse is one of many campus issues that students and parents have trouble accepting. When institutions assumed the role of parents, they regulated curfews, visitors to residence halls (or dorms, as they were called), and alcohol consumption. Campus crime was rare, date rape was undefined, and sexually transmitted disease was not a topic of polite conversation. Personal counseling was an available but less-than-essential component of student services. In the late 1960s, reacting to student demands and the new independence of 18- to 21-year olds, colleges and universities relaxed the rules, and the courts struck down *in loco parentis*.

Now many adults who work on campuses are quick to

observe that students face issues with profound, life-altering consequences—the effects of which are too new for researchers to have investigated. These issues are in fact no different than those facing society as a whole, and they range from nonlife-threatening incidences, such as roommate abuse, to life-and-death issues, such as AIDS and suicide. How do campus officials deal with such threats, and how can students act on their own behalf to protect themselves?

To help the young adult populations assume responsibility for their health and safety, many institutions have increased campus security and routinely educate students about personal safety and physical and psychological wellness. Wellness centers have replaced traditional clinics, and their staffs are trained to promote self-esteem and discuss safe sex and sound nutrition, as well as treat cuts and bruises.

Not surprisingly new approaches to issues involving sexual practice are among the most controversial ones campus health officials face. Some administrators, parents, and alumni have discouraged health centers from distributing condoms and other birth control methods, but others realize that "just say no" is not an effective approach. They believe that education gives students the ability to handle such issues as birth control and the threat of sexually transmitted diseases maturely.

Most campus officials admit that as sensitive as issues of sexual practice can be, they pale in comparison to questions about violent crime, suicide, and sometimes murder. In 1986 a Lehigh University freshman was murdered in her dorm room by another student. Although student life leaders responded to the media outcry by reminding the public that campuses are not secluded from real life, they also worked with professional organizations to help pass the 1990 Student Right-to-Know and Campus Security Act, which requires colleges and universities receiving federal financial aid to distribute annual statistics about on-campus crime and information about campus security to campus inhabitants. In addition universities and colleges must warn students of other crimes that may threaten them.[39] Although the act only requires reporting on-campus crime, students are more likely to be cautious when they know what is going on around them.

Chapel Hill recently funded a safe escort service. One young woman, who is a junior, says, "Now I call the escort service when I leave the library late at night. It's better than riding the bus alone to my dorm. I did this my freshman year, and it was scary." Precautions are justified: In a 3-year period, more than 4000 violent crimes, including 16 murders and 493 rapes, were committed on 580 of the largest U.S. campuses.[40]

One recently defined crime is date or acquaintance rape. Although not widely discussed a decade ago, in the 1980s one college-age woman in four reported being raped by someone she knew. Although acquaintance rape is not confined to the traditional-age student population, students belong to the age-group most likely to be victimized (women 16–24 years old) and most likely to commit the crime (men under age 25). One study narrows the population even more, reporting that women are most likely to be assaulted and men most likely to commit assaults when they are seniors in high school and freshmen in college.[41]

By legal definition, acquaintance rape is no different from rape by a stranger, but both institutions and individuals often find the former more difficult to address. Experts believe that cultural ambiguity about the roles of men and women in society and the sexual scripts the media sends to adolescents contribute to the frequency of acquaintance rape and to the disturbing fact that many more rapes are committed than are reported. Such circumstances have led both college and university officials and student leaders to support information blitzes and ongoing education about acquaintance rape.

Students need to know that 80 percent of all rapes on campus are acquaintance rapes, and 50 percent of these occur on dates. More than half of all assailants have been drinking, and many view a woman who has been drinking as more likely to have sex. Education about rape links assault to drinking and presents strategies to reduce risk. The most progressive colleges and universities coordinate efforts to educate male and female students, prevent violence, and support victims consistently.

From 1991 to 1992 the University of Maryland student suicide rate was a startling 3–6 times the national average of 4–8 of every 100,000 college students. Stress seemed to be at a high, and economic conditions were poor; due to budget cuts, fewer classes were offered per subject, and some departments had been eliminated, leaving students facing uncertain academic futures.[42] Research suggests that hopelessness and loneliness are related to college student suicide; other factors seem to be low self-esteem, conflict, inner turmoil, and drug abuse. Experts advise institutions not to dismiss students who attempt to take their own life but instead offer campus resources for counseling and rehabilitation. Others urge colleges and universities to offer suicide prevention programs both as stand-alone educational opportunities and as components of courses on health and wellness.

Clearly individual and institutional action is required, especially among a population that routinely describes the campus as lonely and isolated.[43] When asked about the advice he would give a new student, a sophomore at a Midwestern college responded:

> As a freshman, I was really lonely here. Before I came, I pictured myself with friends but never thought about having to make friends. Seeing other students looking like they made friends easily and had fun all the time made it worse. It was really hard to fit in. Now I have made this campus my home, and I love it, but I remember how lonely I was. New students, go out and find your niche. It might take a whole year, but you will be surprised how much difference time can make.

This student, like Maria King, the freshman who encountered roommate abuse, acknowledged his problem and sought a solution. The measures he and Maria took exemplify the new approach to campus health and wellness programs, which is prevention. Their goal is to help students take charge of their lives and their health. These programs include education, physical fitness, and health care, reflecting U.S. trends to acknowledge the power of a positive life-style.

In Chapter 9, we have discussed a few of the innovative learning paths for students outside the college or university classroom. Although college or university type does not determine quality, the quality of college experiences can be quite different. It is up to the student to determine the value of college.

10 From Science to Technology: The Future of Instruction

To say that we live in a scientific and technological age is an understatement. We need look no further than the home to realize that technology determines the quality of life.

Today science and technology also influence how we teach and learn. Technological advances lead experts to believe that U.S. education is on the brink of a revolution. Now we know that teaching does not have to be limited to a professor explaining material on a chalkboard or in a textbook while students record notes. Innovative instructors use technology to bring the outside world into the classroom for students to experience firsthand. Others design self-paced, individualized learning experiences, tailored to meet a student's specific needs. In Chapter 10, we focus on scientific and technological influences in teaching.

THE NATURE OF SCIENCE AND TECHNOLOGY

The word "science" comes from Greek and Latin derivatives meaning knowledge or to know, and science, called *natural philosophy* as late as the early 1800s, was once synonymous with knowing. Scientists, thinkers who spent their time explaining how natural phenomena occurred, employed rigid and prescriptive techniques in the classroom. Students memorized facts but developed little understanding of how scientists work. Harvard, for example, required prospective students to have completed a prescribed list of laboratory experiments, activities that merely confirm certain phenomena or outcomes.

Now science is not only knowledge, a product of our thinking and wisdom, but a process of discovering new knowledge. Science includes observing, measuring, collecting data, experimenting and forming hypotheses. Since the late 1950s, science educators have emphasized learning by inquiry and problem solving.

Science is driven by the human mind and spirit. Curiosity, the propensity to ask questions, and the desire to seek truth are human characteristics that fuel the development of science in modern civilization. If curiosity is the mother of science, then necessity is the mother of technology, and through technology, science improves the quality of life. The more formal or classical part of science driven by curiosity is referred to as pure science—scientific inquiry without concern for immediate application. Scientific inquiry whose goal is improved living conditions is called applied science; technology is applied science.

It is helpful to recall the role of technology in our everyday lives. The discovery of fire and the wheel changed the course of human evolution. More recently electricity, plumbing, and automobiles have become fixtures in our society. Some people remember when radios were more familiar than televisions and engineering students carried slide rules instead of calculators. Many others remember when computers were exotic inventions. Only during the past decade have instructors incorporated computers into teaching and learning. Now the potential of scientific products and processes in education is limitless.

EMERGENCE OF INSTRUCTIONAL TECHNOLOGY

The printing press was the first major technological advancement to affect education, because printing enabled students as well as the instructor to own a textbook. In fact once everyone had access to books, mass education became possible.

Until the advent of television, the United States was a print-based society, education was synonymous with books, and educators often viewed the library as the focal point of the college campus. As television became the dominant medium in U.S. society, many alternative instructional systems evolved: Television monitors became standard classroom equipment as early morning television brought courses to students in individual classrooms. In the Department of Psychology at Pennsylvania State University during the 1960s, a professor could lecture simultaneously to several classrooms, thereby eliminating the necessity of repeating the same lecture to different classes.

In programmed instruction, another forerunner of modern instructional technology, a student reads a passage from print and then answers questions about the material. The computer rewards the student, then moves to the next segment. B. F. Skinner, a behavioral psychologist at Harvard University, made this form of immediate, positive reinforcement popular. With programmed instruction, students progress at their own rate and learn independently. Although educators at first heralded programmed instruction as revolutionary, leading perhaps to the extinction of teachers, the method quickly lost popularity and failed to replace more classical approaches because it was unidimensional and boring. While some students found programmed instruction an attractive, practical, and economical way of learning, most students are social creatures who value interaction. Essentially both programmed instruction and televised instruction had been discarded by the late 1960s.[1]

The arrival of computer-based instruction in the 1970s revived programmed instruction by using computers to guide a student through lessons. For example, if a student reads and successfully answers questions on a section of material, the computer tells the student to proceed to the next task. However if a student has not mastered the content, the computer guides the student through additional exercises designed to supplement the original material.

Through such branching, as the design is called, the student completes many activities. At each wrong turn, the computer explains why the answers selected is incorrect. Computerized instruction, therefore, improves on programmed instruction by enhancing the user friendliness of the delivery system.

The potential of programmed instruction, instructional television, and the early forms of computer-based instruction led some advocates of instructional technology to find ways to replace some traditional, lecture-based instructional formats. Although these three forms influence college teaching, none replaces the instructor, chalkboard, and classroom filled with students. Despite the utility of technology, we have not seen a revolution in teaching, and professional educators believe this is due to one factor: Interaction must take place. Students who watch instructional television become restless after 30–40 minutes; similarly, it is fatiguing to follow computer-guided instruction for an hour or two. From experience and research, educators know that any new method of instruction must be designed with the student in mind.

Today several factors suggest that a technological revolution may be coming. Consider that by using classroom equipment, instructors can deliver material through multimedia presentations; for example an instructor may begin the class with a 15-minute lecture, then present a 10-minute videotape demonstrating concepts from the lecture, which is followed by a 20- to 30-minute discussion. Alternatively an instructor may use a personal computer and a projection screen to show the class charts or graphs that evolve as the class investigates concepts. Many professors incorporate multiple teaching methods in their delivery systems, realizing that no one or two approaches ensure learning. Thus we have moved beyond the earlier notion that programmed instruction or instructional television alone can satisfy instructional needs in the classroom.

Compact disk technology is a second breakthrough in instructional technology. Through disks students can access print, graphics, sound, and video for a wide range of interactive options. Instructors at The University of Georgia, for example, deliver one unit of veterinary pathology to students via interactive videodisk technology. Students individually or in small groups proceed through recorded segments of instruction where they observe tissues, hear statements from experts, watch surgical techniques, and even engage in problem-solving exercises. In many instances, as students progress through units on their own, an instructor is nearby to answer questions or provide technical assistance. The advent of interactive videodisk technology brings together several missing features that kept earlier forms of instructional technology from being complete and practical.

AN INFORMATION EXCHANGE MODEL FOR THE FUTURE

Educational technology is making diverse teaching methods available, as the information exchange model in Figure 10.1 illustrates.

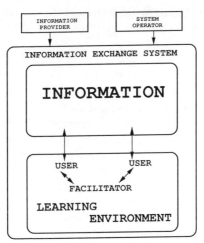

Figure 10.1. An Information Exchange Model.

The model has seven components: information system, information provider, information, user, facilitator, system operator, and learning environment. The *information system* refers to the overall base of technology that houses information. For example if videodisk technology is the basic format, then the information system consists of all the components that make the system work: basic video equipment, videodisk players, monitors, personal computers, and the setting in which the users (students) engage in learning activities.

The *information provider* selects and organizes the material to be learned. The instructor, an information provider, incorporates information produced by others into the learning experience. For example a 5-minute video clip from a local news segment may be part of a presentation on campaign strategies in political races.

The *information* refers to concepts, principles, and data to be learned. Instructional goals and objectives form the learning framework for and often include higher order activities, such as acquiring problem-solving skills and the examining complex attitudes and values.

The *user* refers to anyone engaged in learning; hence user equals student. The term user implies activity and interaction, and within this model students can work individually or with other students.

The *facilitator* offers students individualized or group assistance. The facilitator may play a direct and active role or operate in a more indirect manner. Within some systems, the facilitator administers evaluation measures; that is, the facilitator may distribute, proctor, and collect test materials. As the word implies, facilitator means doing a variety of things to help people learn.

The *system operator* is responsible for overseeing the total system, which may be the course instructor, learning center coordinator, or specially trained instructional technologist. The system operator keeps records, evaluates the system, and controls quality. The system operator is also responsible for handling such problems as scheduling, space allocation, access to courses, and cost factors.

Within the information exchange model, the concept of classroom is a highly modified one. A *learning environment* may be a computer laboratory, a learning center, an office, a dormitory room, or one's home. The most common learning environment in the information exchange model is a learning center or a computer laboratory. As technology advances, learning environments will include just about any space where learning can occur. Instructional technology may prove to be a viable solution to many problems associated with location and space allocation.

TECHNOLOGY LEADS TO CONCEPTUAL CHANGE

Our model represents a departure from traditional approaches to instruction and suggests profound changes in the way teachers and students view responsibility for learning, time, and evaluation.

Responsibility for Learning

Responsibility for learning was addressed over two decades ago when mastery learning became a popular concept among educators. This idea, championed by Benjamin Bloom at the University of Chicago, is based on the premise that the ultimate learning outcome is mastery.[2] In other words, education should consist of carefully formulated objectives, written in terms of performance outcomes, followed by the student's demonstrated ability to perform or master the objectives.

Instructional technology and the information exchange model make mastery learning possible. In a broader sense, responsibility for learning shifts from the instructor to the student, which creates a new environment for teaching and learning.[3] Once instructors communicate course objectives and offer students alternative methods for mastering the objectives, then learning, not teaching, becomes the focus, because students control the technology that directs learning.

Time

Bloom maintains that given ample time and support, almost all students can be successful. However, in traditional classrooms, everyone has the same amount of time to master course content even though students learn at different rates. Therefore when time is constant, the amount learned must vary. When using instructional technology, time becomes a variable, and the amount learned is constant. Formal instruction is not limited to one- or two-hour segments on certain days of the week in a fixed space, and a course is equivalent to mastering a specific amount of material.

Evaluating Learning

Traditionally differences in student achievement, or grades, fall along a bell-shaped curve or normal distribution. Evaluators presume that student behavior (in this case, performance), like other human characteristics or natural phenomena, follows a normal distribution, so that grading on the curve, norm-referenced grading, usually leads to a few As and Fs, a large but close to equal number of Bs and Ds, and then a large cluster of Cs in the middle. By forcing student achievement to fit this normal distribution curve, educators maximize differences, and with norm-referenced grading, one student's grade depends on the achievement of others in the class.

Individualized instruction discourages norm-referenced evaluation in favors criterion-referenced evaluation, which measures progress on the basis of predetermined criteria or standards rather than on classmates' progress. Criterion-referenced evaluation is competency, or performance, based, so that it is compatible with educational models requiring students to demonstrate mastery. In addition criterion-referenced evaluation offers students more control over their learning.

MULTIMEDIA TECHNOLOGY

In the United States, the average 16-year-old has spent more than 15,000 hours in front of a television set.[4] But today's predominant source of entertainment will become tomorrow's predominant method of learning as instructors present material to a group or to individuals in other locations using several kinds of media at once.

Multimedia presentations generally involve three components, one of which is sound. In many disciplines, such as music, speech, and wildlife biology, we study interaction through sound. By storing, delivering, and controlling sound with computers, sound can be incorporated into a multimedia presentation.[5]

Today's most common source of sound is the compact disk (CD). With a CD read only memory (ROM) player and a pair of speakers, computers allow users to manipulate prerecorded music, audio recordings of performances, and foreign language lessons; and stereo headphones permit students to listen without disrupting others in a language or music laboratory.[6]

Graphics is the second multimedia component. Graphics designers can display textual material on a screen and the material with add boxes, typeface, and diagrams to allow instructors to insert art work, figures from books, diagrams, photographs, and frames from videotape.

In addition to sound and graphics, new concepts in video enhance instruction. For example with the advent of digital video—the capability to reduce images to segments that can be edited, stored, and replayed without loss in quality—video can be incorporated into other forms of media. Furthermore videodisk and CD-ROM technologies, permit video, audio, and graphic material to be stored, combined, and presented in a multimedia format.

The videodisk, a larger version of the audio compact disk, stores images that are read by a small laser within the videodisk player. The player converts the digital data into ordinary video and plays it through a video monitor. Since the audio tracks of a videodisk are like those of ordinary CDs, a videodisk can deliver high-quality stereo sound along with visual images. Videodisk players also show still pictures similar to those shown by typical slide projectors.[7]

The videodisk offers three advantages: First the disk can hold a large quantity of information in a multimedia format. Second users can extract the information in any sequence quickly, and third the medium allows individual interaction. For example students who find a concept or problem difficult can access additional information on that topic. Videodisk technology ensures the user's involvement and permits students to control the medium through which they are learning.

Multimedia is becoming a powerful tool for classroom presentations. At the University of North Carolina at Chapel Hill for example several specially equipped master classrooms allow faculty to present material in multiple ways, while at St. Petersburg Junior College, teaching bunkers, consisting of a podium with a built-in MacIntosh computer networked to other on-line campus resources, are being tested.

INSTRUCTION AND THE HUMAN TOUCH

It is important to remember that contact between student and instructor makes learning real. The professor's knowledge is the most important factor, with instructional technology in a supporting role. In the future, teaching and learning will be more cooperative and collaborative as subject matter experts join hands with instructional developers and technologists to create new systems for instruction. Human beings on both sides of the desk will, however, remain the most important factors.

11 📖 Balancing Athletics and Academics

Ronald Smith, in his book *Sports and Freedom*,[1] tells of a meeting in 1852 between the superintendent of the Boston, Concord, and Montreal railroads, James Elkins, and Yale college's James Whiton, a junior and member of the Yale Boat Club. Elkins offered, "If you will get up a regatta on the Winnipesaukee Lake between Yale and Harvard, I will pay all the bills."

Harvard's victory over Yale in this 8-day, all-expenses-paid trip was the first U.S. intercollegiate contest. Commercially the venture was successful: A thousand spectators watched, many of them from a train. But the serenity of that summer day in 1852 is not always repeated in U.S. college sports. Smith notes that seemingly pleasurable and innocent pastimes can lead to strong competition in commercially stimulated collegiate contests.[2]

From that first contest, U.S. collegiate athletics has developed in sophisticated and sometimes disturbing ways. During the turn of the century, the United States expanded, sought wealth, and emerged as a world power, and athletics was both a reflection and symbol of the new, competitive nation. Today lucrative contracts and television coverage have almost completely commercialized college sports. In the past, the relationship between academics and athletics may have received scant attention in a discussion of undergraduate education, but now the situation has changed. No discussion of the undergraduate experience is complete without considering the influence of major sports programs on campus.

THE SEARCH FOR BALANCE

Oxford University was formed in 1167, and Cambridge followed about 40 years later. Because England was the first modern sporting nation and students at these two institutions were the elite of that country, it follows that collegiate sports would reflect society at that time. In England boating, cricket, horse racing, hunting, and tennis prevailed during the sixteenth, seventeenth, and eighteenth centuries; other participant sports included bowling on the green, boxing, bull baiting, cock fighting, fishing, handball, football, and swimming. Fox hunting with hounds was probably the favorite pastime, and students regularly got into trouble when fox hunting and other sports took precedence over Latin and Greek.[3]

Sports in early U.S. colleges developed under the strong influence of England. Rivalries between Harvard and Yale and sporting activities at the College of William and Mary resembled those at Cambridge and Oxford. Between 1636 and the American Revolution, there was considerable tension between academics and sports at the colonial colleges—Harvard, William and Mary, Yale, Columbia, The University of Pennsylvania, Princeton, Dartmouth, Brown, and Rutgers. Because of the curriculum's religious focus, many forms of recreation and sporting activities were prohibited on campus; in fact many colonial institutions were located in small, remote towns away from the negative influences of cities.[4]

After the American Revolution, religious freedom led to some loosening of the rules. Although the classical curriculum at Harvard lasted for two centuries, students began to push for change in the 1800s, and college officials eventually accepted sports as officially sanctioned activities. Later intercollegiate competition emerged in several sports. For male students, the first sporting events, held between 1852 and 1905,[5] were among the Ivy League institutions.

Then just as today, some considered sports to be character building, while others viewed sports as antiintellectual activities.

England, colonial United States, and early industrial United States experienced many of today's stresses as college athletics struggled for control. By 1900 newspapers reported brutality and ruthlessness on playing fields, and in 1905 President Charles Eliot of Harvard described football as "violent attempts to disable opponents with heavy blows." He lamented that "no means could be found to prevent players and coaches from violating the rules of play."[6] Student organizations, college faculties, college presidents, and boards of trustees all failed to control collegiate sports.

Calls for reform by President Theodore Roosevelt, officials at Harvard, Princeton, and Yale, and leaders from other institutions resulted in the formation in 1906 of what was to become the National Collegiate Athletic Association (NCAA). The new and initially weak organization reformed rules, the most notable being the 10-yard first-down rule in football. As the NCAA gained strength, it called attention to several problems facing intercollegiate sports. For example the NCAA favored limiting the number of scholarships offered by an institution, prohibiting professional athletes from college teams, and giving control of athletic policy to local institutions.[7]

The NCAA brought a sense of balance to college athletics. Today about one thousand institutions form the five divisions of the NCAA. Division I institutions (about 300) engage in many intercollegiate sports, offering at least six sports for men and six for women. These schools award grants-in-aid without regard for the financial need of students, but the NCAA limits the number of scholarships awarded to participants in each sport. Institutions of course also have priorities and restrictions based on organizational goals, tradition, and financial resources.

Division I schools are split into three subgroups, with about one hundred schools in each category. Since Division I-A schools have major football programs, these schools have the largest budgets and stadiums, grant the most football scholarships, attract the most spectators, and play the most difficult teams. Another third belong to Division I-AA. These institutions have major athletic programs, but their football programs are smaller

When an ancient human clan went to war against their neighbors, survival for all was at stake. Conflict, ritualized or real, evokes those ancient warlike emotions. Winning this ancient contest was literally a matter of life and death. In these modern surrogates, as the saying goes, "Winning isn't everything; it's the only thing." "Die for dear old alma mater!" say the fight songs. You almost think some people would. These contests are residual combat.

If college sports cannot be reformed by leaders of the academy, it is because these passions evoked by sports are too powerful for the university. To these ancient passions must now, of course, be added greed. Big money is at stake everywhere in college athletics. Television has changed everything in the modern world, including college games. The university is a poor match for the organized influence of the media.

The university was established to manage the passionless but ultimate tasks of teaching the young and searching for truth. The structures of control in the university reflect this central mission. Those structures may well prove too fragile to deal with the passions inflamed by games. Universities manage teaching and learning well. We are no good at fanaticism and passion and money. Our managerial ideology reflects the traditions of collegiality and shared governance.

I sat high in the packed stadium at a bowl game last year. The place was filled with fanatics who had come great distances at great expense for this contest. The parking lot was filled with recreational vehicles, which seemed to me mobile temples, shrines on wheels, to the gods and heroes of the competing schools. The banners of conflict waved, and the bands blared the call to arms. The roar of the crowd was deafening. Sacramental liquors were served to intensify the experience of the conflict. Satellite dishes beamed this spectacle to millions elsewhere. It was spectacular in the literal sense. What is the university against these passions?

Thomas K. Hearn, Jr., president, Wake Forest University, from a speech delivered at the NCAA meeting in Kansas City, Missouri (8 Oct. 1990) than those in Division I-A. The third category is Division I-AAA for schools with major basketball programs and small football programs.

Division II schools offer at least four men's and four women's sports programs and have the option of offering grants-in-aid to student athletes. Division III schools must also sponsor at least four men's and four women's programs, but these schools offer scholarships based only on need. Division III, the largest NCAA division, includes small colleges with sports programs and universities with small programs.

FROM SPORTS PAGE TO FRONT PAGE

When an institution makes sports headlines with positive news, alumni are happy, regional pride is high, enrollment rises, revenue for the athletic department goes up, and donors increase their universitywide support.

But some of these advantages may be problematic. In his foreword to *The Old College Try* by John Thelin and Laurence Wiseman,[8] Jonathan Fife identifies three potentially negative effects on the institution as a whole. The first is financial: In periods of restricted funding, nonacademic expenses divert funds from the educational activities. The second effect is academic: favoritism. When student-athletes appear to have more important nonacademic than academic roles, some suspect that academic standards have been corrupted. The third effect is importance: When nonacademic activities seem more popular and therefore more influential than academics, some fear that the educational mission takes a secondary position.

Thelin and Wiseman illustrate the fickle existence of college sports. In 1985 the *Washington Post* reported on intercollegiate athletics at a major state university that institution had achieved national success in both football and basketball and was cited for having ascended to "within shouting range of the best." Over the next 3 years however, a controversy brought unfavorable news

In our nation sports has been a means of expressing and maintaining our national vitality. Intercollegiate athletic programs have served as the spark of interest for people all over the country and have afforded recognition to many institutions. Historically, college athletic programs have reflected the interests of the institution's students, faculty, and alumni. They have provided a source of enthusiasm and loyalty and have enriched the lives of the entire academic community.

Recently, there has been much written about the direction of college athletics and the need to place the well-being of the student athlete in the forefront. We in college athletics have had to answer growing questions regarding the student athlete's access to the education process, the educational services offered while attending an institution and, of course, those athletes who participate and ultimately graduate.

Roy Kramer, commissioner of the Southeastern Conference, recently stated, "I think it's important for the integrity of athletics for the athlete, within reason, to represent the entire student body." However, college presidents and athletic administrators have come under increased pressure from alumni, fans, and students to win. So, we who are very close to this issue, find ourselves wrestling with the associated issues surrounding the feat of balancing academics and athletics.

Athletic administrators recognize their obligation to the institution, its faculty, alumni, and especially to the parents everywhere who send us their sons and daughters to provide recognized academic achievement and a means for individual as well as social development. Accordingly, athletics departments throughout our nation have developed student athlete support programs that have been designed to assist the student athlete in achieving academically as well as athletically.

These are challenging times for college athletics as many of the nation's brightest minds in the private as well as the public sectors seek to preserve the great pleasure and the excitement, the spectacle of extraordinary effort and color that surround college athletics. It's for these reasons I believe we will continue to see an increasing era of shared responsibility and accountability between the academic and athletic communities. It is important that college athletics, so closely meshed with institutional tradition, continue to enrich the life of our academic communities and serve as a common rallying point for people of all ages and backgrounds.

Vince Dooley, athletics director, The University of Georgia

coverage and internal strain to the entire institution: College athletics appeared on the front page, not the sports page, and the news was not good. Problems with athletics coincided with the university president's decision to resign. Ironically only a small news article in a back section of the paper announced that the interim president sought a new image for the university as he traveled the state to repair its tarnished reputation.[9]

This story is not unusual. Each year prominent U.S. universities are involved in the abuse of intercollegiate athletic regulations, and the entire institution receives unfavorable national publicity. In the past 10 years, stories in *The Wall Street Journal*, *U.S. News and World Report*, and *Sports Illustrated* indicate that athletic scandals are common in college sports.[10]

At one time, the NCAA may be investigating multiple potential violations at over a dozen institutions. At one major university in Pennsylvania, regulators scrutinized the handling of money by the athletics department's booster group. A local paper charged that current players received cash and gifts through an assistant coach. At the same time, a Southwestern Conference basketball coach resigned amid charges that a player from another university had transferred to his school illegally. At another institution, three athletes were allowed to play despite failing to meet academic standards. A highly visible university in the South faced allegations that athletes received federal aid by fraudulent means, and a former university counselor admitted to falsifying federal financial aid applications for athletes and charging them $85 each to support his cocaine habit.[11]

Situations such as these lead to the conclusion that intercollegiate athletics can no longer be dismissed as a peripheral college or university activity.[12] Scandals in college and university sports tarnish the image of higher education. Because college presidents are dismissed because of such matters and millions of dollars are involved, academic leadership is taking a strong position.

Each year the NCAA publishes its constitution and by-laws, operating procedures, and membership rules. Consistent with the early concept of the NCAA, the association attempts to give considerable power and control to member institutions and the conferences to which most members belong. Some believe however that the NCAA is too controlling, while others believe that a high degree of control is necessary. Most agree on one point: A more reasonable balance between academics and college athletics should be found.

Today NCAA officials call for increased self-regulation by institutions, recommending that colleges and universities adopt a high moral tone regarding recruitment and academic standards. College presidents speak forthrightly about academic integrity and intellectual honesty. Faculty members are also concerned and many bringing autonomous athletic associations under the careful scrutiny of the central administration to ensure that profits from athletics support the entire university.

On campuses athletic boards that report to presidents or chancellors most often regulate institutional action. Each conference commissioner in turn monitors the conference just as athletic boards monitor institutions. Technically the president of each institution is the only representative who can vote on NCAA policies, rules, and other practices. In reality most college presidents are too busy to stay abreast of the matters at hand and rely on their athletic directors for guidance. At some institutions, faculty want to control policy, while on other campuses, administrators, including head coaches, athletic directors, or chief academic officers, make policy decisions.

ATTEMPTS AT REFORM

Pressure for reform comes primarily from two sources: The NCAA Presidents Commission and related NCAA activities attempting to bring about change from within the system and some members of the U.S. Congress pursuing change through forced legislation. Forty-four college presidents elected by their peers form the NCAA Presidents Commission[13]; 22 members are presidents of Division I schools, 11 of Division II schools, and 11 of Division III schools. College presidents can vote only for members within their division, and members are limited to two 4-year terms. The commission is empowered to examine any policies or procedures it desires and to bring before the convention or special meetings any concerns or proposals it deems necessary. Perhaps the commission's two most significant areas of influence are the studies presidents initiate and their control over the order of a meeting, which enables presidents to influence the issues the group considers.

In 1991 the NCAA began a voluntary certification process to assess the performance of university sports programs in seven areas, including governance, finance, and academics. By 1992 the association had adopted more stringent academic standards than those held in the past. For example sports officials reduced cost and time demands on student athletes, and presidents reestablished themselves as the dominant force in the NCAA. Presidents of NCAA schools acknowledge that their reform work is not done, but they plan an aggressive course of action for the rest of the 1990s. Critics note that the "megaquestions" of commercialism and links to television revenues remain unaddressed.[14]

Meanwhile Congress has taken a different approach. In 1992 perceiving that the NCAA and its member institutions were reluctant to initiate significant reforms, Representative Tom McMillen, a Democrat from Maryland, former Rhodes Scholar, and college and professional basketball player, proposed that the NCAA remain exempt from antitrust laws only if major rule changes, including those involving financial issues, were forthcoming.

Other lawmakers joined McMillen's efforts to control the salaries of professional athletics and to support higher academic standards for athletes. Regardless of the position one takes on these matters, balancing athletics with academics is a socially and politically charged issue.

The Knight Commission is another visible force for reform. In 1992 the 22-member group, including Lamar Alexander, former U.S. Secretary of Education, and Representative McMillen, recommended that college presidents use their power to reform the "fundamental premises" of college sports.[15] The Knight Commission suggested broad guidelines for college presidents and the NCAA to follow.[16] The Rev. Theodore M. Hesburgh, president emeritus of the University of Notre Dame and a member of the commission, expected the report to make a difference, but some critics believe the commission should make more specific suggestions, while others view the report as a road map to reform in college sports.

The Knight Commission recommended that governing boards give total authority for sports programs to college presidents. Presidents should, in turn, seize control of NCAA decision making and ensure that their sports programs comply with federal statutes barring sex discrimination. The NCAA should require incoming freshman athletes to complete 15 high school core subjects. The academic performance of all athletes should be reviewed each semester and athletes declared ineligible if they are not making progress toward a specific degree. Colleges should require athletes in all sports to graduate at the same rate as other students, they recommend, and scholarships for athletes should last for 5 years with grants for needy athletes covering the full cost of attending college. The Knight Commission also recommended that all athletics revenues—including booster club gifts and coaches' outside income—go to the university's general financial system, with coaches having long-term contracts. Each college should conduct an annual academic and financial audit of its sports program, and results of the audits should be made public.

In addition to the NCAA, alumni, faculty, and administration, there is another key player in the story of college athletics: the athletic director. Previously institutions attracted a popular football or basketball coach by offering the title of athletic director. This practice is less common today, since athletic directors must operate, much like college presidents, as both internal managers of multiple teams and programs as well as external managers in charge of public relations, fund raising, and other development activities. The athletic director, like the president, is caught between producing winning teams and operating a clean and fair athletic program in all sports. This requires competent, full-time leadership.

REFORM AND THE FUTURE

At most institutions where athletics is of prime interest, the athletic director reports directly to the president. Financial and administrative details of the athletic program are important and distinct enough to warrant a separate unit outside the control of academic deans, other vice presidents, or faculty. Today some athletic directors are providing more academic assistance to athletes and contributing funds to support universitywide academic programs. No matter how the administrative structure is arranged, athletic directors play an increasingly complex role in higher education.

However, college presidents are ultimately responsible for athletics, and many campus CEOs are taking a more aggressive role. It is clear that the NCAA and other educational organizations want academic leaders to govern athletics, but this is easier said than done.

Many proposals were debated at the 1992 NCAA meeting in Anaheim, California; some involved increasing core academic courses from 11 to 13, raising the minimum high school core grade point average from 2.0 to 2.5, and allowing freshmen to be eligible with lower entering test scores if offset by higher grade point averages. Other proposals involved phasing out scholarships to nonqualifiers in all sports by 1996 to 1997 and strengthening satisfactory progress rules. Further proposals included requiring junior college transfers who were nonqualifiers to wait a year before becoming eligible at a 4-year school, requiring institutions to provide graduation rates to a prospective athlete's guidance office, and requiring institutions to pay tuition for athletes formerly on full scholarship if their eligibility expires before they have completed degree requirements. Institutions would pay athletes' tuition until they received a degree or were dismissed for academic or disciplinary reasons. Other proposals would allow scholarship aid for incoming freshmen to attend summer school prior to the first academic year, prohibit Division I schools from housing athletes in privately owned dormitories or apartments, and reduce Division II scholarships 10 percent across the board.

Like other proposed regulations, raising the grade point

During the National Collegiate Athletic Association's (NCAA) Annual Conference, the Presidents Commission introduced legislation to enhance the student life environment of the student-athlete. Earlier, policies had been adopted that raised minimum admission standards for freshman as well as for student-athletes transferring from junior college. These were initiatives that were aimed at increasing the probability for academic success by student-athletes.

A study commissioned by the NCAA found that had the tougher rules been in force in 1981, nearly 60 percent of football and basketball recruits would have been ineligible. But when it took effect in 1986, after a 3-year warning period, only 9 percent of football players and 13 percent of basketball players were ineligible. This supports my thesis that when you provide standards, people will usually try to attain them. I believe in the past, some athletes made lower scores simply because there was little pressure to achieve a certain standard. Today, it's exciting to see, first-hand, those athletes who have risen to the test.

Vince Dooley, athletics director, The University of Georgia

average from 2.0 to 2.5 is significant, since coaches across the country estimate that more than half of today's football players would not qualify under this stricter ruling. Such recommendations will take years to evaluate, and other modifications will be forthcoming, but regardless of specific changes, it is clear that educational leaders are serious about raising academic standards for athletes and changing how athletic programs are financed and held accountable. The balance between academics and athletics is changing, but the problem of balance forms an integral part of our collegiate history and will continue to challenge higher education in the future.

A GLANCE AT THE STUDENT ATHLETE

Considering the role of the student athlete is an appropriate way to end this chapter. Yolanda Pittman gets up at 6:00 A.M. sharp each morning for a grueling run and workout before breakfast and class. Yolanda, a 19-year-old African-American member of the women's basketball team at a prominent Western university, is very much like any student working her way through college. She spends 20–36 hours a week practicing, traveling, and competing in basketball at a school that takes this sport seriously. But unlike her classmates who work at Burger King or in the university bookstore, she is never free of her job because wherever she goes, classmates want to talk about the next big game or about their last win over UCLA.

This emerging star athlete also has other challenges that go beyond those faced by most of her peers. As a youngster growing up in Los Angeles, she spent countless hours at the local playground playing basketball and grooming her physical skills. She could outrun, outjump, and outplay other children her age. In high school, she enjoyed an enviable reputation, but the long hours devoted to basketball decreased her study time, and Yolanda fell behind in mathematics and language arts. So while working her way through college and handling the attention that follows her everywhere, Yolanda also has to work to catch up in English and mathematics.

This situation is common for many college athletes. Like Yolanda they have additional challenges that other students do not face. Some are unable to cope with the glitter and challenge of major college sports, and when they finally discover the price of winning and being successful in college, it is too late to survive.

There is of course a bright side of athletics, and numerous sterling athletes are also stars in the classroom. Although many believe that athletes are less intelligent and less motivated to learn than other students, participation in athletics often leads to the development of values, work habits, and commitment that are important assets in an individual's personal and professional lives.

Mike McKenzie, a successful attorney in Atlanta, is an example. Mike recognizes that his success as a defensive back on Georgia Tech's football team during the early 1970s helped prepare him for a successful career in litigation. For McKenzie a win on Saturday afternoon in Bobby Dodd Stadium came when "I was better prepared than my opponent." Today Mike says, "I can win for my client when I am better prepared than the opposing attorney. For me, playing college athletics was the best preparation possible for my career. I learned how to cope with defeat and how to get back up after being knocked down."

Other stories about athletes in other sports are equally stirring. Many young women and men who have played collegiate golf, tennis, or competed in gymnastics have gone on to professional careers directly or indirectly related to their athletic experience. Todd Simpson for example won the Flint Junior Championship in golf after high school. He enrolled at Central Michigan University, where he is majoring in speech communication. Todd hopes for a career in golf after college.

Of course there is another side: Some athletes face such intense pressure to win that they use steroids or other performance-enhancing drugs. Dick Bestwick, former head football coach at the University of Virginia says, "College athletes taking drugs is not unlike white-collar crime. The motivation is the same.

People think that if I just do a little of this or a little of that, it will help me succeed and nobody will know that I cheated just a little." Other athletes speak privately about how marginally prepared students search for ways to cheat academically. Intense pressure to win at all costs can lead young men and women to seek ways of beating the system, not realizing that in doing so, they shortchange themselves for life.

Many of life's joys and disappointments are depicted in sports, and many of these highs and lows mirror life itself. We encourage students to learn how to live in responsible ways. College athletics, like other enterprises in our society, are neither good nor bad. It is how one chooses to handle the challenges embodied in collegiate sports that is good or bad. How one learns to accept responsibility, make commitment, and deal with adversity makes the difference.

12 🎓 The World: The New U.S. Classroom

In 1785 Thomas Jefferson offered this advice to a young American seeking an education that would prepare him to serve his country:

> Cast your eye over America: who are the men of most learning, of most eloquence, most beloved by their countrymen and most trusted and promoted by them? They are those who have been educated among them, and whose manners, morals, and habits are perfectly homogeneous with those of the country. . . . The consequences of foreign education are alarming to me, as an American.[1]

Jefferson, writing from Paris, where he had succeeded Benjamin Franklin as resident minister, captured the spirit of a newly independent United States in which some states assigned alien status to citizens who went abroad to be educated.[2] Today our attitudes toward international education are quite different. As a candidate, President Clinton declared that leadership for the new millennium should be leadership for change, leadership that recognizes the United States need not run the world but should meet the competition and win.[3] The United States cannot afford to respond from a culturally, educationally, or economically isolationist position; we must recognize our world interdependence and work to create global linkages for a productive future. In *Megatrends 2000*, futurists John Naisbitt and Patricia Aburdene name the "booming global economy of the 1990s" as the first trend of the new millennium. Despite forecasts of doom by economists,

Naisbitt and Aburdene predict that the world is entering a period of growth in which no single influence defines the new order. Rather, accelerated change fuels prosperity. Today the United States, Japan, Western and Eastern Europe, and the Third World no longer have their own economies. They are instead parts of a global structure that defies national borders and promises increased democracy, freedom, trade, opportunity, and prosperity. In the 1980s, economies became more important than ideologies, and today economic considerations transcend political considerations, telecommunications drive growth, and human resources provide the competitive edge for countries and companies.[4] Today's economic competition is a global race in which innovative ideas define success.

This state of affairs opens new vistas for business and political leaders, educators, and college students across the nation and around the globe. The twenty-first century will be the era of the

---

Let's look at what the world will be like in the early twenty-first century. I believe that we will be well along in the information age—an age characterized by the vast amounts of information available. We will no longer take our know-how and apply it to low-cost natural resources from third-world countries, turn it into products, and sell it back to them—as we do in a hierarchical economy. Rather, we'll be only one member in a global dynamic economy with tremendous network interdependency between countries.

We're going to have to come up with new kinds of industries, and those industries, in my opinion, are not going to be ones that we had in the industrial age if we are to be competitive with the rest of the world. They will be industries very much tied to innovation, using America's ability to create new technology, ideas, and services. That has always been one of our strengths. Established companies will be reinventing themselves, and new ones will be appearing all the time.

John Sculley, chairman, Apple Computer from "A Perspective on the Future," *Change* (Mar./Apr. 1988)

individual as hierarchies flatten, and the value of personal contribution grows. Perhaps more than ever before, creative, imaginative individuals will be courted, hired, and advanced in companies that recognize the value of superior employees. Job-specific international competencies are critical skills in the U.S. work place. For example, managers in banking and transportation need to speak the language of their clients, negotiators in business need to understand the culture of their competitors, and researchers need to build on the work of their international colleagues.

In exploring unique learning experiences on today's college and university campuses, we have described the new and diverse undergraduate mix and examined innovative curricula and programs designed to customize learning. In Chapter 12, we expand the learning stage from a single classroom or campus by considering the effect of the global economy and worldwide competitiveness on individual learning. Sven Groennings of the American Express Company underscored the importance of the coming global economy when he observed that it rivals the civil rights movement as the most important long-term development in this country since World War II. The new scheme is not only a U.S. phenomenon; everyone will be affected.[5]

How will the United States become more competitive in a global economy? Certainly individuals and their ideas and energy will make the difference. Professor Rosabeth Moss Kanter of the Harvard Business School compares the global economy to a corporate Olympics with domestic and international competitors who compete as individuals in some contests and as team members in others. Collaboration will play a key role. Kanter advises business leaders to keep doing all they are doing, only better and to become dedicated visionaries.[6]

Who are these visionaries and how do they lead? In 1991, *Fortune* magazine searched the country to identify the most exciting U.S. visionaries for the new century. One person selected was Ralph Gomory, president of the Alfred P. Sloan Foundation. According to Gomory, cooperation between the industrial and academic communities in Japan and Germany feeds new ideas into their economies. Such cooperation is lacking in the United States, but Gomory is working to link the academic community to industry. In recent years, the Sloan Foundation has given millions of dollars to Carnegie-Mellon, Harvard, and other universities to develop expertise in various industries. For example, Sloan backed a Massachusetts Institute of Technology (MIT) study of the global auto industry. Gomory expects the partnership to result in new products and new manufacturing methods. Ultimately his strategies should encourage U.S. business leaders to adopt winning attitudes by realizing that last year's competitive stance is this year's fallback position. By today's definition, progress is the process of constantly accelerating change.[7]

In the new world order, the concept of linkage is critical for business and for education. Many U.S. students acquire facets of a competitive education but fail to link them; for example students major in a foreign language or study in a foreign country, but few use their time abroad to complete internships with international companies. Thus they forfeit opportunities to make valuable international connections and learn firsthand about competing in other cultures. At home many students study geography, business, and sociology, but few combine work in these disciplines with an international focus. In Chapter 2, we consider the power of integrated links. We do not dwell on traditional study abroad or foreign language majors but look instead at awareness-expanding international and domestic experiences that prepare students for tomorrow's boundless opportunities. First we examine the critical need for such knowledge, then investigate the link between international education and the competition in our society.

INTERNATIONAL EDUCATION: A FRAMEWORK FOR GLOBAL PERSPECTIVES

As Jefferson indicated, formal U.S. education has traditionally included foreign, and predominantly Western European, travel and study. Perhaps this predilection reflects our cultural debt to

Europe for our unique system of higher education. Early U.S. colleges patterned themselves after English colleges, where professors lived with their students and prescribed a standard classical curriculum. Later the German ideal of pure learning led to the U.S. notion of pure science, and research became the focus of the U.S. university.[8] At first small numbers of U.S. students studied abroad. Then in 1919, higher education leaders and proponents of internationalization joined forces to found the Institute of International Education, an organized effort to exchange knowledge about and with other nations. By 1930 more than 5000 U.S. students were studying abroad.[9] The trend caught on and grew.

After World War II, the Fulbright educational program expanded the opportunity for international education for U.S. college students. The Fulbright program was designed to increase the mutual understanding of U.S. citizens and citizens of other countries through educational and cultural exchange. Originally the sale of surplus war property abroad funded Fulbright travel grants. In 1961 the Fulbright–Hays Act took over and extended the focus on people and their need to understand one another. Each year about 3000 U.S. citizens apply for a thousand Fulbright awards.

To meet growing national interests in the international community, the federal government has also created other opportunities for learning, such as technical assistance programs administered by the Agency for International Development and the Peace Corps, which aids in building the infrastructure of developing nations. Federally funded foreign language and area studies on our campuses aim at improving foreign relations by enhancing our understanding of others.[11]

The Peace Corps, originally intended to combine public service with a global experience, today attracts students who have the skills most needed by foreign countries. Some institutions offer "Peace Corps tracks" in the curriculum to prepare students for service abroad, while other institutions grant credit to students for service when they return to the United States.[10] In 1990, 3500 people served in the Peace Corps, and another 13,000 applications could not be accommodated.

By the early 1980s, many higher education, business, and political leaders had recognized our growing world interdependence, and the future of international education seemed bright. New and traditional offerings fared well, and international education programs, originally authorized as Title VI of the National Defense Act of 1958, were moved to Title VI of the Higher Education Act. About 75 percent of the total Title VI appropriation went to foreign language and area studies centers and fellowships for study at these centers. Perhaps the most exciting development, the Business and International Program, attracted grant proposals from a variety of institutions.[12]

The 1972 amendments to the Higher Education Act made grants available to help institutions give an international focus to their undergraduate offerings. Colleges and universities of all sizes planned international additions to the curriculum, and appropriations increases seemed assured. Then federal budget cuts threatened recent gains, and progressive programs in international education were halted.[13]

Although the Fulbright program, the Peace Corps, and other government-sponsored offerings continue to expand, they are not sufficient to meet the changing world order, and U.S. students continue to know less about the world outside U.S. borders than their counterparts in other countries know about the United States. While domestic companies move to capture shares of foreign markets and decision makers in U.S. business schools agree that the absence of language training is a critical weakness in U.S. business, only 1 percent of all U.S. undergraduate students major in a foreign language. While the global society becomes more knowledge-based in technology, U.S. citizens earn less than 40 percent of the doctorates conferred by U.S. universities in engineering and about 55 percent of the doctorates in the physical sciences.[14] Because educational competitiveness is a principal component of economic competitiveness, U.S. business, government, and higher education leaders have reason to worry: They know that U.S. students must have knowledge and skills at least commensurate with those of our competitors to become future leaders in a global society, and far too few U.S. students graduate from college with such proficiencies.

Meanwhile the world order is changing more rapidly than ever before: In the course of a few months, the Berlin Wall came down, the United States waged war in the Persian Gulf, and the Soviet Union was dissolved. Today global challenges await U.S. citizens in all walks of life, and business, political, and education leaders face a dilemma. While the need for a global perspective is escalating, initiatives to strengthen the international focus of the higher education curriculum are lagging. But students who persevere in their search for global training and experience will not be disappointed with the opportunities they discover.

ECONOMIC COMPETITIVENESS AND EDUCATIONAL COMPETITIVENESS

If U.S. workers do not possess knowledge and skills at least equal to those of our competitors in the world market, how can the United States remain strong? The question is a good one because the United States is not moving quickly toward educational competitiveness. Many people espouse economic competitiveness, but too few focus on educational competitiveness, which is an integral component.[15]

To become educationally competitive, teaching and research must foster an atmosphere in which what we know and not merely what we have learned is important. In such an environment, colleges and universities contribute to competitiveness on two fronts: technical know-how and international knowledge.[16]

Most U.S. business leaders today depend on technological superiority to reach and maintain strong competitive positions, but what good are their efforts if we are less effective than our Japanese competitors in selling the same product to European markets? How can we sell to the Dutch? Should we negotiate in their language or require them to negotiate in ours? How can we learn to interact with the business leaders of China? Should we stress classroom discussion and study abroad in Western Europe, or should we encourage students to intern in Chinese corporations? Carefully constructed solutions to these problems are needed to support U.S. economic competitiveness, and the best solutions should exemplify an educationally competitive stance.

Unfortunately the best solutions are not chosen often enough by U.S. businesses and students. Because we expect and require others to adopt our language, customs, and outlooks, we lack sufficient global perspective to convert opportunities into competitive positions. We fail to link economic change, competitiveness, and international education or to recognize the opportunities for links afforded by a U.S. undergraduate education.

Educational Competitiveness: What Are We Doing?

In the late 1980s, one higher education organization, the New England Board of Higher Education (NEBHE), became so concerned about U.S. performance worldwide that it commissioned a major investigation of the relationship between a global economy and higher education. The project had three empirical bases: the internationalization of the New England economy; the opinions of the region's corporate, governmental, and higher education leaders about how higher education should prepare students for the global economy; and actual practices at 40 New England colleges and universities. The study identified higher education and global economic relationships and proposed an action plan for progress. One finding—a global perspective is fundamental.[17]

How do U.S. citizens develop a global perspective? Before we can compete successfully with people from other cultures, we must understand them: We must know their political and religious ideologies and their business, community, and family structures. We must communicate effectively both verbally and nonverbally. Higher education is an invaluable resource in this learning process: In addition to teaching U.S. students the history, politics, and language of other countries, colleges and universities bring large numbers of international students to U.S. campuses each year. While learning about the United States firsthand, these visitors teach their U.S. peers more than can be learned in a classroom. The campus is a natural forum for cross-cultural learning. In addition many international students obtain a U.S. education before assuming positions of importance in their home countries, so that friendships and acquaintances they establish as students can become the basis for future international networks.[18]

Economic Competitiveness: Direct Links to Higher Education

Higher education also has a more direct stake in U.S. competitiveness: Colleges and universities draw revenues from state and local taxes; private-sector corporations support endowment drives, scholarships, and academic research; employed families contribute to the tax base and make direct donations to institutions; and endowment funds are invested in U.S. companies. Thus higher education depends on a strong national economy, as events of the last few years demonstrate all too dramatically: In October 1987, the endowment portfolios of U.S. institutions lost more than 13 percent of their value when the stock market crashed, and the recession of the early 1990s took a more serious toll on the fiscal health of colleges and universities. For example in 1990–1991, the state systems of Massachusetts, New Jersey, and Virginia lost 30, 27, and 15 percent, respectively, of their state funding, and cutbacks continue. Without question the academy's health depends on the economy's health. (For a more complete discussion of the effects of the recession on higher education, see Chapter 13.)

Colleges and universities contribute to a healthy economy in several important ways. First higher learning is a major U.S. export: Each year U.S. institutions attract more than 400,000 international students, with an export value of $4 billion. Second colleges, universities, and their employees and students spend and invest billions of dollars in this country each year; for example total revenues and expenses of the more than one thousand institutions in the 15 Southern states begin a $60 billion annual spending cycle. In all higher education contributes about $100 billion to the economy of the South annually. New England is another case in point: In 1988 260 institutions with an aggregate budget of $8 billion generated more than $20 billion in spending and respending.[19] Without the economic activity generated by higher education, these regions would be less healthy economically.

Today U.S. higher education, business, and political leaders recognize the vital link between the academy, the economy, and global competitiveness. We look to the brightest and the best of U.S. youth to generate new solutions, and we depend on their college years to prepare them for the challenge.

UNDERSTANDING THE WORLD STAGE

Up to this point, we have discussed the critical need for U.S. educational competitiveness and its tie to international education, but fundamental questions regarding specific routes to success remain. Just what are the components of international education, and how are these components incorporated into the college curriculum? How can students use these components to their maximum advantage? In investigating specific programs for international education, we find many answers to these questions; in fact college students on 10 different campuses in the United States may find 10 different but equally justifiable definitions of international education and just as many international components of specific courses and majors. They may also identify interdisciplinary programs and various opportunities to learn in other countries, since some especially progressive state and regional systems of higher education have required all the institutions under their control to increase the international focus of their offerings. Even less progressive schools are discussing international perspectives and no longer depend on foreign language instruction and isolated Western European study abroad programs to accomplish narrowly defined objectives. Today state systems, public and private institutions, and individual instructors are taking the lead. Here we look at a sampling of their efforts to give undergraduates the perspective they need to work with our neighbors around the world.

Pennsylvania Responds

In Pennsylvania long-term, statewide efforts to provide an international focus to education began in 1971. In that year, 43 public and private colleges and universities in Pennsylvania joined the Pennsylvania Council for International Education (PaCIE), which was formed to foster long-term growth of international education throughout Pennsylvania. The PaCIE soon joined with the Pennsylvania Department of Education to identify international education as a statewide priority. In 1987 the department of education brought together more than 300 business, government, labor, college, university, and school leaders to work for dramatic improvements in international education.[20] The resulting Partnership for International Competence works to ensure Pennsylvania's place as a major participant in the world economy.

Learning is the basis of the partnership. Because education provides international knowledge and the competence for economic success, a competitive education in Pennsylvania must include basic reading, writing, quantitative, and analytic skills; an understanding of today's international economic order and the languages, cultures, and markets of other countries; and the capacity to develop and transfer new technology.

The goal of the partnership is to strengthen all three components of education for all students in Pennsylvania.[21] Institutions address the goal in different ways. At the University of Pittsburgh's Center for International Studies, the program on regional change in international perspective links structural changes in Western Pennsylvania to transformations in the industrial regions of Western and Eastern Europe, China, Japan. High school and college students study languages not usually taught through independent study with native-speaking partners hired specifically to teach these languages. Grades are awarded by outside evaluators who are competent in the languages. Students participating in the program not only study the language, they also interact with people who are familiar with the culture of the country they are studying.

Global Learning Firsthand

In Pennsylvania students also develop international competence through study in the United States, where the classroom can become a global arena. Other students serve as interns in the foreign offices of international companies or study at foreign universities and focus on specific issues related to the development of the host country.

At the University of Massachusetts at Amherst (UM/A), international exchange began in 1876 when its president traveled to Japan to help establish the University of Hokkaido. Today it continues through the International Programs Office, which coordinates over 50 overseas study programs in Denmark, Israel, Japan, Egypt, Germany, Kenya, Australia, Sweden, or Ireland.

In 1988 while 700 students studied in other countries, faculty members at home investigated how to make foreign study more accessible, more flexible, and more meaningful to students. Their goal was to expand the international focus of undergraduate degree programs. As a result of their work, UM/A students who study abroad meet degree and major requirements by enrolling in foreign universities, not by participating in programs only for U.S. or other foreign students. Students in all disciplines can choose to study in non-Western or developing countries. Because international programs at UM/A focus on greater involvement between university learning and the global business community, graduates are in a good position to contribute to the globalization of U.S. business when they begin their careers.

Engineering students at the University of Rhode Island work as interns in the foreign offices of international corporations as participants in a U.S. Department of Education sponsored program to help prepare for careers in the international marketplace. These students spend 5 years qualifying for two degrees, a bachelors of science in engineering and a bachelor of arts in German. After studying German language and culture, they serve as professional interns in Germany, Austria, or Switzerland.[22] In addition to providing unique global perspectives for engineering students, the program offers bachelor of science and bachelor of arts students opportunities to participate in an innovative approach to global education.

Still other international learning experiences combine classroom learning in the United States with wide-ranging experiences in other countries. An example is the Global Awareness Program at Agnes Scott College, which combines classroom study; a cross-cultural experience organized around home stays in Greece, Eastern Europe, Burkina Faso, India, or Japan, for example; and follow-up seminars to expand and deepen new perspectives. Students who choose to increase their awareness of Japan also concentrate on international economics as they learn about world markets and global competition. Then they spend several weeks, a semester, or a year in Nagoya, Japan's fourth largest city, where they study interconnections that transcend borders and work to gain intimate knowledge of the world outside the United States. One student at Agnes Scott remarked that she could think of no better way of knowing another country and in fact, her own, than by understanding another culture. She discovered that although people have fascinating differences on the surface, we are very much alike.[23] Such a perspective will help this student as she completes her degree and begins work in the global marketplace.

Internationalizing the Disciplines

On campuses where broad-based international learning is not so well-defined or readily available, many undergraduates find at-home ways of adding an international dimension to their major or career objective. One alternative involves classroom learning experiences within the academic disciplines; here we find global, discipline-based responses to resource shortages, the population explosion, environmental crises, arms competition, increasing numbers of refugees, terrorism, human rights issues, and worldwide inflation.[24] Discipline-based approaches assure that all students gain international perspectives within their major fields of study. Unlike campus-based approaches, discipline-based response to international study is organized across institutional lines.

In the early 1980s, Groennings identified four innovations in internationalizing academic disciplines: the business curriculum, foreign language proficiency testing, teacher education, and the liberal arts curriculum.[25] Later the National Council on Foreign Language and International Studies expanded the list when it commissioned 40 scholars in the areas of geography, history, journalism, philosophy, political science, psychology, and sociology to investigate what undergraduates should learn about international perspectives in these fields. The project resulted in the book *Group Portrait: Internationalizing the Disciplines* in which scholars refocus the relatively domestic view presented in most mainstream college courses to determine what undergraduate majors should study about the world before leaving the university.[26] Although it is easy to identify the general knowledge needed to develop broad-based international perspectives, specific material for each subject is more difficult to determine.

Despite difficulties important advances are under way, so that today, the international component of certain disciplines contributes to a student's global perspectives. For example at the University of North Carolina (UNC), students study theories of evolution and ecology, development from prehistory to industrialization, and life in contemporary capitalist, socialist, and Third World societies in an introductory sociology course. Students compare the United States to other industrial societies to determine if the United States is more or less democratic, more or less dependent on foreign imports, and offers more or fewer opportunities. In the course syllabus, Professor Francois Neilson tells students that preconceived ideas about U.S. superiority will be proven false, and he reminds them to look at comparative material objectively and logically when evaluating the United States and global competitors.

At the University of Michigan, students incorporate global perspectives into the political science curriculum on the undergraduate level by examining historical developments, political processes, and international organizations. They study issues that arise from increasing interdependence among nations by investigating, for example, the economic issues on the bargaining table at summit meetings. Because competence in an academic discipline requires a global perspective, internationalization of the disciplines is one important step in our move toward educational competitiveness.

Collaborating across Disciplines

Another approach to at-home internationalization relies on interdisciplinary courses, also called global or comparative studies, which present global concepts across disciplinary lines. At The University of Georgia, the Center for Global Policy Studies offers courses in anthropology, human geography, comparative politics, and the religious perspectives of mankind. Foreign area studies are devoted to the history, culture, and political systems of Africa, Asia, Canada, Europe, or Latin America and the Caribbean. Functional specialties include agricultural economics, business and economics, communications, and linguistics, among others. Students who study in these areas also identify career goals, which serve as a focus for an individualized curriculum.

Success in such a broad-based and comprehensive program requires careful planning, but the rewards are substantial, since graduates earn credentials in both a major and international specialties.

At Indiana University, the interdisciplinary approach is part of teacher education: Future elementary teachers must enroll in 13 courses offering an international perspective. This program strives to improve specific international course content as well as to produce teachers who can interact effectively with people from other cultures, work cooperatively in group settings, and apply critical thinking skills to both international and instructional issues.[27] The importance of an international perspective in teacher education cannot be overstated if education is going to prepare students for the world in which they live.

When we reflect on Jefferson's advice to U.S. students to be educated at home and thus avoid the alarming consequences of foreign education, we realize that the world is a strikingly different place today. Fortunately higher education is also strikingly different, and many learning opportunities replace the somewhat narrow curriculum of Jefferson's day. To prepare for the new century, students in every discipline have a number of ways of gaining the international perspectives they need. Whether students elect to study abroad, work as corporate interns in other countries, join the Peace Corps, compete for a Fulbright, or enroll in interdisciplinary courses at home, they can enhance their education by developing a global perspective.

PART III

INVESTING IN THE FUTURE

13 ◤ The Price of Learning

Steve Albright is a bright, hardworking honors graduate of a public high school in the Southeast; he is also an experienced leader, debate team member, and ranking tennis player. In high school, he was president of the student council and received state recognition for his academic achievements. At graduation the high school faculty named him the best all-around member of the graduating class. Because Steve wants to develop his leadership skills in a large, diverse arena, he applied to one of the "public ivy" universities as an out-of-state student. Steve did not request financial aid or plan to look for part-time work. His parents encouraged him to become involved in college life, and they expected to pay his expenses. But the university Steve chose did not accept him even though he meets the admissions criteria, because the university received 2000 more applications than usual. The university can select from top-ranking applicants but it cannot accept more than the state-legislated quota of out-of-state students. Admissions officials advise Steve to attend another high-profile school, then transfer his junior year.

Marianne Garcia is one of the top-ranking applicants who will attend a public ivy university, but that is not her first choice. Marianne is a high school senior at the top of her class in her public Northeastern high school who wants to attend a highly competitive private college to prepare for medical school. Her dream is to attend an Ivy League school, but because these schools reject more applicants than they accept, Marianne applies to three Ivy League schools, an out-of-state public ivy university, and her home state university. Two of the Ivy League schools and both public universities accept Marianne. She and her parents, who are teachers, are thrilled, but their euphoria is short-lived, since even with student loans and a part-time job Marianne cannot afford the annual Ivy League cost of more than $20,000. Financial aid is Marianne's only alternative, but the level of assistance based on her parents' income is not enough, so she declines the Ivy League offers and attends the public ivy university.

Jonathan Ahmad attends a private high school in a small city in the Midwest. He is in the middle of his class and wants to attend a small college. Jonathan applies to three schools for different reasons: One is his "safe" choice—he is sure to get in; considering his test scores, the second is a bit of a stretch. The third is Jonathan's dream school, a regionally well-known private college with about 5000 undergraduate students. To the amazement of Jonathan's high school counselor, all three schools accept him. Both the safe choice and the dream school offer partial academic scholarships and invite Jonathan to participate in special weekend activities for scholarship recipients. Jonathan is thrilled with his options; he selects his dream school and accepts the scholarship offer.

Steve, Marianne, and Jonathan are three participants in the college admissions game, and the constantly changing playing field makes the game difficult for students and their families. Faced with budget deficits in the early 1990s, many states slashed higher education allotments and began a chaotic fiscal cycle for public colleges and universities. At the same time, economic conditions influenced students' ability to pay college costs, forcing many to choose less expensive institutions. Thus some freshmen who would have attended expensive private schools in good economic years applied to highly selective but less expensive state universities (see Table 13.1), while those who had planned on a large university readjusted their sights to include affordable state colleges, and former state college aspirants turned to community colleges.

Tuition increases affected freshman class profiles across the

TABLE 13.1. Admissions Categories by Average Test Score

Admissions Category	Test Score Averages Reported by Colleges	
	SAT total[a]	ACT composite[b]
Open (all high school graduates accepted to limited of capacity)	680–810	17–20
Liberal (some freshmen from lower half of high school graduating class)	720–860	18–21
Traditional (majority accepted freshmen in top 50% of high school graduating class)	810–950	20–23
Selective (majority of accepted freshmen in top 25% of high school graduating class)	920–1090	22–27
Highly Selective (majority of freshmen in top 10% of high school graduating class)	1120–1290	27–31

SOURCE: *American College Testing Program College Planning/Search Book 1991–1992* (Iowa City: American College Testing, 1991).

[a]Combined score on verbal and math sections.

[b]Estimate for Enhanced ACT Assessment administered after 1989.

country. Students who chose highly selective public universities instead of Ivy League schools had higher test scores and high school grade point averages than did former applicants. Such students raised admissions criteria, thereby making students like Steve ineligible and forcing them to attend less selective but very competitive schools. Admissions criteria rose in less competitive schools also, so that other students were not admitted to, for example, state universities. These students chose traditional private colleges and state colleges, or community colleges, which have lower admissions requirements or accept all high school graduates. Therefore better students applied to state and community colleges along with a less well-prepared population. Some excellent private colleges had places to fill, so they admitted students like Jonathan, who were at or below long-held admissions standards, which initiated another chain of events.

Confused? You have plenty of company. Situations like these contribute to ever-changing cost factors in higher education. From the end of World War II through the 1970s, costs were not so difficult to predict. The baby boom produced record numbers of traditional-age college students, enrollment increased fourfold, and family income levels kept up with tuition rates. Federal and state programs funded new and expanded student aid offerings, and opportunities for minority students increased, so that more students shared college operating costs. But in the 1980s, difficulties emerged: The traditional-age student population declined sharply; tuition and fees increased more rapidly than inflation or family incomes; and growth in state support and student aid declined.[1]

At the same time government policy changed. The Higher Education Act, first passed by Congress in 1965, was a federal commitment to reduce barriers to higher education for financially disadvantaged students. The primary component of the act was a need-based grants program, or tuition funds that would not require repayment. Congress also authorized loans for middle-income families that students would repay after graduation. Only a portion of the actual interest had to be repaid because the federal government subsidized the program and guaranteed repayment in the event of default. Today heavily subsidized loans, not outright grants, are the largest source of federal financial aid. With thousands of students beginning their working lives with large debts to repay and loan default rates over 35 percent at many institutions, policy makers agree that new regulations are overdue.[2] In 1992 Congress authorized a new Higher Education Act. Provisions in the 600-page law make the cost of higher education more manageable for some students but intensify competition for aid by making more students eligible for inadequately funded programs.

Tuition rates and financial aid policies are cost factors that concern individual students directly. Higher education decision makers share their concerns, but they must also consider other cost issues. For example operating expenses and faculty and staff compensation require more of the total institutional budget, state funding is precarious, new endowment dollars (savings that institutions count on to provide permanent income) are difficult to obtain, and some colleges are using their savings to meet operating costs. Like students and parents, decision makers at the highest levels must consider factors outside their control as they plan high-quality education for students and fund other higher education programs.

How do individuals and institutions handle critical questions concerning cost? First we look at student issues, namely, tuition and how to pay it, then we examine some institutional issues and investigate the relationship of price and quality in higher education.

STUDENT ISSUES

Tuition: A Universal Concern

From 1991 to 1992, two important statistics ran contrary to recent trends: Tuition increases at private colleges and universities were the lowest in years, yet they still outstripped inflation, and tuition increases at private colleges seemed meager when compared to those at many public institutions. From 1990 to 1991, average tuition rates at private institutions rose 7–8 percent, while many public colleges and universities increased their rates by 10–12 percent. From 1991 to 1992, private institution rates increased by another 6 percent, and public rates rose another 8 percent (see Table 13.2). These increases were necessary to help offset fiscal gaps due to state budget deficits.

Such deficits were one of several circumstances in the early 1990s that led to difficulty in financing a college education. The economy entered a recession as fees for tuition, room, and board rose. Many parents and adult students who lost jobs or watched their incomes decline had fewer dollars to invest in college. At the same time, the declining pool of traditional-age college students meant that some colleges had a smaller number of students to bear the costs; that is many colleges asked fewer students with fewer

TABLE 13.2. Average Costs at Public and Private
Institutions (1991–1992)[a]

Expenses	Public College		Private College	
	Resident	Commuter	Resident	Commuter
4-Year college				
Tuition and fees	$2,137	$2,137	$10,017	$10,017
Books and supplies	485	485	508	508
Room and board[b]	3,351	1,468	4,386	1,634
Transportation	464	793	470	795
Other	1,147	1,153	911	1,029
Total	$7,584	$6,036	$16,292	$13,983
2-Year college				
Tuition and fees	$1,022	$1,022	$5,290	$5,290
Books and supplies	480	480	476	476
Room and board[b]	—	1,543	3,743	1,529
Transportation	—	902	519	786
Other	—	966	895	925
Total	—	$4,913	$10,914	$9,006

SOURCE: *The Chronicle of Higher Education Almanac* (Washington, D.C.: The Chronicle of Higher Education, Inc., 1992), 34.
[a]The figures are weighted by enrollment to reflect charges incurred by the average undergraduate enrolled at each type of institution.
[b]Room not included for commuter students.

dollars to bear increasing costs. Suddenly a safe college became an affordable one, not one a student counted on for admission.

While external funds were decreasing, college officials worked to manage rising operating costs. Like individuals and businesses, colleges must pay more for utilities, insurance, and supplies, which increase in cost each year. Faculty and staff salaries are increasing although real levels of faculty and staff compensation still lag behind inflation from the 1970s (see Table 6.1). Although wage freezes imposed by desperate state governors in the early 1990s slowed or canceled recent gains in college and university faculty compensation, salaries for chief executives increased by 6 percent a year from 1988 through 1991. (See Tables 13.3

TABLE 13.3.   Median Salaries of College and
University Administrators (1991–1992)

Position	Median Salary
Chief executive of a system	$99,452
Chief executive of a single institution	95,500
Chief academic officer	72,676
Director, library services	47,064
Chief business officer	68,500
Chief development officer	64,000
Chief student affairs officer	60,662
Registrar	40,000
Director, admissions and financial aid	48,550

SOURCE: *The Chronicle of Higher Education Almanac* (Washington,
D.C.: The Chronicle of Higher Education, Inc., 1992), 16.

TABLE 13.4.   Median Salaries of Chief Executive
and Academic Officers (1991–1992)[a]

Type of Institution by Full-Time Equivalent Enrollment	Chief Executive Officer	Chief Academic Officer
Public		
Up to 2012	$ 78,960	$ 58,227
2013–4498	89,444	70,103
4499–10,743	98,000	82,272
10,744 or more	121,850	103,000
Total	93,547	76,425
Private, Independent		
Up to 653	$ 87,365	$ 57,963
654–1316	98,950	69,833
1317–2784	122,500	84,254
2785 or more	150,206	107,646
Total	114,114	78,440

SOURCE: *The Chronicle of Higher Education Almanac* (Washington, D.C.: The Chronicle of Higher
Education, Inc., 1992), 32.

and 13.4 for median salaries of college and university administrators.)[3]

Colleges and universities also spend more on each student now than in the past, because today most institutions provide, for example, computer labs and learning centers for students, and students expect comprehensive counseling, health, and recreational services. At the same time, aging buildings need repair, equipment to support the sciences must be current, and most instructors require technological support. To remain competitive in a buyer's market, many institutions increase fees and improve their offerings rather than cut tuition to the bone. Decision makers know that today's students are careful shoppers who expect sophisticated services. As parents of toddlers wonder how they will afford college in 12–15 years, officials look for funds to meet the huge gap in annual income and actual costs per student.

College: An Unaffordable Necessity?

Before we decide that college will be unaffordable in the next century, let us take a closer look at the financial picture. In 1989 the investment firm of Paine, Webber predicted that tuition could climb to $62,894 by the year 2005. Harvard, with its $4.1 billion endowment, raised tuition by 6.5 percent to $19,395, but at state-supported schools, tuition, room, board, and books for in-state students averaged $6671. Although writers report that parents are raging over "sticker shock at the Ivory Tower,"[4] many colleges remain affordable. Each year about 78 percent of all college students attend public colleges and universities, where students at 4-year schools spend an average of $7584 for tuition, books, room and board, and other items. As shown in Table 13.5, about 78 percent of the students at public colleges and universities pay less than $2000 each year in tuition and fees (excluding room and board). Students at only 60 public 4-year schools pay $3000 or more in tuition per year, and they comprise less than 12 percent of

TABLE 13.5. Tuition Range at 4-Year Institutions (1991–1992)[a]

Tuition Range ($)	Number of Colleges	Average Tuition and Fees ($)	Proportion of Total Enrollment (%)
Private institutions			
15,000 or more	73	16,141	12.9
14,000–14,999	30	14,404	3.2
13,000–13,999	25	13,522	2.8
12,000–12,999	44	12,459	4.4
11,000–11,999	63	11,431	6
10,000–10,999	96	10,448	9.2
9,000–9,999	120	9,462	13.7
8,000–8,999	130	8,438	9.7
7,000–7,999	132	7,482	8.7
6,000–6,999	129	6,474	9.1
5,000–5,999	99	5,449	6.3
4,000–4,999	94	4,467	4.4
3,000–3,999	90	3,479	3
2,000–2,999	55	2,512	6
1,000–1,999	12	1,602	0.3
Less than 1,000	6	440	0.3
Total	1,198		100
Public institutions			
3,000 or more	60	3,672	11.1
2,500–2,999	54	2,738	10.9
2,000–2,499	113	2,283	23.8
1,500–1,999	148	1,754	26.6
1,000–1,499	128	1,275	25
Less than 1,000	18	753	2.6
Total	521		100

SOURCE: *The Chronicle of Higher Education Almanac* (Washington, D.C.: The Chronicle of Higher Education, Inc., 1992), 34.

[a]Includes only those institutions that provided final or estimated 1991–1992 tuition and fees by 10 Sept. 1991.

the enrollment at public 4-year institutions. Nine 4-year public institutions charge less than $1000 per year.[5]

On the other hand, more students than ever before choose private institutions, 72 percent of which charge yearly tuition rates under $10,000.[6] Contrary to predictions, many private colleges and universities flourished in the 1980s and early 1990s; in fact some private school enrollments increased as much as 600 percent. While this figure is certainly the exception, growth has been the norm in the private sector, with small colleges, selective colleges, women's colleges, and historically black colleges faring particularly well during this period.[7] Financial analysts say that elite, expensive institutions continue to underprice their services, since demand exceeds supply.[8]

Regardless of tuition rates, college follows housing as the second most significant purchase in a lifetime for many families. How do students and families finance a college education? Financial aid from a variety of sources is the traditional source of help, while more recent avenues include prepaid tuition plans, individual savings plans, and other financing schemes.

Federal Financial Aid: A Shrinking Source of Help

Most colleges offer qualifying students a financial aid package that includes federal and state grants and loans, campus employment, and funds supplied by the college. The size of the package is based on such factors as family income, the number of family members, and the number of family members in college. Recently internal financial aid (scholarship funds supplied by the institution) has become so plentiful in the private sector that critics accuse some schools of using aid packages to discount tuition randomly. This practice can result in hidden costs for paying students: When internal aid comes from the operating budget, replacement dollars come from tuition increases.

Today more than 70 percent of all financial aid dollars come from federal funds, and 70 percent of federal funds flow through two programs, the Pell grant program and the Stafford loan program, named for U.S. Senators Claiborne Pell and Robert Stafford, long-time friends of higher education. These two programs benefit almost 7 million students each year.

The Pell grant program,[9] intended as the basis for federal financial aid, provides support for needy students who are working toward a first bachelor's degree. From 1990 to 1991, almost $5 billion went to 3.3 million undergraduates who received Pell grants ranging from $100–$2400 for the academic year (see Tables 13.6 and 13.7). Most recipients come from families with annual incomes under $35,000.

TABLE 13.6. Student Financial Aid (1990–1991)

	Total Spending ($)
Federal programs	
Generally available aid	
Pell grants	4,915,000,000
Supplemental Educational Opportunity grants	439,000,000
State student incentive grants	59,000,000
College Work–Study	823,000,000
Perkins loans	860,000,000
Income contingent loans	6,000,000
Stafford student loans	9,844,000,000
Supplemental loans for students	1,630,000,000
Parent loans for undergraduate students	942,000,000
Subtotal	19,517,000,000
Specially directed aid	
Veterans	701,000,000
Military	378,000,000
Other grants	119,000,000
Other loans	349,000,000
Subtotal	1,547,000,000
Total federal aid	21,065,000,000
State grant programs	1,870,000,000
Institutional and other grants	4,915,000,000
Total federal, state, and institutional aid	27,850,000,000

SOURCE: *The Chronicle of Higher Education Almanac* (Washington, D.C.: The Chronicle of Higher Education, Inc., 1992), 9.

TABLE 13.7.   Recipients and Amount of Student
Financial Aid (1990–1991)

Program	Recipients	Amount
Pell grants	3,300,000	$1,489
Supplemental Education Opportunity grants	678,000	648
College Work-Study	876,000	940
Perkins loans	804,000	1,070
Stafford student loans	3,633,000	2,709
Supplemental loans for students	576,000	2,828
Parent loans for undergraduate students	293,000	3,213
State grants and state student incentive grants	1,681,000	1,148

SOURCE: *The Chronicle of Higher Education Almanac* (Washington, D.C.: The Chronicle of Higher Education, Inc., 1992), 9.

From 1990 to 1991, 3.6 million students received almost $10 billion through the Stafford loan program (formerly the Guaranteed Student Loan program), which permits students to borrow money for educational expenses from private sources, such as banks and credit unions, then repay the loan after graduation. Originally a subsidized loan program for students who demonstrated financial need, in 1992 Stafford loan funds became available to all students who complete financial aid forms. Students demonstrating need still receive financial federal subsidies. Stafford loan funds represent about one-third of all financial aid to college students.

While Pell grants and Stafford loans are the largest sources of federal support, they are by no means the only ones. Other federal funds flow from the three campus-based programs intended to supplement Pell grants for the neediest students. Individual institutions receive and distribute these funds, some of which they are required to supplement.

The Supplemental Educational Opportunity grant program (SEOG) gives to institutions federal funds for first-time undergraduates with exceptional financial needs; SEOG funds do not have to be repaid. About 678,000 students received SEOG awards from 1990 to 1991; the total dollar amount was $439 million.

The College Work–Study program provides on-campus employment for first-time undergraduates who demonstrate financial need. Students earn at least the minimum wage for their work in departmental offices, libraries, or laboratories, for example. From 1990 to 1991, 876,000 students received $823 million from the College Work–Study program and at the same time met critical employment needs on college campuses.

Formerly the National Direct Student Loan program, the Perkins loans program provides federal dollars to institutions for student loans. Although interest rates are not subsidized, borrowers must meet more stringent standards for need than those who receive subsidized Stafford loans, but the interest rates are lower. Repayments is used for future loans; the federal government repays loans for students who choose certain public service occupations. Because funds for Perkins loans have remained fairly constant in recent years, inflation has reduced the impact of the program. From 1990 to 1991, 804,000 students received $860 million in Perkins loans.

Such funds as Parent Loan for Undergraduate Student (PLUS) loans for parents and Supplemental Loans for Students (SLS) provide additional dollars for college expenses. Third-party lenders supply the funds. Before 1993 the maximum PLUS loan was $4000. In 1993 however, new regulations allowed parents to borrow the entire cost of college and repay the funds at less than going rates.

Various federal loan programs provide funds for students with different levels of need. Congress originally intended to divert more money to grants than loans, but as tuition increases, family income declines, and federal regulations change, more students become clients of the financial aid office at their institution. In the early 1990s, statistics brought attention to the growth, abuse, administrative cost, and default rate statistics associated with government-backed student aid. For example in 1991, several states reduced support for vocational and college courses for prisoners and encouraged inmates to apply for Pell grants to pay for postsecondary education. In Illinois alone, 16 of the 18 colleges and universities with which the prison system has contracts helped inmates apply for Pell grants.

Other abuses involved Stafford loans. About 23 percent of first-year postsecondary students receive Stafford loans, but many who benefit are not college students. About a third attend vocational schools and represent half of those schools' enrollment. Higher default rates for vocational school students than college and university students led a senate committee investigating financial aid issues to recommend that the government limit funds for students attending vocational schools.[10]

Can better ways to manage federal financial aid for students be found? Recent deficits in state budgets and large reductions in higher education funding highlight the need to revitalize the educational system. Some of the most radical changes in the 1992 Higher Education Act were designed to solve problems leading to fraud and abuse in federal financial aid programs. However some financial aid officials fear that recent regulations will only increase default rates and create a new population of borrowers.

In addition to federal programs, other avenues exist for students who need help in financing college. For example all states provide some form of assistance to qualified residents who attend public or private institutions in the state, and most institutions offer scholarships, loans, and grants. From 1989 to 1990, 1.6 million students received more than $1.7 billion in state grant programs, while aid awarded by colleges and universities exceeded $4.9 billion. Corporations and private foundations also make college funds available to students. Each year impressive numbers of students who are diligent about seeking funds and flexible in their college choice are find some assistance in paying for college.

At the same time, experts are looking for new ways of meeting college costs. Among these are federal loan plans that guarantee against default but do not subsidize interest rates, loans whose repayment figures are based on the income of the student borrower after graduation, and loans whose repayment can be canceled or reduced by volunteer services. Other plans award funds to students based on need and merit.[11] All of these plans are in the formative stage, but they represent an important step. We look to them to provide solutions for the growing financial aid crisis in the next century.

The Return to Savings

Some refreshing new ideas to help families pay for college are in keeping with a national move to encourage individual savings. Today a number of states and individual institutions offer organized plans to prepay tuition or save systematically for future payments. The plans, designed for families with children younger than college age, assume that today's interest rates are surely better than tomorrow's. In 1990 parents invested over $1 billion in plans designed to help finance college costs for their children.[12]

Presently both state systems and private institutions sponsor tuition plans. While such plans vary, most require parents to make cash payments based on two variables: today's tuition rates and the number of years before the student enters college. State-supported plans usually cover tuition costs at an institution of the student's choice within the system. Prepayment dollars remain in a state-managed investment fund until the student is ready to enroll, then the money goes directly to the institution. Plans offered by private institutions work in much the same way, but they represent an added advantage for the school, since the money can be used before the student enrolls.

Tuition plans have developed in two directions: prepayment combined with loans and tuition guarantees. Parents who choose the prepayment option usually borrow enough to cover today's cost of college and repay the amount before the student enters college. Tuition guarantees allow parents to invest college funds when the student is young. The investment fund guarantees to pay some or all of the costs of college when the student is ready to enroll. Duquesne, a private university in Pittsburgh, offered the first tuition guarantee but suspended the offer during the 1987 stock market collapse. The Duquesne plan eliminated future choice for the student, but it attracted the attention of James Blanchard, governor of Michigan, who altered the concept so that state-tax-deductible payments to a state-managed investment fund cover the costs of college at any school in the Michigan system to which a student is admitted.

Savings bond plans are another alternative for parents who begin saving early for college. Participants purchase tax-exempt municipal bonds that mature when the student enrolls in college. The invested money and the interest earned can be used at any school the student chooses. Parents in certain income brackets receive tax breaks when they invest in bonds for tuition.

A few moments reflection on these schemes brings many "what ifs" to mind. If tuition rates increase more rapidly than return on invested funds, how will future tuition costs be subsidized? If parents purchase a tuition plan from a school to which the student is not admitted, how are payments refunded? If the institution should close before the student enters college, is the investment lost? If the student chooses not to attend the school or the state system, can the investment be recaptured? Most plans have provisions for such situations, and investors should seek answers to these and a host of other questions before investing for future tuition payments.

Perhaps the most important long-term implications of these plans rest on the concept of systematic saving for college. Prepayment and savings plans are based on the premise that students and their families, not federal and state governments, should pay for college. To do so requires early, methodical planning. These payment concepts foreshadow a time when individuals will be required to bear more of the burden for educating themselves or their children.[13]

INSTITUTIONAL ISSUES

Each year higher education decision makers work to contain operating costs and to strengthen state and federal support. Although costs and support have direct implications for schools, they affect students, parents, and taxpayers, consumers of education who fund federal and state support for higher learning.

Containing Costs: Doing More with Less

In 1991 Georgia Tech shelved student computers worth $4000 each because the school could not afford repair bills of $100 per computer. At Dartmouth College, insurance benefits for employees and their families rose by 50 percent in 1988, and health care costs accounted for $6.2 million, or 2.8 percent of Dartmouth's total budget. In 5 years the fuel bill at Mount Holyoke College jumped from $159,000 to $452,000.[14] While these situations seem unusual, college and university administrators have no trouble believing them, for they are part of daily life for budget officers, deans, presidents, and trustees who must annually do more on campus with less (See Table 13.8). Such situations led 71 percent of college and university administrators to identify issues of adequate financing as their primary concern for the new decade (See Table 13.9).

Containing costs on campus is an issue that families can understand. Anyone who manages even a small personal budget knows that costs are rising at alarming rates, and many people spend less on nonnecessities to make ends meet. But in today's competitive higher education market, this practice is rarely applicable. Because students pay dearly for college, they seek quality in academic and student service programs, and if they fail to find it, they look elsewhere. In a controversial review of the financial profile of Mount Holyoke College, Barry Werth suggests that college is expensive because the United States wants it that way.

TABLE 13.8. Revenue and Expenditures of Colleges and
Universities (1989–1990)

| | Percent of Total Budget | |
	Public	Private
Revenues		
Tuition and fees	15.5	39.6
Appropriations		
Federal	1.8	0.5
State	39.2	0.7
Local	3.3	*a*
Government grants and contracts		
Federal	8.3	9.4
State	2.4	1.8
Local	0.4	0.7
Federal research and development center	0.2	6
Private gifts, grants, and contracts	3.8	8.7
Endowment income	0.5	5.3
Sales and services		
Educational activities	2.7	2.4
Auxiliary enterprises	9.5	10.8
Hospitals	9.5	9.4
Other	2.7	4.6
Total current fund revenues	100	100
Expenditures		
Instruction	34.1	26.4
Research	10	8.1
Public service	4.3	2
Academic support	7.6	5.9
Student services	4.7	4.8
Institutional support	8.7	10.6
Plant operation and maintenance	7.4	6.4
Scholarships and fellowships	2.8	8.7
Mandatory transfers	1.1	1.5
Auxiliary enterprises	9.7	10.1
Hospitals	9.5	9.3
Other	0.2	6.1
Total current fund expenditures	100	100

SOURCE: U.S. Department of Education.
[a]Indicates less than 0.1 percent. Due to rounding, individual entries may not add
up to totals.

TABLE 13.9. Administrative Challenges Facing Institutions in the Next 5 Years[a]

Challenge	Total	Administrator's Affiliation			
		Doctoral	Baccalaureate	Comprehensive	2 Year
Adequate finances	71%	53%	57%	91%	87%
Fund raising	13	25	12	9	5
Maintain enrollment	30	40	31	28	22
Enrollment growth	11	8	11	7	15
Assessment	16	22	7	5	16
Maintain quality	27	21	48	32	23
Strengthen curriculum	21	25	16	18	20
Serve new needs and populations	5	4	12	5	4
Effective faculty	14	14	13	18	14
Recruitment and faculty member retention	3	7	0	2	2
Other faculty issues	28	26	41	18	26
Diversity	17	19	21	32	13
Facilities and technology	27	29	17	18	30

SOURCE: *Campus Trends*, ed. E. Khawas (Washington, D.C.: American Council on Education, 1991), 43.

[a]Figures are based on responses to a new survey sent to senior administrators at 444 colleges and universities in spring 1991. The response rate was 81 percent.

The University of Massachusetts at Boston started the 1988 academic year with a state allocation of $62,000,000. We opened the 1991 academic year with a state allocation of $41,000,000—a freefall of 35%!

What has this meant for the functioning of the university? Most dramatically, it has shifted us from incremental growth and the related style of managing resources to a period of decline and a management style focused on preserving the best and making some very tough choices. Education is a people-intensive enterprise, so a loss in dollars means an enormous loss of faculty and staff. Most expense accounts have been cut; services have been cut, and several administrative areas have been eliminated.

What has this meant for students? First, they have incurred the loss of available courses and reductions in a variety of student services. Second, it has meant an enormous increase in tuition and fees. We are a public institution, but we have gone from being state-supported to being only state-assisted, with the additional burden being shifted to students and their families. We are very concerned about the issue of affordability, particularly for poor and working class students, many of whom are the first in their families to go to college. Our reputation has always been one of high quality and low cost, but now large numbers of students simply don't consider the university as an option.

For 1991–1992, we are pleased to say that we are experiencing some stability. We have embarked on a successful major fundraising campaign, we have increased our revenue from other grant and contract sources, and we have made major changes in the administrative structure of the institution. We have not given up our vision of a great urban, public university serving a diverse student body, providing low-cost and high quality education as well as conducting valuable research and service to the community in which we live.

Sherry H. Penney, chancellor, Jean MacCormack, vice chancellor, University of Massachusetts at Boston and coauthors of "Managing On the Edge: Massachusetts after the Miracle," *Journal of Higher Education Management* (winter/spring, 1992)

Colleges and universities compare themselves to clusters of peer institutions with similar tuition rates. Within the cluster, top-priced schools have more applicants than less expensive schools, which suggests that price equates to quality. Kalamazoo College president David W. Breneman agrees with the cluster theory for schools in the private sector, which he describes as a Chivas Regal marketing mentality. As a result, college officials base budgets on reasonable cost increases but inflate these when they find that peer institutions are more expensive. Such practices cause price increases that are difficult to control.[15]

Public institutions recently found themselves in equally dire circumstances. In fiscal 1990 to 1991, 30 states reduced higher education budgets by an average of 3.9 percent. Virginia's reduction was 10 percent. These reductions midyear meant decreased funding for libraries and staffing, temporary and part-time faculty salaries, and critical equipment purchases. Allan Ostar, former president of the American Association of State Colleges and Universities, said the reductions were the largest he had seen in 26 years with the association.[16] In states where midyear reductions were made, tuition increases averaged 12.9 percent.

To make matters worse, the budget reductions began a multi-year trend in some states: From 1988 to 1991, public support for higher education declined 9.5 percent in California, 15 percent in Virginia and Rhode Island, 27 percent in Maryland, and 30 percent in Massachusetts.[17] What do budget reductions of this magnitude mean to the economic health of the region? The 260 New England colleges and universities, with an aggregate budget of over $8 billion, typically contribute about $30 billion annually in direct and indirect spending to local economies.[18] Budget reductions have decreased the flow of dollars as bans on hiring and wage increases, and layoffs have caused consumer spending reductions.

In the face of declining support, what can be done to contain costs? Michael O'Keefe, president of the Consortium for the Advancement of Private Higher Education, analyzed the cost situation at six public and private institutions and raised questions about the dual meaning of cost. For students costs are tuition, fees, room, and board; for administrators costs are what the college pays for goods and services; ideally both must be controlled.

O'Keefe was not surprised to find rising costs at all six institutions he investigated. As the schools changed to offer broader educational experiences, both instructional and administrative costs increased, but generalizations about causes are difficult to draw. Colleges and universities respond to their constituencies; among other things, they improve the quality of instruction, research, and student services constantly. Colleges and universities also compete, which can be expensive.[19] O'Keefe cites many reasons for increased competition in higher education; we have discussed two of these: demographics and the economic picture. Another stems from the Higher Education Amendments of 1972. When Congress passed the act, it decided that federal dollars for financial aid would go to students, not colleges. Today colleges and universities receive federal financial aid dollars only when students elect to attend them; therefore they compete for students who qualify for financial aid. In the process, institutions respond to the needs of their constituencies. Most colleges and universities resist cost reductions that would produce less relevant and rich educational experiences; instead they improve their offerings and count on students to recognize and pay for high-quality programs.

Federal Dollars Fund More Than Financial Aid

Financial aid dollars are not the only federal funds to reach colleges and universities: Federal funds for research, programs benefitting special populations, and facilities go directly to institutions, and such funds make a significant difference to many schools. How will budget decisions affect higher education in the future? From 1980 to 1990 expenditures for national defense and interest on the national debt grew from 7 to 8.9 percent of the gross national product (GNP), a measure of the goods and services produced by the United States. Entitlement spending for such programs as Social Security and Medicare held its own at 10.7 percent, while spending for domestic discretionary programs fell sharply from 5.9 to 3.8 percent. With the exception of the Stafford loan program and defense department research dollars, most federal funds for higher education are in this category. Funding for the Stafford loan program is on the rise, but the decrease in research funding is alarming. In 1967 more than $700 million went to colleges and universities to construct academic and research facilities; in 1990, $70 million was the outlay. Because we are losing ground in areas of expanding knowledge, rebuilding academic research facilities could cost as much as $10 billion.[20] These funding patterns warrant close security, because the future of our system, and perhaps of our country, hangs in the balance.

Although many federal dollars go to students for tuition at the institution of the student's choice, the government traditionally is not involved in tuition matters. Now this trend may be changing. In 1991 members of both houses of Congress began investigating incentives to moderate tuition increases, control the alarming reliance and subsequent defaults on Stafford loans, and to simplify the paperwork necessary to apply for federal financial aid. Also in 1991, the U.S. Justice Department ended a long-term arrangement for comparing financial aid and tuition to the same students at Ivy League schools and the Massachusetts Institute of Technology (MIT).[21] Such interest is encouraging because it signals new and widespread concern about the quality and affordability of higher education in this country.

PRICE VERSUS QUALITY

In the past, the issues we raise in this chapter were separate from questions about institutional operating costs and federal support for higher education. Few people have investigated the relationship between the cost of attending college and the quality of the education offered. Students used to choose a college aware of its cost, and find ways of paying the bill. Today this trend is changing, as tuition increases and uncontrollable institutional costs cause many to wonder about the relationship between price and quality.

In 1989 the Department of Education joined the discussion by asking if the quality of a college is reflected in its tuition and fees. Some surprising answers surfaced: Researchers investigated 593 private liberal arts colleges and found that higher prices may not represent real differences in quality. Sometimes higher prices result from operational inefficiencies, costly marketing strategies, support for goals unrelated to learning, or low endowments. It does seem however that price and graduation rates are related, because paying more for college appears to strengthen a student's commitment to completing a degree.[22]

While the Department of Education study was not based on a representative sample of all colleges and universities in the United States, it is an early look at the relationship of student costs to certain measures of quality. For example researchers asked institutions if parents and students count on more costly institutions to provide a superior education or does it pay to shop around? Researchers also asked if students who attend expensive institutions are more likely to graduate than students enrolled in less expensive colleges and universities. Researchers gave expensive schools high marks in resources, selectivity, reputation, and educational results. It seems however that desirable faculty student ratios and the number of remedial programs offered are not linked to high tuitions. Expensive schools generally seem superior, but 31 percent of the schools in the study contradicted this assumption, so perhaps it pays to shop around.

What should you look for in a college or university? Some expensive colleges with low endowments channel tuition dollars into programs of little benefit to students, so that fewer institutional dollars are available to make up the difference in tuition costs and federal and state financial aid. Despite this funding gap, colleges electing to raise tuition beyond the inflation rate gain in two ways: Applicants and revenue increase.

What about educational results? Here more expensive colleges seem to shine, since findings show that students at expensive schools are more likely to graduate than students at less expensive schools. Academic enrichment experiences, student activities programs, and faculty interaction with students outside the classroom benefit students also. If expensive colleges encourage students to become involved in campus life and especially with faculty members, then the investment may be a sound one.

The Department of Education is not alone in asking questions about price and quality in the 1990s. Researchers Ernest Pascarella and Patrick Terenzini took a different approach to the question in their book *How College Affects Students*. As part of a review of some 2600 studies involving millions of college students, they investigated the impact of college on an individual's lifetime earnings. Pascarella and Terenzini estimate that the bachelors degree provides a 20–40 percent advantage in earning over a high school diploma, but future earnings are not determined by college choice. Attendance at only the most selective colleges and universities may enhance earnings significantly.[23]

Pascarella and Terenzini also found little evidence to suggest that college choice or prestige influences students' learning and intellectual development. Variation in learning depends on the individual student, the influence of other people in a student's life, and the nature of the learning environment. Students learn best when they are involved with others and the institution they attend.[24]

How then is price related to quality? Students, such as Steve Albright, Marianne Garcia, Jonathan Ahmad, and their parents, must answer this question. Adult students who are paying their own way to college also have to answer this question. Traditionally students have responded indirectly by taking tuition into account as one factor in their decision. But in today's economic climate, indirect responses may not be sufficient. Considering the escalating cost of attending any college, questions about direct relationships between price and quality are essential.

14 ⬛ Connections for Learning

If there are heroes in U.S. higher education, undergraduate students should be counted among them. The student is at the heart of the undergraduate experience. Some researchers declare that colleges and universities are not all that different, but the experiences and perceptions of individual students are quite different, and these differences compose the mosaic of U.S. higher learning.

Today more people are considering college from the student's perspective. College presidents, deans, and faculty members, as well as scholars and researchers, want to know exactly what happens to a student as a result of attending college, and they are investigating the factors that define students' experiences. On many campuses, this process of investigation has become an assessment of the effectiveness of educational programs. A number of colleges, universities, state systems, and regional accrediting agencies require systematic assessment; in some states, it is required by law.

Those who work in higher education are not the only ones asking questions about educational outcomes: Parents want to know what measures colleges take to ensure that life-enriching opportunities and career-related skills will result from the investment of time, energy, and dollars. Business leaders want to know which schools and academic programs produce graduates who can contribute to their companies in positive ways. Legislative bodies want to know if education funds are well spent. Answers to these questions require careful planning, measuring, and evaluating; the results form the basis for improvements.

But what about students? Are they, too, planning for effective college experiences? Are they measuring, evaluating, and acting with purpose? In previous chapters, we considered research findings and expert opinions about undergraduate learning. Now we turn to experts of a different sort—students themselves—to hear what they have to say about the challenges they face, the successes they celebrate, and their growth in today's collegiate environment. But first we investigate some tools they may use as they investigate their futures.

MISSION AND PLANNING: KEYS TO INVOLVEMENT

When a college or university subscribes to the concept of effectiveness, everyone on campus becomes involved. Student experiences, both inside and outside the classroom, become the focus of the learning process. Students who want to maximize the effectiveness of their college experiences would do well to become involved in planning their futures, thinking about their goals, and creating ways of achieving these goals. How do students begin to approach college in this way? One way is to ask questions that lead to planning, for example:

- □ What is my mission for my college years?
- □ What goals can I adopt that will help me achieve my mission?
- □ What are the unique opportunities available to me that can contribute to achieving my goals?

The following questions can help students measure progress:

- □ How is each course I take an opportunity to achieve my goals?
- □ What is the best way for me to spend my time outside the classroom?

□ How can some of the many unique opportunities available in or through my college or university be linked for maximum advantage?

These questions should precede others that evaluate progress:

□ How has my participation in a particular course, program, or experience contributed to my short- and long-term goals?
□ What have I learned that can help me plan my next steps?

In more familiar language, where am I, where do I go from here, and how do I arrive there?

In their best seller *Smart Moves*, Sam Deep and Lyle Sussman marvel at such accomplishments as the NASA space missions, the Panama Canal, and the Hoover Dam,[1] and these group achievements of vast proportions justify the attention they receive. But many other accomplishments of a more individual nature are just as momentous, for example many artists, heads of state, corporate presidents, or humanitarians have reached lofty heights through thoughtful planning. Most often these people focused on means as well as ends and elicited the ideas of others as they constructed plans to reach challenging but achievable goals.

Success-oriented college students would do well to pay attention to these models of success. After determining why they are in college, students should plan a relevant course of study. Activities outside the traditional classroom, volunteer efforts, and summer employment can be used as part of the exploration and planning processes. Ideally most college experiences lead students closer to their goals.

To make good choices, students must broaden their experience. Before choosing a major or a course of study, we encourage students to plan deliberate encounters with a variety of people, explore unusual activities, and deepen their understanding of their goals. For most students, a picture of the future and a plan for achieving goals and measuring progress lead to success.

These suggestions may be obvious to students who know

what they want to do with their lives, but what about students who enter college with unclear objectives? To them, we suggest that college is the ideal place to explore future possibilities. Most students who are undecided about majors and careers do not lack determination to succeed; in fact many are high achievers. They are in the right place to discover, define, and focus their goals. For them, as for students who come to college with definite ideas about the future, planning is a critical early step.

EVALUATING OPTIONS

Most college students would agree that they are constantly being evaluated. They receive grades on papers and tests, they must satisfy prerequisites before proceeding to more difficult courses, and many must pass examinations to be accredited in their professions after graduation. But how often do students evaluate college? For students with a mission and a plan for achieving objectives, "How am I doing?" is a vital question, and one to ask frequently.

People who measure progress use two kinds of measuring devices: formative evaluations and summative evaluations. The distinction here is important, because formative evaluation contributes to future action, while summative evaluation gauges past performance. Summative evaluations, such as most quizzes, final course exams, and standardized tests, are end-point or gate-keeping devices. They answer such questions as: Has the student learned enough to pass the course? Has the student mastered the concepts required to proceed to the next level of learning? Answers to these questions reveal little about the future.

Formative evaluations measure past mastery for the purpose of improving future teaching and learning. Some examples of questions with a formative approach include: What is the most important thing you have learned? Why is this most important to you? What would improve your learning in this course? Such questions cause students to reflect on past experiences, make important judgments about the present, and focus on the future through midcourse corrections. Formative questioning acknowledges the power of changing environments and maturing aspirations, both hallmarks of productive college years. Why is the formative approach the most useful? Perhaps because the process suggests that new beginnings are always possible.

MIDCOURSE ADJUSTMENTS

After reviewing 20 years of higher education research, Pascarella and Terenzini reached some important conclusions about the changes college students experience. One change concerns how students perceive the external world. Pascarella and Terenzini found that college students move from authoritarian, dogmatic, and ethnocentric thinking, becoming more tolerant of others' views; that is, their thinking becomes more flexible.[2] The freshman who sees only black and white becomes the senior who considers many shades of gray and consequently thinks in global terms when making personal decisions.

Considering these findings, we expect college students to make numerous and sometimes highly significant midcourse corrections during college. In fact change is a hallmark of the college years, and students who enter college firmly committed to a major or a career should not be surprised to find their preferences changing; they are in the majority. Today many adults change careers two, or three times. Changes in personal and career goals are normal, and well-educated people welcome such changes and challenges.

LINKING OPPORTUNITIES FOR MAXIMUM ADVANTAGE

In Chapter 1, we discussed the decision of William Desmond, a high school senior choosing a college. After being accepted at Harvard and Princeton, William decided to attend a small college in his hometown Baltimore. This incident made the newspapers and, as William describes it, created repercussions for which he was not prepared.

Like many other high school seniors who struggle with choosing a college, William may have thought his most difficult decision was behind him, but selecting a college is only the first of many decisions that confront a college freshman. Other difficult choices influence a student's decision about remaining in college, a decision many students make during the first 6 weeks of college.

Susannah Frost had to make such a decision. She left the security of her family and circle of friends for a strange, new world at The University of Georgia. Long lines, unfamiliar faces, sorority rush, and dormitory life challenged Susannah as she struggled to survive at a university of over 28,000 students. Although she expected to find a new environment at the university, she did not expect to be lonely among so many of her peers. After a few weeks, she was seriously considering leaving the university, a situation she would never have imagined a few months earlier. But by becoming involved, Susannah managed to alter her first disappointing impressions of university life.

Not all freshmen are like Susannah—18 years old and just out of high school; many are adults who return to college despite numerous other commitments. As JoAnn McKenzie, wife, mother of two, full-time research assistant, and part-time student at Emory relates, life is anything but lonely! After waiting 11 years to begin college, JoAnn's first day in philosophy class was exciting. By the third day of class however, the excitement had turned to confusion. As assignments increased, JoAnn found herself working day and night just to get by.

Like Susannah, JoAnn survived her first term by making a midcourse correction. After abandoning the idea of being a "supermom," JoAnn learned to draw on her family for support; now she finds college easier to manage, and her 11-year-old daughter is benefitting from JoAnn's dedication to her studies. Both Susannah and JoAnn took control of their situations early. Rather than allowing seemingly uncontrollable circumstances to alter their

Leaving home and going to college is an adjustment for any 18-year-old. Although most students find the adjustment difficult, it is especially hard on the campus of a large university. In the close community of my high school, I was very involved, but I knew I did not want the same kind of experience in college. I wanted to share a large campus with lots of different kinds of students, but I was not prepared for just how different university life would be. At Georgia I realized quickly that I was a very, very small fish in a huge ocean of unfamiliar faces. The crowds of people overwhelmed me, and even though I was almost never alone, I was very lonely. Soon I wondered if my decision to attend Georgia had been the right one.

To become more at home in my new environment, I decided to get involved. To begin I went through sorority rush—an endurance test in itself. Then I decided to get involved by competing for a spot on the Freshman Council. The third aspect of my involvement was academic. I tried to become absorbed in my classes, even though many new students seemed to be partying most of the time. I was blessed with small classes. I attended class every day, sat on the front row, and got to know my professors. Frequently I met with them for extra help.

Even though I got involved in sorority life, Freshman Council, and my studies, surviving my first quarter was a struggle. Without involvement I would not have made it. I will continue to be involved, because meeting and learning from all types of people is one of the most valuable lessons a large university has to offer. Becoming lost quickly is an easy thing to do. For me involvement has been the way to become a person instead of a number and feel at home on a big university campus.

Susannah Frost, freshman, The University of Georgia

My daily schedule consisted of getting up at three or four in the morning, reading two chapters of text and doing homework, waking my children up and getting them ready for school, dropping them off, and then going to work. By the time I arrived at work, I was up for five hours already and exhausted. By the end of the day, I felt like a zombie, and my day was just beginning again when I had to pick up the kids, cook dinner, do laundry, and prepare both them and myself for the next day. By the time I collapsed into a deep sleep at midnight, it was time to do it all over again. I decided before Thanksgiving break that I would have to rearrange my life if I wanted to continue going to school and maintain a family and job. I started by asking for additional help from my family. My husband was a big contributing factor to my being able to continue going to school. He shortened his working hours so that he would be able to pick the kids up from school, which allowed me to stay at work for an extra hour to do homework. I found that this worked out better, because I was able to concentrate uninterrupted. He prepared several meals on Sunday evening and froze them, so that the only thing I had to do was warm them up. I also tried to set aside one day out of the weekend to spend time with my family without worrying about school. As I became more comfortable with my class, the easier the homework and the studying became. I started to notice that it didn't require so much of my time.

If I had to sum up what the hardest part of going back to school for me was, it would be time. At first I felt guilty because I was taking time away from my family by having to study so much. Because the course was not an easy one for me, I had to do extra studying to try and understand the subject. I spent hours in the library as well as in my professor's office going over homework. As time went on, I developed a pattern that so far has worked for me and my family. I still get up before the crack of dawn to study, but my family and I are adjusting. They even help by quizzing me before each test.

JoAnn McKenzie, working mother and student, Emory University larger goals, they managed those variables they could control. Both students may find that their new, more acceptable circumstances are only one result of their actions: They may have discovered a useful model for future decision making.

Students who have successfully coped with freshman survival can learn valuable lessons from involvement of a different sort. For example every 4 years, students at Washington and Lee University host Mock Convention, a universitywide event that attracts major political figures to the campus and receives coverage in the national press. At the convention, student delegates attempt to predict correctly the presidential nominee of the national political party currently out of the White House. Mock Convention has been part of the Washington and Lee experience since 1908 when William Jennings Bryan addressed the student body; in 1992 Mock Convention speakers included Michael Dukakis, Jesse Jackson, and Tip O'Neil.

A group of students who compose an executive board spends 2 years organizing and running Mock Convention and approximately 1200 of the university's 1600 students are involved. For 2 years, student John Darden, a board member and convention treasurer, managed the convention budget of $150,000. Through his participation in this unique activity, John acquired valuable skills and enriched his educational experience. No other member of John's class will experience quite the same combination of classes and activities as those to which John committed his energy.

John benefitted from opportunities for involvement available on his campus. Theresa DiRaimo, an engineering student at the University of Rhode Island, planned early in her college career to take advantage of an opportunity for a global learning experience. As a sophomore, Theresa learned of the International Engineering Program (IEP), a joint effort between Rhode Island's College of Engineering and College of Arts and Sciences. Graduates of the 5-year program receive two degrees: a bachelor of science in engineering and a bachelor of arts in German. A unique part of the program is the 6-month internship with a German engineering

> It is impossible to articulate how much one learns from making an idea a reality. Putting on a successful convention took figuring out what motivated people. We had to invent ways to hold attention during countless meetings. We discovered, albeit through trial and error, what made the difference between people writing donations for $10 as opposed to $100. We learned to think of what could be wrong beforehand and be ready for it to happen, or better yet, prevent problems from happening in the first place. We learned how to relate to all types of people, be they national political leaders who are on the news every night, small town city councilmen, or fellow classmates.
>
> I can't help but think that after doing this, any of us involved with Mock Convention are prepared to take on whatever responsibility may come our way in the future. And none of this was learned in the classroom. It was skill acquired totally by doing. Lastly, the most valuable things I have gained from Mock Convention are the friendships I made by spending time with people. These friendships, along with other skills, I can cherish for the rest of my life.
>
> John S. Darden, student and treasurer for Mock Convention, a student-run political convention, Washington and Lee University

firm. Theresa realizes she gained much more than fluency in a foreign language by participating in this demanding program.

Although Theresa chose a program within her area of academic interest while John participated in an activity outside the formal curriculum, both students gained special qualifications while in college. At the same time, Theresa began the career for which she was preparing. Such was also the case for Dorothy Harris Blaise, a hospitality management major at East Carolina University. In her junior year, she learned through her university's cooperative education program that Walt Disney World would be interviewing for a summer work study program. She made initial inquiries, arranged an interview, and won acceptance into the Walt Disney World college program the summer prior to her senior

For my internship, I traveled to Frankfurt, Germany, to work at Hoechst Aktiengesellschaft—a large chemical and pharmaceutical company with satellite companies worldwide. During the first half of my working assignment, I was placed in the environmental department and worked in a chemical laboratory. My final 3 months were spent in the water treatment division conducting tours and assisting with research. It was my responsibility to meet and work with the sales representatives to discuss and evaluate their products.

The internship not only improved my German proficiency but also provided me with valuable insight into my chosen profession. Through my internship, I realized that although people approach problems in different manners, we are all working toward the same end result. The German and American cultures differ greatly, but being different does not mean we cannot work together to achieve the same outcome. An internship is a valuable experience—an international internship is even more so. All students should be as fortunate as I was and have the opportunity to embark on an internship.

Theresa DiRaimo, student in the International Engineering Program, University of Rhode Island

year. During the 10-week program and an internship that followed, Dorothy attended business seminars, prepared a presentation for management, and worked 40 hours a week cross-training in the hotel industry. She combined classroom learning with practical experience outside of college to graduate with a position at Walt Disney World waiting for her. Her on-the-job training provided her with an essential introduction to the new perspectives needed in the workaday world.

Susannah, John, Theresa, and Dorothy expanded their education by involving themselves in particular offerings at their college or university. In addition to this type of involvement, most schools offer exchange opportunities with other schools; for exam-

The experience I received through both the college program and my internship with the Walt Disney World Company will be one I will carry with me forever. Being able to join the book knowledge acquired in school with the work experience allows the past four and a half years of study to correlate as a whole. There is more to studying than taking tests and completing projects. Nothing will outweigh the benefits associated with on-the-job training. Having an education and work experience will certainly ensure a foot in the door to a promising job in the future.

I am now employed full-time as a Walt Disney cast member (as Disney refers to its employees). I was able to stay on after completing my internship. I do not feel that I have the perfect job, and I don't think there is one. No job will ever just fall into my lap. I do know that my education and experience will one day help me move to a better and more challenging job.

Dorothy Harris Blaise, student and intern with the Walt Disney World College program, East Carolina University

ple students can study on other U.S. campuses or abroad without withdrawing from their home institution. Some exchanges however involve truly unusual opportunities as was the case for Catherine Little, a University of Georgia student who participated in a international exchange organized by another university.

To celebrate the two-hundredth anniversary of the ratification of the U.S. Constitution, the University of South Carolina, the U.S. Information Agency, and its Israeli counterpart arranged for 10 U.S. students and 10 Israeli students to study one another's country through an exchange visit. While in Israel, Catherine met with representatives of various factions and became acquainted with the different perspectives of each situation. Although Catherine's experience in Israel lasted only a short time, its lessons affected her understanding of world politics and later her view of the Persian Gulf war.

Larry Battertin also gained new perspectives from an off-

We talked with Palestinians in Jerusalem, Copts in the Golan Heights, U.S. envoys in Tel Aviv, members of the Knesset, Orthodox Hasidic Jews, as well as Ethiopian Ashkenazi Jews. We met Holocaust survivors and Arab residents on the West Bank and Gaza Strip. We exchanged political views with U.N. peace keeping forces from Fiji and generals in the Israeli army. Not only were we encouraged to discuss issues with judges, lawmakers, and professors, but we were allowed to carry on lengthy talks with ordinary people we met. Once people knew who we were and what we were studying, everyone had a story to tell. Naturally I was moved.

Now looking back, I realize how much my perceptions of the Mideast situation were affected by my limited understanding of world politics and my naive trust in the American press. I cannot say that my experience radically changed my view of the world, but it did open my eyes to the variety of possible perspectives on any single event. I now realize that the 30-minute newscast we watch each night may not tell the whole story.

Catherine Little, exchange student to Israel, The University of Georgia

campus experience that took place in the United States by simultaneously student teaching in high schools and studying educational theory at Colorado State University. According to Larry, the mix was valuable. Teaching and learning at the same time enabled him to see the logic behind the theory. But Larry was particularly captivated by an opportunity to experience different kinds of student teaching situations. In one year, he taught in a high school in a large town, in an inner-city high school, and in a rural school. While teaching in the rural community, Larry lived with a local family and became involved with the community. He decided to stay and make his career there.

Many students have difficulty choosing a major. In Chapter 4, we discussed the advantages of being undecided for freshman and sophomores. Most junior and senior students however decide

From the very first, students and staff went out of their way to make us feel comfortable. At first I was surprised at how readily the students accepted us and how eager they were to learn what we had to offer. It soon became apparent that this acceptance was a direct result of both the teachers and parents working together to prepare the students for our arrival. There was a real feeling that we had something to offer and the students were ready. It made us feel proud to be teachers and not just a little concerned that we had to deliver. This closeness of the community probably could have made us feel like outsiders. However I found everyone used this closeness to help us feel accepted.

Probably the most interesting aspect of this experience was living in the community with families. I, for one, worried about imposing on the family. The family I stayed with never gave me any reason to feel this way, it was strictly self-imposed. As a matter of fact, the family was open, easygoing, and created a relaxed atmosphere in its home in spite of my intrusion. I was included in the family activities including the weekly volleyball games, trips to the store, and the birth of a child.

The advantage of this opportunity was to allow me a close-up look at community life in a small town. I liked what I saw. From the start, it was apparent the school and the children were the focus of the community. Every person in the community knows what is happening at the school and is interested. We were made to feel that what we were doing and going to do was important.

Larry Battertin, student teacher, Colorado State University

on a field of study and pursue one degree, but like Theresa DiRaimo, Valerie Goetz of Stanford University is an exception. She obtained two degrees in different fields, even though achieving her goal required an extra year of college.

How did Valerie reach her decision to extend her undergraduate years for a second major? She admits that as a freshman, the dedicated students at Stanford intimidated her. Most entered college knowing exactly what they would study and why; they even divided themselves according to their interests: technical experts and creative types. Was she the exception or the rule in the larger world? Were most 18-year-olds sure of their goals, or was she by chance in the middle of a large group of unusually decided peers? Although she wondered about this, Valerie came to feel at home in both camps. Because she pursued her interests and made an extraordinary commitment to her goals, she will begin her professional life with a special set of qualifications.

Many students move directly from undergraduate to graduate work. In Elizabeth Anderson's case her employer, a major technological corporation, offered to send her to the university of her choice to pursue a master of business administration (MBA) degree. She chose Harvard with the understanding that she would return to her company after completing her degree. Although she was a top-ranked undergraduate, Elizabeth found it difficult to adjust to the case method of teaching at Harvard (see her discussion of the case method in Chapter 7).

This innovative and individualized way of teaching challenged Elizabeth as she had not been challenged in the undergraduate classroom. For Elizabeth graduating from college was not the end of classroom instruction but the beginning of a new way of learning.

INVESTING IN THE FUTURE

As these students' experiences suggest, colleges and universities are changing how they relate to the outside world, and as a result, many schools are developing outside their walls, as their architecture indicates. While ivy-covered towers rising amid mossy structures typify older, more traditional colleges, new campuses are an eclectic mix of open spaces, covered plazas, and inviting buildings that acknowledge the power of multifaceted relationships both on campus and with external communities. The learning experiences today's colleges and universities offer have also changed. In the past, most courses of study were completed

At Stanford you are immediately introduced to two types of people: "fuzzy" and "techy." If you are fuzzy, you are a liberal arts major—you write papers and are creative. If you are techy, you are an engineer or premed student—you have a calculator and you know how to use it. And so the beginning of my sophomore year, I declared industrial engineering as my major and became a techy. I chose industrial engineering because of the practical, yet very technical, background it would give me.

In the fall of my junior year, after a summer in Europe, I threw everyone for a loop and declared art history as my second major: a techy delving into the fuzzy side of things. In Europe I realized that my interests did not solely lie in number crunching and problem solving; I was intrigued with art and how important it was to understanding different cultures.

Surprisingly I have found that I do not have to make a conscience change in mind set when moving from one subject to the other. At first I thought it was going to be difficult to adjust to the extensive reading and writing required of a liberal arts degree. I have found though that it is actually more of a relief: When my engineering classes get too burdensome, I can pick up one of my art books for some refreshing reading. It has also been interesting for me to see these two degrees mesh together as I get more creative in recommendations and reports given to executive boards and as I become more efficient at expressing myself in limited time on an art history exam.

So what will I do with these two degrees? On hearing of my two different courses of study, people often assume that I know exactly why I'm pursuing both degrees—or why else would I be pushing myself to complete the two polar opposites? But there really is no clear-cut reason why I declared both majors except an equal interest in both.

Valerie Goetz, double major, Stanford University

on campus, in classrooms, and in 4 years; now many students seek global experiences, and some expect to spend more than 4 years completing a degree.

Why have institutions changed such basic and long-held views about their orientation toward the rest of society? George Keller, author of *Academic Strategy: The Management Revolution in Higher Education*, suggests that the change is not one of choice but one of crisis.[3] We have discussed many of the factors that point to a crisis in U.S. higher education due to shrinking budgets, changing student populations, the disintegration of the liberal arts curriculum, the need to expand technological resources, the aging professoriate, and increasing criticism from external constituencies. Today institutions compete for dollars, students, and the best faculty members.

In Chapter 14, we have seen how a few students have circumvented crisis to take advantage of the best of U.S. higher education. Some have done so by taking control of their personal situations; others have welcomed once-in-a-lifetime opportunities, both at home and abroad. Still others have taken a new view of everyday circumstances and created individual learning experiences suited to their needs.

What makes the experiences of these and other enterprising students different? Many sacrifice, along with their families, short-term gains for long-term achievement. In diligent and focused ways, they invest in the future. Although the rewards of such investments sound exciting, even glamorous, unexciting tasks and hard work are the foundation of their achievements. Long lines, completed forms, visits to advisers, and requests for special consideration accompanied detailed library research, successfully completed quizzes, and well-done term papers that contributed to their success. While the experiences of these students are unique, the students themselves are not. We know many others like them whose stories could also have been told. Successful students are inventive, industrious, enterprising, and persistent; they are among the heroes of U.S. higher education.

15 ⬛ New Issues, New Agendas

At 35 Stanley Barron cannot decide how to spend the rest of his life. In college Stanley had many interests, among them art, politics, and travel, but eager to succeed in the work place, Stanley chose advertising as his major. After graduation he found a high-paying job and began creating his future—or so he thought. Now Stanley wants to change the direction of his life, but he does not feel equipped to do so.

Stanley has not made the most of the opportunities available to him. He began college as an aspiring artist or politician, and he could have studied in Europe, worked on a major drama production, or served as a summer intern with a candidate for governor. Stanley declined these offers because they did not seem related to his major. When he graduated, he did not regret his decisions because he had met the goals he set for himself.

Bright, articulate, and talented, Stanley wonders if he missed the point of college altogether. He did not know then, as he does now, that college is more than choosing a major, going to class, and doing well on exams. Learning to think in broad and global ways and being open to learning experiences throughout life are important. Stanley regrets not having been more involved in what could have been the most enriching experience of his life.

Those who work in the university setting enjoy broad responsibility for the advancement of knowledge. Charged not only to teach individual students, but to learn for all of society, we have the opportunity to influence the future far more than many other institutions in our nation. Teaching and research at the frontiers of knowledge open up new worlds for all. But each of these missions must pull its own weight if the university's potential is to be realized in full.

Our historic commitment to instruction, directed now to non-traditional as well as traditional undergraduate students and, increasingly, the public-at-large through a wide variety of outreach activities, is a much needed foil to the more recent growth of research activity that has expanded the knowledge base immensely. The importance of the teaching mission in a world dependent on knowledge and technology is obvious. It is also apparent in the urgent need for effective leadership and creative solutions to address serious problems existing in so many areas of concern. What is more difficult to establish, however, is a vision of teaching and learning that measures up to these needs.

As we develop a broader and sharper vision of how teaching must change, we are challenged to use appropriately new resources and technologies and to balance appropriately knowledge transmission and knowledge utilization. More importantly, we are challenged to find the energy and the courage to respond to the urgencies and demands for change that our new vision clarifies, and our technologies make possible. Our approach must visualize far more than simply mass producing a product that is trained to perform a task or enter a profession; it must visualize the development of people—people with disciplined minds, trained in the processes of analysis, testing, evaluation, discrimination, and communication; minds cultivated for a lifetime of intellectual growth.

The societal issues we face now are so urgent in their time, so global in their scope, and so awesome in their potential effect on human lives that we can ill afford either to dilute or to compromise on the issue of what constitutes an educated person. This is a central priority for universities and the public they serve.

Joab Thomas, president, The Pennsylvania State University

CHANGING THEMES OF HIGHER LEARNING

Although they may not know it, the students whose stories we shared in Chapter 14 are quite different from Stanley: Because they are involved in learning, they benefit from higher education in immeasurable ways. They are not only making the most of the opportunities available to them, they are establishing patterns for lifelong growth. But even collectively, these students have experienced only a few of the numerous benefits available to college students, which calls into question Allan Bloom's condemnation that the academy lacks distinction.

After looking at higher education from the inside, reflecting on the issues that guide change, and considering tomorrow's requirements for the college educated, we are convinced that many distinctive learning opportunities exist in today's academy. Although trends and predictions foreshadowing positive change are important, students can benefit from new opportunities before these possibilities become reality. On any campus in the United States, students can seek learning experiences inside and outside the classroom. The learning opportunities available to students reflect the potential of the academy and predict the future needs of students.

Diversity has taken on new meaning as U.S. higher education has developed. Early leaders created a diverse system by nurturing all types of institutions: colleges and universities, public and private, large and small; but now diversity among institutions is diminishing. As 2-year colleges become 4-year colleges, 4-year colleges become universities, universities become research universities, and research universities become world-class research universities, institutions become more alike. Instead of valuing the unique talents of faculty members, universities and many colleges focus on research productivity. Consequently many faculty members who were hired for their teaching skills are evaluated for promotion and tenure on the basis of grants obtained, articles published, and books written, and excellent teachers spend little time with undergraduates. As the critics charge, an essential balance is missing.

In Chapter 2, we considered the critics' charges. Most declare that undergraduates lose in the United States, where instructors pay little attention to them, and institutions slight their learning needs. Just when society demands more from each member of the work force, college is supplying less. Although these charges concern us, we find evidence of positive change.

In colleges and universities, impressive efforts to right the teaching-research imbalance are under way. Contrary to past rhetoric, even the presidents of leading research universities comment publicly on the critical role of teaching. As Joab Thomas, president of The Pennsylvania State University, proclaims, we must reenvision teaching and learning in broader and sharper ways.

Although we applaud the new tone of university leaders and acknowledge that liberal arts colleges and 2-year institutions have affirmed the teaching mission over the years, teaching will not occupy its position of central importance until reward systems reflect the high status of teaching and value different kinds of scholarly achievement. Evidence suggests that academic leaders who are serious about rethinking reward systems may be joining together to bring about positive change. Ernest Boyer, among others, recommends ways of achieving a new balance, and some administrators and faculties are giving attention to his ideas. Institutions are funding efforts to improve the quality of instruction and providing routes to continued development for faculty. In 1993 for example, over 500 college and university leaders from across the country and world met to consider faculty roles and rewards. They questioned how in the future institutions and individuals can more thoughtfully balance teaching, research, and service. Perhaps for the first time in decades, teaching is gaining ground in the hierarchy. Will this new agenda lead to renewed diversity within the academy?

Although diminished on the institutional level, diversity among student populations is increasing. Once largely homogeneous, student populations are now quite diverse, and their histories and viewpoints are a valuable source of strength.

Though coming from different backgrounds, students share a common purpose—learning—and this purpose can become a route to understanding others. We urge students not to remain isolated, but to seek out their peers, learn about other perspectives, and adopt personal attitudes that welcome differences.

Individuals make possible many of the changes from which students benefit, and we find the most exciting innovations on the individual level. In Chapter 14, we described students who are taking charge of their education by recognizing opportunities, finding new routes, and creating distinctive learning experiences. Just as diversity defines the population, it also defines individual needs and how students meet these needs. We applaud students who take the lead, create their futures, and foreshadow possibilities for those who follow them. Perhaps this pattern is the most rewarding consequence of diversity.

Closely related to diversity is how colleges and universities view the larger world. For years the academy, the curriculum, and students were inwardly focused; now external factors, and some critics, demand change. While some critics call for a return to the more traditional past, we believe that just as the external world is changing, so should the curriculum change to address new concerns and new orientations. Formerly most U.S. citizens viewed the world through filters defined by Western perspectives, but new issues demand more inclusive learning agendas. Discipline-based courses of study that fail to incorporate broad outlooks are inadequate. No informed member of a college community can ignore questions about the curriculum that pervade campus conversations and appear in the popular press. Such questions concern our understanding of knowledge and the larger world. To prepare for a future where facts and methods become obsolete quickly, students must understand the cultures and viewpoints of their future colleagues, customers, competitors, and neighbors. As the critics point out, students who are not involved in learning must learn how to learn and develop new skills throughout their lives by becoming involved.

In broader ways, faculties are addressing questions about the curriculum, and these issues will concern them for a number of years. Soon global, multicultural, and pluralistic perspectives will infuse all parts of the curriculum, and future programs of study may no longer be organized around the disciplines but around other, more integrated ways of thinking. Students are creating distinctive learning experiences from the central components of future curricula that exist on many campuses as special programs waiting for curricular crises to be resolved.

Another area requiring change involves how teaching and learning take place. Traditionally instructors have taken active roles while students have been more passive participants in the learning process. Now technological advances make new roles possible, as students have access to vast systems of information and to new ways of understanding and using knowledge. At the same time, classrooms are becoming only one of many places to learn, and time is becoming a student-controlled variable. In labs, homes, and dorm rooms, students access video, sound, data, and graphics at their convenience. Rather than primarily disseminating knowledge in a classroom, future instructors will facilitate learning, over which students will have more control.

Other innovative methods involve new paths to learning, such as learning through interdisciplinary approaches, creative advising relationships, and special residence arrangements. Such learning paths give students increased responsibility and offer teachers and students multidimensional ways of teaching and learning.

FORECASTING CHANGE

What new directions do these changes foreshadow? In our view, the academy is redefining itself in ways that have occurred only rarely in the past. Formerly students felt privileged to attend college, and faculties took pride in effective teaching. Then dedication to growth, research productivity, and technological advances overshadowed dedication to academic values. Now faculties and students are reassessing basic questions about learning and its place in the academy. By pressing colleges and universities to redress their most basic commitments, they are influencing the culture of the academy.

How is this redefinition emerging? Some instructors are discarding lecture notes and designing interactive learning environments, thereby exchanging class-based instruction for more personal learning. Ideas, formerly shared through print only, now reach others through multimedia, and course credit depends on achievement, not class contact hours.

Academic communities are also redefining their relationships to one another and the larger world. Today with broad segments of the population attending college, other questions about availability are in order, since students must know about such opportunities and understand the processes that lead to participation before they can take advantage of curricular innovations, special programs, or unique learning experiences.

Those who describe the global economy speak of linkages, and we think their term is appropriate, because it describes not only the alliances that define new societal norms but also the connections students need to consider as they examine opportunities and the advantages of involvement. In the larger world of work, these new connections will serve students well as they learn to examine options, discern meaning, make decisions, and become productive in tomorrow's environment.

Institutions, too, need linkages. Some colleges and universities are already working together and with business, government, and other educational enterprises in ways not considered possible in the past. As other institutions follow this trend opportunities for collaboration will increase. The most vital institutions will define and nurture linkages, thereby setting good examples for students and society.

MOVING TOWARD RESPONSIBILITY

If the ideas of this book converge on one concept, it is that of responsibility—for individuals and institutions. As institutional structures change to meet the new and varied needs of students, the responsibility for teaching and learning shifts. To benefit most from the new flexibility, students, with the help of knowledgeable people inside and outside the academy, must plan for their future. Although colleges and universities tend toward sameness, students can enhance their learning and their futures by taking advantage of opportunities available on virtually every campus in the United States.

Faculty members and administrators should rethink the purpose of the academy and the place of higher education in society. Important questions about balancing the elements of a liberal education with the needs of the marketplace, reconciling the Western view of civilization with more broad-based perspectives, appropriately evaluating faculty talent, and redistributing responsibility for learning must be addressed.

Institutional responsibility, influenced by diversity and economics, is contributing to a new vision of higher education. No longer do bricks and mortar define the academy; information is taking over. Of course institutions still invest in buildings and books, but, more importantly, they also invest in students, faculty, ideas, networks, and systems. Due to shrinking resources, these investments will become more critical in the future.

In our view, the richest resources in the United States are found in colleges and universities. Nowhere else does such a wealth of knowledge, experience, and energy exist; nowhere else is this knowledge and experience focused on enhancing the potential of others; and nowhere else can individuals or society find a better investment for tomorrow.

UNANSWERED QUESTIONS

A young student once remarked, "There is something refreshing about an unanswered question." The notion is a good one on which to end our investigation. Who are the caretakers of excellence in the academy? How will we know when we achieve excellence? Will the college educated lead the United States to new pinnacles of greatness, or will limited perspectives and resources confine us?

The question of excellence is a vital one for individuals and institutions. For enterprising students, the outlook is bright; they need not wait for institutions to point the way. Colleges and universities also have bright futures, and even in times of economic crisis, many are defining new paths to distinction. We urge them to intensify their efforts, and we urge other colleges and universities to join them.

The questions we pose have challenged the United States in the past and will continue to challenge our society in the future. Fueled by a commitment to learning and belief in human potential, U.S. citizens have designed an unparalleled system of higher education. Now perhaps our most challenging question is, Why do we learn? To become clear-thinking, problem-solving individuals is part of the answer; to know oneself, believe in oneself, and approach the future in self-directed ways are other compelling reasons. There is however more: Dreaming, having ideals, and caring about society make life even richer.

Collectively higher education is our greatest national treasure, and individually higher education is our greatest investment. Although we predict with confidence that college enhances each student's potential, college also prepares people to address tomorrow's unpredictable questions. As we end this look at undergraduate education for the future, what about the questions that remain? These we leave unanswered, for they serve as a warrant for new challenges and new learning agendas. On many campuses, visionaries are already addressing some of them. Others wait for today's college students to become the thinkers, parents, and leaders of tomorrow. Like those who have gone before them, they will conceive solutions and define new measures of excellence for higher education. Meanwhile, students do not have to wait for change. Students with initiative will find creative ways to use today's opportunities to prepare for tomorrow.

Endnotes

Chapter 1

1. For a social history of U.S. colleges and universities, see F. Rudolph, *The American College and University: A History* (New York: Knopf, 1962). For a discussion of colonial college governance patterns, see J. Herbst, *From Crisis to Crisis: American College Government, 1636–1819* (Cambridge, MA: Harvard University Press, 1982).
2. F. Rudolph, Ref. 1, 1–7.
3. *Ibid.*, 23–37.
4. *Ibid.*, 22.
5. D. B. Potts "American Colleges in the Nineteenth Century: From Localism to Denominationalism," *History of Education Quarterly* **11** (winter 1971), 363–80. Rudolph, 34–36, 85–91.
6. *Ibid.*, 243, 251–63.
7. R. L. Geiger, *To Advance Knowledge: The Growth of American Research Universities, 1900–1940* (New York: Oxford University Press, 1986), 18–19.
8. Rudolph, 362–63, 462–63.
9. D. Bok, *Universities and the Future of America* (Durham, NC: Duke University Press, 1990), 1.
10. Geiger, 255–67.
11. J. Evangelauf, "Enrollment Projection Revised Upward in New Government Analysis," *The Chronicle of Higher Education* (22 Jan. 1992), A1, A36.
12. W. Desmond, "Other Voices: Tell Harvard I'm Not Home," *The Evening Sun* (21 May 1991), A9. *Ibid.*, "Voices of the New Generation: I'm Not Going to Harvard," *The New York Times* (22 May 1991), A19. Desmond's columns prompted respondents to question his motives for choosing Loyola. For a complete account of the episode, see W. Altman, "On Rejecting Harvard," *The New York Times* (25 May 1991), 22; M. Bowler, "The Calls of Ivy," *The Evening Sun* (31 May 1991), A11; Desmond, "Why I Chose Loyola," *The Evening Sun* (4 June 1991), A19.

Chapter 2

1. A. Bloom, *The Closing of the American Mind: How Higher Education Has Failed Democracy and Impoverished the Souls of Today's Students* (New York: Simon and Schuster, 1987), 19, 337–44.
2. D. Bok, *Higher Learning* (Cambridge, MA: Harvard University Press, 1986), 1–34.
3. C. J. Sykes, *Profscam: Professors and the Demise of Higher Education* (Washington, DC: Regnery Gateway, 1988), 3.
4. Sykes, *The Hollow Men: Politics and Corruption in Higher Education* (Washington, DC: Regnery Gateway, 1990), 15, 36, 46, 313.
5. *Ibid.*, 4–5, 103.
6. M. Anderson, *Imposters in the Temple* (New York: Simon and Schuster, 1992). P. Starr, "Pummeling the Professors," *The New York Times Book Review* (9 Aug. 1992), 10–11.
7. R. Kimball, *Tenured Radicals: How Politics Has Corrupted Our Higher Education* (New York: Harper and Row, 1990), xi–xiii.
8. P. Smith, *Killing the Spirit: Higher Education in America* (New York: Viking Penguin, 1990), 6.
9. *Ibid.*, 20.
10. E. L. Boyer, *College: The Undergraduate Experience in America* (New York: Harper and Row, 1987).
11. Boyer, *Scholarship Reconsidered: Priorities of the Professoriate* (Princeton, NJ: Carnegie Foundation for the Advancement of Teaching, 1990), 25, 27.
12. *Ibid.*, 56–57.
13. T. Short, "Higher Education?" *Commentary* **89** (July 1989), 68.
14. F. M. Hechinger, "Vandals With Ph.D.s," *The New York Times Book Review*, 9 Dec. 1990, 28.
15. A. W. Lindsay and R. T. Neumann, *The Challenge for Research in Higher Education* (Washington, DC: ASHE-ERIC Higher Education Report No. 8, Association for the Study of Higher Education, 1988), 38, 46. J. F. Volkwein and D. Carbone, "A Study of Research and Teaching Orientations in Twenty-Seven Academic Departments: The Impact on Undergraduates," paper presented at the annual meeting of the *Association for the Study of Higher Education* (Boston, 1991), unpaginated.
16. A. W. Astin, W. S. Korn, and E. R. Berz, *The American Freshman: National Norms for Fall 1990* (Los Angeles: Cooperative Institutional Research Program, 1990), 4. R. Wilson, "Quality of Life Said to Have Diminished on U.S. Campuses," *The Chronicle of Higher Education* (2 May 1990), A1.
17. E. Jayne, "Academic Jeremiad: The Neoconservative View of American Higher Education," *Change* (May/June 1991), 30–42. Jayne reviews the books by Bloom, Kimball, Smith, and Sykes, among others.

Chapter 3

1. D. C. Reynolds, "Next Stop Twenty-First Century: A Look at the Future As an Extension of the Past," *Association Management* (Dec. 1990), 96. J. F. Coates and J. Jarratt, "What Futurists Believe: Agreements and Disagreements," *The Futurist* (Nov./Dec. 1990), 23.
2. J. Naisbitt and P. Aburdene, *Megatrends 2000: Ten New Directions for the 1990s* (New York: William Morrow, 1990), 14.
3. D. B. Bostian, Jr., "Paradigms for Prosperity: Economic and Political Trends for the 1990s and Early Twenty-First Century," *The Futurist* (July/Aug. 1990), 33–35. Coates and Jarratt, 23–28.
4. J. Waldrop, "You'll Know It's the Twenty-First Century When . . ." *The Saturday Evening Post* (Apr. 1991), 69–70.
5. *Ibid.*, 68.
6. Naisbitt and Aburdene, 216–29.
7. J. Castro, "Get Set: Here They Come," *Time* Special issue: "Women: The Road Ahead" (fall 1990), 52.
8. R. M. Kanter, *When Giants Learn to Dance: Mastering the Challenges of Strategy, Management, and Careers in the 1990s* (New York: Simon and Schuster, 1989), 343–72.
9. A. Bernstein and A. Levine, "The Unfinished Academic Revolution," *Change* (Mar./Apr. 1990), 6.
10. J. Hillkirk, "Execs Focus on Resurrecting Education," *U.S.A. Today* (3 Feb. 1989), B1.
11. M. Minow, "On Neutrality, Equality, and Tolerance: New Norms for a Decade of Distinction," *Change* (Jan./Feb. 1990), 17–25.
12. *Changing Patterns of Finance in Higher Education* (Paris: Organization for Economic Cooperation and Development, 1988), 60 (monograph).
13. L. R. Veysey, *The Emergence of the American University* (Chicago: University of Chicago Press, 1965), vii.
14. Commonwealth of Virginia Commission on the University of the Twenty-First Century, *The Case For Change* (undated).
15. Hillkirk, B1.
16. R. J. Wood, "Toward Cultural Empathy: A Framework for Global Education," *Educational Record* (fall 1991), 10–13.

Chapter 4

1. *Changing Patterns of Finance in Higher Education* (Paris: Organization for Economic Cooperation and Development, 1988), 66 (monograph).
2. Carnegie Foundation for the Advancement of Teaching, "New Strategies Keep Enrollments Growing," *Change* (Jan./Feb. 1989), 39.

3. A. W. Astin, K. C. Green, and W. S. Korn, *The American Freshman: Twenty Year Trends* (Los Angeles: University of California Press, 1987), 7–27.

4. *The Chronicle of Higher Education Almanac* (26 Aug. 1992), 3, 11. U.S. Department of Education, National Center for Education Statistics, *National Indicators of Education Status and Trends* (Jan. 1985), 14.

5. A. W. Astin, *What Matters in College? Four Critical Years Revisited* (San Francisco: Jossey-Bass, 1993), 429–31.

6. Astin, Green, and Korn, 7–27.

7. *Ibid.*, 7–28. A. W. Astin, W. S. Korn, and E. R. Berz, *The American Freshman: National Norms for Fall 1990* (Los Angeles: Cooperative Institutional Research Program, 1990), 4–7. *Chronicle Almanac*, 3.

8. Astin, Korn, and Berz, 4–7.

9. V. Tinto, *Leaving College: Rethinking the Causes and Cures of Student Attrition* (Chicago: University of Chicago Press, 1987), 93–99.

10. *Chronicle Almanac*, 11.

11. C. J. Polson and J. P. Eriksen, "The Impact of Administrative Support and Institutional Type of Adult Learner Services," *NACADA Journal* **8.2** (1988), 7. J. C. Polson, *Advising Adult Learners* (Seattle: National Academy Advising Association, 1986), 50.

12. L. A. Daloz, *Effective Teaching and Mentoring: Realizing the Transformational Power of Adult Learning Experiences* (San Francisco: Jossey-Bass, 1986), 43.

13. D. E. Champagne, *Planning Developmental Interventions for Adult Students* (Chicago: American College Personnel Association, 1989), 22.

14. C. J. Polson, *Advising Adults in Transition Implications for Developmental Advising* (ERIC 1988) 19–50 (ED 298 825).

15. *Ibid.*, 2.

16. J. P. Bean and B. S. Metzner, "A Conceptual Model of Nontraditional Undergraduate Student Attrition," *Review of Educational Research* **55.4** (1985), 485–40. Polson, 9. C. J. Polson, "Adult Learners: Characteristics, Concerns, and Challenges to Higher Education, a Bibliography," *NACADA Journal* **7.2** (1989), 86–112. D. Sloan and M. B. Wilmes, "Advising Adults from the Commuter Perspective," *NACADA Journal* **9.2** (1989), 67–75. J. S. Swift, Jr., "Retention of Adult College Students," *NACADA Journal* **7.2** (1987), 7–19.

17. Sloan and Wilmes, 67–75.

18. D. Richter-Antion, "Qualitative Differences between Adult and Younger Students," *NASPA Journal* **23.3** (1986), 58–62.

19. *Ibid.*, 61.

20. F. Barringer, "Census Shows Profound Change in Racial Makeup of the Nation," *The New York Times* (11 Mar. 1991), 1.

21. L. R. Estrada, "Anticipating the Demographic Future: Dramatic Changes Are on the Way," *Change* (May/June 1988), 14–19.

22. S. Arbeiter, "Black Enrollments: The Case of the Missing Students," *Change* (May/June, 1987), 6–7, 14–19. Barringer, A1, A12.

23. M. A. Cibik and S. L. Chambers, "Similarities and Differences among Native Americans, Hispanics, Blacks, and Anglos," *NASPA Journal* **28.2** (1991), 129–39. M. S. Hughes, "Black Students' Participation in Higher Education," *Journal of College Student Personnel* **28** (1987), 533–45. B. Mallinckrodt, "Student Retention, Social Support, and Dropout Intention: Comparison of Black and White Students," *Journal of College Student Development* **29** (1988), 61–64. D. P. McCauley, "Effects of Specific Factors on Blacks' Persistence at a Predominantly White University," *Journal of College Student Development* **29** (1988), 49–51. S. McPhee, "Addressing the Attrition of Minority Students on Predominantly White Campuses: A Pilot Study," *College Student Affairs Journal* **10.1** (1990), 15–22. W. E. Sedlacek, "Black Students on White Campuses: 20 Years of Research," *Journal of College Student Personnel* **28.6** (1987), 484–95. T. J. Tracey and W. E. Sedlacek, "The Relationship of Noncognitive Variables to Academic Success: A Longitudinal Comparison by Race," *Journal of College Student Personnel* **26.5** (1985), 404–10. T. M. Williams and M. M. Leonard, "Graduating Black Undergraduates: The Step beyond Retention," *Journal of College Student Development* **29** (1988), 69–75.

24. W. R. Allen, "Black Colleges vs. White Colleges: The Fork in the Road for Black Students," *Change* (May/June, 1987), 34.

25. C. Fields, "The Hispanic Pipeline: Narrow, Leaking, and Needing Repair," *Change* (May/June, 1988), 22. *Chronicle Almanac*, 3.

26. *Ibid.*, 20–27. E. B. Fiske, "The Undergraduate Hispanic Experience: A Case of Juggling Two Cultures," *Change* (May/June 1988), 28–33.

27. Fields, 25.

28. *Ibid.*, 20–27.

29. B. H. Suzuki, "Asian Americans As the 'Model Minority' Outdoing Whites? Or Media Hype?" *Change* (Nov./Dec. 1989), 13.

30. Barringer, A1, A12.

31. J. Hsia and M. Hirano–Nakanishi, "The Demographics of Diversity: Asian Americans and Higher Education," *Change* (Nov./Dec. 1989), 25.

32. *Chronicle Almanac*, 11.

33. Hsia and Hirano–Nakanishi, 20–27.

34. D. T. Nakanishi, "A Quota on Excellence? The Asian American Admissions Debate," *Change* (Nov./Dec. 1989), 39–47.

35. P. Y. Bagasao, "Student Voices Breaking the Silence: The Asian and Pacific American Experience," *Change* (Nov./Dec. 1989), 28–37.

36. A. Levine, "On Campus, Stereotypes Persist," *U.S. News and World Report* (28 Mar. 1988), 53. Nakanishi, 39–47.

37. *Ibid.*, 39–47.

38. *Ibid.*, 39–47.

39. *Ibid.*, 39–47.

40. R. Wilson, "Foreign Students in U.S. Reach a Record 386,000," *The Chronicle of Higher Education* (28 Nov. 1990), A1, A36. P. G. Altbach, "The New Interna-

tionalism: Foreign Students and Scholars," *Students in Higher Education* **14.2** (1989), 125.

41. U.S. Department of Education, National Center for Educational Statistics, *Race/ Ethnicity Trends in Degrees Conferred by Institutions of Higher Education: 1978–79 through 1988–89* (Jan. 1991), 16.

42. S. Groennings, *The Empires of the Mind: The Global Economy and Higher Education's Agenda* (presentation at the CASE Annual Assembly, Anaheim, CA, 1988), 3.

43. Altbach, 125. R. A. J. Cadieux and B. Wherly, "Advising and Counseling the International Student," *Guiding the Development of Foreign Students*, ed. K. R. Pyle (San Francisco: Jossey-Bass, 1986), 51–63.

44. J. D. Bulthius, "The Foreign Student Today: A Profile," *Guiding the Development of Foreign Students*, ed. K. R. Pyle (San Francisco: Jossey-Bass, 1986), 19–27. Cadieux and Wherly, 51–63.

45. S. M. KaiKai, "Accommodating Diversity," *College Teaching* **37.4** (1989), 123–25.

46. F. T. L. Leong and W. E. Sedlacek, "Academic and Career Needs of International and United States College Students," *Journal of College Student Development* **30** (1989), 106–11.

47. K. S. Kalivoda and J. L. Higbee, "Students with Disabilities in Higher Education: Redefining Access," *Journal of Educational Opportunity* **4.1** (1989), 14.

48. "Report Shows Increase of Freshman with Disabilities," *Higher Education and National Affairs* **36.6** (23 Mar. 1987), 1, 6.

49. K. S. Kalivoda, F. S. Young, and D. L. Wahlers, *Students with Disabilities: A Guide for Faculty and Staff* (Athens: The University of Georgia, 1989), 7–8. D. N. Stilwell, W. E. Stilwell, and L. C. Perrit, "Barriers in Higher Education for Persons with Handicaps: A Follow-up," *Journal of College Student Personnel* **24.4** (1983), 337–43.

50. H. J. Burbach and C. E. Babbitt, "Physically Disabled Students on the College Campus," *Remedial and Special Education* **9.2** (1988), 18.

51. C. Hoy and N. Gregg, "Learning Disabled Students: An Emerging Population on College Campuses," *Journal of College Admissions* (summer, 1986), 11. J. M. McGuire and J. M. McDonnell, "Helping Learning-Disabled Students to Achieve," *College Teaching* **37.1** (1989), 29–32.

52. Hoy and Gregg, 11, 13.

53. A. Abraham, *College-Level Study: What Is It?* (Atlanta: Issues in Higher Education, Southern Regional Education Board, No. 22, 1988), 2.

54. Astin, Green, and Korn, 7–27.

55. L. M. Tomlinson, *Postsecondary Developmental Programs: A Traditional Agenda with New Imperatives* (Washington, DC: ASHE-ERIC Higher Education Report No. 3, 1989), 3–4.

56. *Ibid.*, 5–6. U.S. Department of Education, 14.

57. Tomlinson, v.

58. Astin, Green, and Korn, 25.

59. J. Castro, "Get Set: Here They Come," *Time* Special issue: "Women: The Road Ahead" (fall 1990), 50. *Chronicle Almanac*, 14.

60. J. Bernard, "Introduction: College Women in a Changing Society," *Facilitating the Development of Women*, ed. N. J. Evans (San Francisco: Jossey-Bass, 1985), 5.

61. D. J. Levinson, *The Seasons of A Man's Life* (New York: Knopf, 1978).

62. C. Gilligan, "In a Different Voice: Women's Conceptions of Self and of Morality," *Harvard Educational Review* **47.4** (1977), 481–517.

63. R. M. Hall and B. R. Sandler, *Out of the Classroom: A Chilly Campus Climate for Women?* (Washington, D.C.: Association of American Colleges, 1984), 22.

64. B. McVicker Clinchy, "The Development of Thoughtfulness in College Women," *American Behavioral Scientist* **32.6** (July/Aug. 1989), 649.

65. *Ibid.*, 647–57.

66. M. A. Eisenhart, "Women Choose Their Careers: A Study of Natural Decision Making," *Review of Higher Education* **8.3** (spring 1985), 247–70.

67. Castro, 51.

68. A. Bernstein, "Women As Student Leaders," *Change* (Mar./Apr. 1986), 43–49.

Chapter 5

1. *A Classification of Institutions of Higher Education* (Princeton, NJ: Carnegie Foundation for the Advancement of Teaching, 1987), 7–8.

2. E. L. Boyer, "Foreword," in *A Classification of Institutions of Higher Education* (Princeton, NJ: Carnegie Foundation for the Advancement of Teaching, 1987), 1–6.

3. *Ibid.*, 1.

4. *Ibid.*

5. L. R. Veysey, *The Emergence of the American University* (Chicago: University of Chicago Press, 1965), 264–341.

6. H. Rosovsky, *The University: An Owner's Manual* (New York: Norton, 1990), 159–212.

Chapter 6

1. H.R. Bowen and J. H. Schuster, *American Professors: A National Resource Imperiled* (New York: Oxford University Press, 1986), 24–27.

2. *Ibid.*, 27–29.

3. *Ibid.*, 11–29.

4. P. H. Crosson, *Public Service in Higher Education: Practices and Priorities* (ASHE-ERIC Higher Education Report No. 7, 1983), 11–29.

5. E. H. Shein, "The Individual, the Organization, and the Career: A Conceptual Scheme," *Journal of Applied Behavioral Science* **7** (1971), 401–26.

6. Bowen and Schuster, 235–40.
7. *Ibid.*, 235.
8. *Ibid.*, 235–40.
9. G. M. Sheehy, *Passages: Predictable Crises of Adult Life* (New York: Dutton, 1976), 5–15.
10. Bowen and Schuster, 30–44.
11. *Ibid.*, 69–75.
12. *Ibid.*
13. *Ibid.*, 30–54.
14. *Ibid.*, 49–54.
15. R. G. Ehrenberg, "The Future of Academic Salaries: Will the 1990s Be a Bust Like the 1970s or a Boom Like the 1980s?" *Academe* **77**:2 (1991), 9–32.
16. R. G. Baldwin, "Faculty Career Stages and Implications for Professional Development," in *Enhancing Faculty Careers: Strategies for Development and Renewal*, ed. J. H. Schuster and D. W. Wheeler (San Francisco: Jossey-Bass, 1990), 29–40.
17. *Ibid.*, 49–54.
18. J. H. Schuster, "Meeting the Challenge of Personal and Professional Renewal for Faculty," *Proceedings of Second Conference on Professional and Personal Renewal for Faculty* (Athens, GA: Office of Instructional Development, The University of Georgia, 1988), 1–22.
19. *Ibid.*
20. Ehrenberg, 5–6.
21. Schuster, 4–5.
22. *Ibid.*
23. R. D. Simpson and W. K. Jackson, "A Multidimensional Approach to Faculty Vitality: The University of Georgia," in *Enhancing Faculty Careers: Strategies for Development and Renewal*, ed. J. H. Schuster and D. W. Wheeler (San Francisco: Jossey-Bass, 1990), 167–87.

Chapter 7

1. H. Peterson, ed., *Great Teachers: As Portrayed by Those Who Studied under Them* (New Brunswick, NJ: Rutgers University Press, 1946), 134.
2. C. R. Christensen, *Teaching and the Case Method: Text, Cases, and Readings* (Boston: Harvard Business School, 1987).
3. A. W. Astin, *What Matters in College? Four Critical Years Revisited* (San Francisco: Jossey-Bass, 1993), 425–29.
4. R. Yeany, Jr., "A Case from the Research for Training Science Teachers in the Use of Inductive/Indirect Teaching Strategies," *Science Education* **59** (1975), 520–21.
5. K. P. Cross, "College Teaching: What Do We Know about It?" *Innovative Higher Education* **16** (fall 1991), 7–26.

6. P. M. Treisman, "A Study of the Mathematics Performance of Black Students at the University of California, Berkeley," *DAI* **47** (1986), 1641.

7. The inventories were developed by A. W. Chickering of George Mason University, Z. F. Gamson of the University of Massachusetts at Boston, and L. M. Barsi of the American Association of State Colleges and Universities (AASCU). The guide was prepared by S. J. Poulsen of the Johnson Foundation, with support from the Lilly Endowment.

8. Personal communication with W. F. Prokasy, vice president for Academic Affairs, The University of Georgia, Athens, Georgia, September 1990.

9. R. D. Simpson and W. K. Jackson, "A Multidimensional Approach to Faculty Vitality: The University of Georgia," in J. H. Schuster and D. W. Wheeler, ed., *Enhancing Faculty Careers: Strategies for Development and Renewal* (San Francisco: Jossey-Bass, 1990), 167–87.

10. *The Third National Conference on Professional and Personal Renewal for Faculty Proceedings* (Athens, GA: Office of Instructional Development, The University of Georgia, 1991).

Chapter 8

1. H. Spencer, *Education: Intellectual, Moral, and Physical* (New York: Appleton, 1860), 11–16.

2. E. Boyer, "The Undergraduate Experience: Critical Issues for the '90s," address given at the annual meeting of *The Freshman Year Experience* (Columbia, SC: University of South Carolina, 22 Feb. 1992).

3. R. W. Tyler, *Basic Principles of Curriculum and Instruction* (Chicago: University of Chicago Press, 1949), 1–25.

4. W. G. Perry, Jr., *Forms of Intellectual and Ethical Development in the College Years: A Scheme* (New York: Holt, Rinehart, and Winston, 1970), 1–34.

5. R. Driver, *The Pupil As Scientist?* (Milton Keynes, England: Open University Press, 1983).

6. D. Bok, *Higher Learning* (Cambridge, MA: Harvard University Press, 1986), 54–72.

7. *Ibid.*, 158–201.

8. *Ibid.*

9. J. S. Stark and M. A. Lowther, *Designing the Learning Plan: A Review of Research and Theory Related to College Curricula* (Ann Arbor, MI: University of Michigan Press, 1986), 38–40.

10. *Ibid.*, 23–27.

11. A. Levine, "A Time to Act," *Change* (Jan./Feb. 1992), 4–5.

12. A. Levine and J. Cureton, "The Quiet Revolution: Eleven Facts about Multiculturalism and the Curriculum," *Change* (Jan./Feb. 1992), 25–29.

13. H. Collins, "PC and the Press," *Change* (Jan./Feb. 1992), 12.

14. J. W. Scott, "The Campaign against Political Correctness: What's Really at Stake?" *Change* (Nov./Dec. 1991), 30–43.
15. Boyer, "The Undergraduate Experience."

Chapter 9

1. A. W. Astin, W. Korn, and K. Green, "Retaining and Satisfying Students," *Educational Record* **68**(1) (1987), 39.
2. E. L. Dey, A. W. Astin, and W. S. Korn, *The American Freshman: 25-Year Trends, 1966–1990* (Los Angeles: Higher Education Research Institute, UCLA, 1991), 1–38. Statistics in the following paragraphs have been taken from this report.
3. A. W. Astin, *What Matters in College? Four Critical Years Revisited* (San Francisco: Jossey-Bass, 1993), xiv, 365–95. A. W. Astin, "Student Involvement: A Developmental Theory for Higher Education," *Journal of College Student Personnel* **25** (1984), 297–307.
4. V. Tinto, *Leaving College: Rethinking the Causes and Cures of Student Attrition* (Chicago: University of Chicago Press, 1987), 1.
5. *Ibid.*, 5.
6. *Ibid.*, 6–7.
7. R. Levitz and L. Noel, "Connecting Students to Institutions: Keys to Retention and Success," in *The Freshman Year Experience: Helping Students Survive and Succeed in College*, ed. M. L. Upcraft and J. N. Gardner (San Francisco: Jossey-Bass, 1989), 65. E. Myers, *Unpublished Attrition Research Studies* (St. Cloud, MN.: St. Cloud State University, 1981). Tinto, 97–98.
8. *Ibid.*, 98.
9. *Ibid.*, 119.
10. *Ibid.*, 66. J. J. Endo and R. L. Harpel, "The Effect of Student–Faculty Interaction on Students' Educational Outcomes," *Research in Higher Education* **16** (1982), 115–35.
11. Tinto, 7.
12. E. T. Pascarella and P. T. Terenzini, *How College Affects Students: Findings and Insights from 20 Years of Research* (San Francisco: Jossey-Bass, 1991), xv–xvii.
13. *Ibid.*, 557, 611.
14. M. N.-K. Collison, "Nonelite Colleges Measure up to Prestigious Institutions, Authors Say," *The Chronicle of Higher Education* (17 Apr. 1991), A38.
15. F. Rudolph, *The American College and University, a History* (New York: Random House, 1962), 460. H. M. Bullock, *A History of Emory University* (Nashville, TN: Parthenon, 1936), 313.
16. M. L. Upcraft and J. N. Gardner, *The Freshman Year Experience: Helping Students Survive and Succeed in College*, (San Francisco: Jossey-Bass, 1989), 2. M. L. Upcraft, *Residence Hall Assistants in College: A Guide to Selection, Training, and Supervision* (San Francisco: Jossey-Bass, 1982). M. L. Upcraft, "Residence Hall

and Student Activities," in *Increasing Student Retention: Effective Programs and Practices for Reducing the Dropout Rate*, ed. L. Noel, R. Levitz, and D. Saluri (San Francisco: Jossey-Bass, 1985). S. H. Frost, "Academic Responsibility: Can It Be Taught?" *NACADA Journal* **9**(2) (1989a), 17–24. S. H. Frost, "The Effects of Academic Advising and the Frequency of Faculty Contact on the Cognitive Development of College Freshman," *DAI* **51** (1989), 87A.

17. Upcraft and Gardner, 3.

18. G. L. Kramer and R. Washburn, "The Perceived Orientation Needs of New Students," *Journal of College Student Personnel* **24** (1983), 311–19. M. A. D. Sagaria, L. C. Higginson, and E. R. White, "Perceived Needs of Entering Freshman: The Primacy of Academic Issues," *Journal of College Student Personnel* **21** (1980), 243–46.

19. P. P. Fidler and D. S. Fidler, *First National Survey on Freshman Seminar Programs: Findings, Conclusions, and Recommendations* (Columbia, SC: National Resource Center for the Freshman-Year Experience, 1991), 10–11, 19. Questionnaires were completed by 1699 of the 3168 institutions receiving the survey. We report percentages of actual respondents.

20. J. H. Banning, "Impact of College Environments on Freshman Students," in *The Freshman Year Experience: Helping Students Survive and Succeed in College*, ed. M. L. Upcraft and J. N. Gardner (San Francisco: Jossey-Bass), 58–59.

21. M. A. Okun, C. A. Kardash, W. A. Stock, I. N. Sandler, and D. J. Bauman, "Measuring Perceptions of the Quality of Academic Life among College Students," *Journal of College Student Personnel* **27** (1986), 447–51.

22. Astin, Korn, and Green, 41. E. L. Boyer, *College: The Undergraduate Experience in America* (New York: Harper and Row, 1987), 52–54.

23. A. W. Chickering, *Education and Identity* (San Francisco: Jossey-Bass, 1969), 20–142.

24. B. B. Crookston, "A Developmental View of Academic Advising As Teaching," *Journal of College Student Personnel* **13** (1972), 12–17.

25. S. H. Frost, *Academic Advising and Student Success: A System of Shared Responsibility* (Washington, DC: ASHE-ERIC Higher Education Report No. 3, 1991), 15–21.

26. Frost, *Academic Responsibility*, 17–24.

27. R. B. Winston, Jr., and J. A. Sandor, "Developmental Academic Advising; What Do Students Want?" *NACADA Journal* **4.1** (1984), 5–13. L. L. Fielstein, "Student Priorities for Academic Advising: Do They Want a Personal Relationship?" *NACADA Journal* **9.1** (1989), 33–38.

28. S. H. Frost, *Educational Improvement through Academic Advising: Advisor Attitudes and Practices That Make a Difference* (F. Lauderdale: Southern Association for Institutional Research, 1990), 8–9.

29. W. R. Habley and D. S. Crockett, "The Third ACT National Survey of Academic Advising," in *The Status and Future of Academic Advising: Problems and Promise*, ed. W. R. Habley (Iowa City: ACT National Center for the Advancement of Educational Practices, 1988), 74–76. Frost, *Educational Improvement*, 8–9.

30. A. W. Astin, W. S. Korn, and E. R. Berz, *The American Freshman: National Norms for Fall 1990* (Los Angeles: University of California, American Council on Education, 1990), 15, 31, 47.

31. A. W. Astin, *Achieving Educational Excellence* (San Francisco: Jossey-Bass, 1985), 147–48.

32. A. W. Astin, "The Impact of Dormitory Living on Students," *Educational Record* **54** (1973), 204–10.

33. Rudolph, 86.

34. *Ibid.*, 89.

35. Upcraft, 321.

36. *Ibid.*

37. E. T. Pascarella and P. T. Terenzini, "Residence Arrangement, Student/Faculty Relationships, and Freshman-Year Educational Outcomes," *Journal of College Student Personnel* **22** (1981), 149.

38. J. H. Clarke, K. M. Miser, and A. O. Roberts, "Freshman Residential Programs: Effects of Living–Learning Structure, Faculty Involvement, and Thematic Focus," *Journal of College and University Student Housing* **18**(2) (1988), 7–13.

39. W. J. Johnson, "Crime Report," *CASE Currents* (Jan. 1992), 30–32.

40. S. Burd, "Colleges Issue Federally Required Reports on Campus Crime Rates, Arrests, Policies," *The Chronicle of Higher Education* (2 Sept. 1992), A25, A36. M. N.-K. Collison, "4000 Violent Crimes Occurred on 580 Campuses in Past 3 Years: Use of Data Questioned," *The Chronicle of Higher Education* (23 Sept. 1992), A32.

41. A. Abbey, "Acquaintance Rape and Alcohol Consumption: How Are They Linked?" *JACH* **39** (Jan. 1991), 165–69. D. Benson, C. Clarkton, and F. Goodhart, "Acquaintance Rape on Campus: A Literature Review," *JACH* **40** (Jan. 1992), 157–65. These articles are sources for the succeeding paragraphs on acquaintance rape.

42. "Notebook," *The Chronicle of Higher Education* (15 July 1992), A29.

43. L. M. Range, "College and University Suicide: Trends and Implications," *Counseling Psychologist* **18**.3 (July 1990), 464–76.

Chapter 10

1. R. D. Simpson and N. D. Anderson, *Science, Students, and Schools: A Guide for the Middle and Secondary School Teacher* (New York: Wiley, 1981).

2. B. S. Bloom, *Human Characteristics and School Learning* (New York: McGraw-Hill, 1976), 1–21.

3. W. F. Prokasy, "The New Pedagogy: An Essay on Policy and Procedural Implications," *Innovative Higher Education* **15** (spring/summer 1991), 109–15.

4. P. Lynch, *Multimedia: Getting Started* (Sunnyvale, CA: PUBLIX Information Products for Apple Computer, 1991), 1–3.

5. *Ibid.*, 4–5.
6. *Ibid.*, 8–9.
7. *Ibid.*, 16-21.

Chapter 11

1. R. A. Smith, *Sports and Freedom: The Rise of Big-Time College Athletics* (New York: Oxford University Press, 1988), 1–12.
2. *Ibid.*
3. *Ibid.*
4. *Ibid.*, 13–25.
5. *Ibid.*
6. D. S. Jordan, "Football: Battle or Sport?" in *Portraits of the American University 1890–1910*, ed. J. C. Stone and D. P. Denevi (San Francisco: Jossey-Bass, 1971), 336.
7. J. R. Thelin and L. L. Wiseman, *The Old College Try: Balancing Academics and Athletics in Higher Education* (Washington, DC: George Washington University Press, 1989), 63–84.
8. J. Fife, "Foreword," in Thelin and Wiseman, xv–xvi.
9. Thelin and Wiseman, 1–2.
10. *Ibid.*
11. "Athletics," *The Chronicle of Higher Education* (4 Sept. 1991), A50–A53.
12. Thelin and Wiseman, 1–2.
13. *Ibid.*, 71.
14. D. Lederman, "College Sports Brace for Rigorous External Examination as Demands Mount for Accountability and Accreditation Mount," *The Chronicle of Higher Education* (20 Feb. 1991), A43–A44. D. Lederman, "NCAA's Leaders See Big Strides in Effort to Reshape Sports," *The Chronicle of Higher Education* (22 Jan. 1992), A38, A40.
15. *Ibid.*, A40.
16. D. Lederman, "Emboldened Presidents' Commission Urges NCAA to Toughen Its Academic Requirements for Athletes," *The Chronicle of Higher Education* (3 July 1991), A25–A26.

Chapter 12

1. T. Jefferson in a letter to J. Banister, Jr., from Paris, 15 Oct. 1785, in *The Life and Selected Writings of Thomas Jefferson*, ed. A. Koch and W. Peden (New York: Random House, 1944), 387–88.
2. S. E. Fraser and W. W. Brickman, "The Comparative Advantages of an American Rather Than a European Education," *A History of International and Compara-*

tive Education: Nineteenth-Century Documents (Glenview, IL: Scott, Foresman, 1968), 26.

3. Governor B. Clinton and Senator A. Gore, *Putting People First: How We Can All Change America* (New York: Random House, 1992), 191–92.

4. J. Naisbitt and P. Aburdene, *Megatrends 2000: Ten New Directions for the 1990s* (New York: William Morrow, 1990), 20, 31–39.

5. S. Groennings, "Public Policy and National Imperatives" (position paper for the Invitational Seminar on Planning Imperatives for the 1990s, The University of Georgia, Athens, GA, 21–22, Nov. 1988), 5.

6. R. M. Kanter, *When Giants Learn to Dance: Mastering the Challenges of Strategy, Management, and Careers in the 1990s* (New York: Simon and Schuster, 1989), 18.

7. L. Kraar, "25 Who Help the U.S. Win," *Fortune* (spring/summer 1991), 36.

8. L. R. Veysey, *The Emergence of the American University* (Chicago: University of Chicago Press, 1965), 128–29.

9. R. T. Arndt, "Rethinking International Education," in *International Education: The Unfinished Agenda*, ed. W. C. Olson and L. D. Howell (Indianapolis, IN: White River Press, 1984), 11–12.

10. S. Jaschik, "Administration Outlines Plans to Expand Several International Education Programs," *The Chronicle of Higher Education* (8 Nov. 1989), A25, A31.

11. S. Groennings, "The American Democracy in the Global Community: Federal and University Roles in the International Education Triad," in *International Education: The Unfinished Agenda*, ed. W. C. Olson and L. D. Howell (Indianapolis, IN: White River Press, 1984), 70.

12. S. Groennings, "The Federal Role in Higher Education: Beyond Access to Competitiveness," draft of chapter for *Knowledge for All Americans: The Third American Revolution*.

13. S. Groennings, "Beachheads in International Education," *ADFL Bulletin* **14**(3) (Mar. 1983), 1.

14. *The Chronicle of Higher Education Almanac* (26 Aug. 1992), 14, 15. In 1990 foreign language majors earned 11,326 of the 1,049,657 bachelors degrees conferred by U.S. colleges and universities, and U.S. citizens earned 55 percent of the 6276 doctoral degrees awarded in the physical sciences and 38 percent of the 5212 doctoral degrees awarded in engineering. J. C. Bednar, "Business Schools Must Make Language Fluency a Top Priority," *The Chronicle of Higher Education* (7 Feb. 1990), B2.

15. Groennings, "Public Policy," 4.

16. *Ibid.*, 8.

17. *Ibid.*, 12.

18. P. C. Altbach, "The New Internationalism: Foreign Students and Scholars," *Students in Higher Education* **14**(2) (1989), 126.

19. S. Groennings, "The Empires of the Mind: The Global Economy and Higher Education's Agenda" (paper presented at the CASE Annual Assembly, Anaheim, CA, 12 July 1988), 3. Groennings, "Public Policy," 12–13.

20. A. Dinniman and B. Holzner, ed., *Education for International Competence in Pennsylvania* (Pennsylvania: Pennsylvania Department of Education and University of Pittsburgh, 1988), 9.

21. *Ibid.*, 3–6.

22. J. M. Grandin, "Developing Internships in Germany for International Engineering Students," *Die Unterrichtspraxis/Teaching German* **24**(2) (fall 1991), 209–14.

23. A. DeWees, quoted in the Agnes Scott College Office of Admission's pamphlet "Agnes Scott: A World of Experience through Agnes Scott's Global Awareness Program."

24. C. Alger and J. E. Harf, "Global Education: Why? For Whom? About What?," in *Promising Practices in Global Education: A Handbook with Case Studies*, ed. R. E. Freeman (New York: National Council on Foreign Language and International Studies, 1986), 1.

25. Groennings, *Beachheads*, 1.

26. D. S. Wiley, "Project Scope and History," in *Group Portrait: Internationalizing the Disciplines*, ed. S. Groennings and D. S. Wiley (New York: American Forum, 1990), 5.

27. A. S. Ochoa, "Internationalizing Teacher Education," in *Promising Practices in Global Education: A Handbook with Case Studies*, ed. R. E. Freeman (New York: National Council on Foreign Language and International Studies, 1986), 48.

Chapter 13

1. A. M. Hauptman, *The Tuition Dilemma: Assessing New Ways to Pay for College* (Washington, DC: Brookings Institution, 1990), 1–2.

2. T. J. DeLoughry, "Up to 300 Institutions May Be Cut by U.S. from Loan Programs," *The Chronicle of Higher Education* (22 May 1991), A1, A25.

3. C. Leatherman, "Salaries of Chief Executives in Higher Education Found to Have Grown by 6 Percent a Year Since 1988, *The Chronicle of Higher Education* (3 July 1991), A11–A13.

4. S. Tifft, "Sticker Shock at the Ivory Tower," *Time* (25 Sept. 1989), 72–73.

5. *The Chronicle of Higher Education Almanac* (26 Aug. 1992), 3, 34.

6. *Ibid.*, 34.

7. M. O'Keefe, "Private Colleges Beating the Odds: Despite Warnings, Enrollments Are up," *Change* (Mar./Apr. 1989), 11–19.

8. A. G. Shilling, "$50,000-a-Year Tuition?" *Forbes* (11 Dec. 1989), 323.

9. U.S. Department of Education, 1992, *Financial Aid from the U.S. Department of Education 1992–93*, 23–40. Financial aid details are current for the 1992 to 1993 academic year. Regulations are subject to annual review.

10. G. Blumestyk, "Use of Pell Grants to Educate Inmates Provokes Criticism," *The Chronicle of Higher Education* (5 June 1991), A1, A20. Hauptman, 41. T. J.

DeLoughry, "Senate Study Sees 'Ultimate Collapse' of U.S. Loan Program Unless Reforms Are Made," *The Chronicle of Higher Education* (22 May 1991), A25.

11. Hauptman, 40–74. Chapter 3 of Hauptman's book discusses these and other innovative versions of traditional financial aid programs.

12. G. Putka, "Anxious Parents Flock to Tuition Schemes," *Wall Street Journal* (1 Nov. 1989), C1.

13. Hauptman, 18–39. The discussion of tuition prepayments and guarantees is drawn largely from this source. See Hauptman for a more detailed description of public policy issues and participation trends.

14. B. Werth, "Why Is College So Expensive? Maybe America Wants It That Way," *Change* (Mar./Apr. 1988), 16.

15. *Ibid.*, 13–25, 19.

16. M. C. Cage, "30 States Cut Higher Education Budgets by an Average of 3.9 Percent in Fiscal 1990–91," *The Chronicle of Higher Education* (26 June 1991), A1, A17.

17. *Ibid.*, A1.

18. S. Groennings, "Implications of the Global Economy for Educational Exchange," invited paper at the *Fortieth Anniversary National Conference of the National Association for Foreign Student Affairs* (2 June 1988), 6.

19. M. O'Keefe, "A New Look at College Costs: Where Does the Money Really Go?" *Change* (Nov./Dec. 1987), 33.

20. T. Hartle, "Federal Support for Higher Education in the '90s: Boom, Bust, or Something in between?" *Change* (Jan./Feb. 1990), 37.

21. S. Jaschik, "Ivy League Agrees to End Collaboration on Financial Aid," *The Chronicle of Higher Education* (29 May 1991), A1, A18. The Ivy League schools, the Massachusetts Institute of Technology, and 14 other schools, known as the Overlap Group, have met each year since 1956 to compare financial aid offerings to students. In essence each school agreed not to compete for the same student by offering more attractive aid and scholarship packages than other schools in the group. The U.S. Justice Department charged that students were being denied the right to compare prices and discounts among schools. To resolve the dispute, the Ivy League schools and MIT agreed not to comply with other institutions on matters of financial aid, family contribution to tuition, students fees or faculty salaries.

22. J. L. Gilmore, *Price and Quality in Higher Education* (U.S. Department of Education, Office of Educational Research and Improvement, 1991), 1–110.

23. E. T. Pascarella and P. T. Terenzini, *How College Affects Students: Findings and Insights from Twenty Years of Research* (San Francisco: Jossey-Bass, 1991), 530.

24. *Ibid.*, 592, 648.

Chapter 14

1. S. Deep and L. Sussman, *Smart Moves: 14 Steps to Keep Any Boss Happy, 8 Ways to Start Meetings on Time, and 1600 More Tips to Get the Best from Yourself and the People around You* (New York: Addison-Wesley, 1990), 191–93.
2. E. T. Pascarella and P. T. Terenzini, *How College Affects Students: Findings and Insights from Twenty Years of Research* (San Francisco: Jossey-Bass, 1991), 214–68.
3. G. Keller, *Academic Strategy: The Management Revolution in Higher Education* (Baltimore: Johns Hopkins Press, 1983), 3–26.

Index

About the Authors

Ronald D. Simpson, Ed.D., is Director of the Office of Instructional Development at The University of Georgia, where he is also professor of science education and higher education. Formerly head of the Department of Mathematics and Science Education at North Carolina State University, he holds degrees from the University of Tennessee and The University of Georgia. The author of over 100 scholarly publications, Dr. Simpson has taught college students at all levels. The father of two children who are college graduates, he lives in Athens, Georgia.

Susan Henson Frost, Ed.D., is Director of Institutional Planning and Research and adjunct assistant professor of educational studies at Emory University. A graduate of Agnes Scott College and The University of Georgia, she investigates undergraduate learning and patterns of institutional decision-making. Dr. Frost's earlier book, *Academic Advising for Student Success: A System of Shared Responsibility*, is a best-seller for the ASHE-ERIC Higher Education Reports Series. The mother of a college student and a high school student, she lives in Gainesville, Georgia.